Challenging Psychological Issues

We would like to dedicate this course to the memory of Brenda Smith, Psychology Staff Tutor and member of the course team, who died during the final year of the course's production. She had been a Psychology Staff Tutor since 1995, first in Scotland and then most recently in Ireland, but her close association with the Open University stretches back much further than this. She was an Open University student herself and then later returned to teach and was a tutor who enthused and supported very many students throughout their social science studies. At her funeral one of these students spoke very movingly of her warmth and energy and of the fact that she had really 'made a difference' to their lives. She certainly also made a difference to our DSE212 course team, where her commitment to education for mature students was clear in everything that she said and did, and her immensely hard work influenced many of our plans for the teaching and learning strategy of the course and the content of the texts. She contributed enormously at both a professional and personal level, particularly to the early work of the course team, and we hope that her influence on the course will shine through, helping it in turn to 'make a difference' to the lives of all the students who will study it in the coming years.

Challenging
Psychological Issues

Edited by Troy Cooper and Ilona Roth

The Open University

Cover and title page images: Guillem Ramos-Poqui

This publication forms part of an Open University course DSE212 *Exploring Psychology*. Details of this and other Open University courses can be obtained from the Course Information and Advice Centre, PO Box 724, The Open University, Milton Keynes MK7 6ZS, United Kingdom: tel. +44 (0)1908 653231, email ces-gen@open.ac.uk

Alternatively, you may visit the Open University website at http://www.open.ac.uk where you can learn more about the wide range of courses and packs offered at all levels by the Open University.

To purchase this publication or other components of Open University courses, contact Open University Worldwide Ltd, The Open University, Walton Hall, Milton Keynes MK7 6AA, United Kingdom: tel. +44 (0)1908 858785; fax +44 (0)1908 858787; email ouwenq@open.ac.uk; website http://www.ouw.co.uk

The Open University
Walton Hall, Milton Keynes
MK7 6AA

First published 2002. Reprinted 2003

Edited, designed and typeset by The Open University.

Printed in the United Kingdom by The Bath Press, Bath.

ISBN 0 7492 5355 X

1.2

Contents

DSE212 course team

Open University staff

Dr Dorothy Miell, Senior Lecturer in Psychology, Faculty of Social Sciences (Course Team Chair)

Dr Paul Anand, Lecturer in Economics, Faculty of Social Sciences

Peter Barnes, Lecturer in Centre for Childhood, Development and Learning, Faculty of Education and Language Studies

Pam Berry, Key Compositor

Dr Nicola Brace, Lecturer in Psychology, Faculty of Social Sciences

Dr Nick Braisby, Lecturer in Psychology, Faculty of Social Sciences

Maurice Brown, Software Designer

Sue Carter, Staff Tutor, Faculty of Social Sciences

Annabel Caulfield, Course Manager, Faculty of Social Sciences

Lydia Chant, Course Manager, Faculty of Social Sciences

Dr Troy Cooper, Staff Tutor, Faculty of Social Sciences

Crystal Cunningham, Researcher, BBC/OU

Shanti Dass, Editor

Sue Dobson, Graphic Artist

Alison Edwards, Editor

Marion Edwards, Software Designer

Jayne Ellery, Production Assistant, BBC/OU

Dr Linda Finlay, Associate Lecturer, Faculty of Social Sciences, co-opted member of course team

Alison Goslin, Designer

Professor Judith Greene, Professor of Psychology (retired), Faculty of Social Sciences

Celia Hart, Picture Researcher

Professor Wendy Hollway, Professor of Psychology, Faculty of Socia Sciences

Silvana Ioannou, Researcher, BBC/OU

Dr Amy Johnston, Lecturer in Behavioural Neuroscience, Faculty of Science

Dr Adam Joinson, Lecturer in Educational Technology, Institute of Educational Technology

Sally Kynan, Research Associate in Psychology

Andrew Law, Executive Producer, BBC/OU

Dr Martin Le Voi, Senior Lecturer in Psychology, Faculty of Social Sciences

Dr Karen Littleton, Senior Lecturer in Centre for Childhood, Development and Learning, Faculty of Education and Language Studies

Dr Bundy Mackintosh, Lecturer in Psychology, Faculty of Social Sciences

Marie Morris, Course Secretary

Dr Peter Naish, Lecturer in Psychology, Faculty of Social Sciences

Daniel Nettle, Lecturer in Biological Psychology, Departments of Biological Sciences and Psychology

John Oates, Senior Lecturer in Centre for Childhood, Development and Learning, Faculty of Education and Language Studies

Michael Peet, Producer, BBC/OU

Dr Ann Phoenix, Senior Lecturer in Psychology, Faculty of Social Sciences

Dr Graham Pike, Lecturer in Psychology, Faculty of Social Sciences

Dr Ilona Roth, Senior Lecturer in Psychology, Faculty of Social Sciences

Brenda Smith, Staff Tutor, Faculty of Social Sciences

Dr Richard Stevens, Senior Lecturer in Psychology, Faculty of Social Sciences

Colin Thomas, Lead Software Designer

Dr Kerry Thomas, Senior Lecturer in Psychology, Faculty of Social Sciences

Dr Frederick Toates, Reader in Psychobiology, Faculty of Science

Jenny Walker, Production Director, BBC/OU

Dr Helen Westcott, Lecturer in Psychology, Faculty of Social Sciences

Dr Clare Wood, Lecturer in Centre for Childhood, Development and Learning, Faculty of Education and Language Studies

Christopher Wooldridge, Editor

External authors and critical readers

Dr Koula Asimakopoulou, Tutor Panel

Debbie Balchin, Tutor Panel

Dr Peter Banister, Head of Psychology and Speech Pathology Department, Manchester Metropolitan University

Clive Barrett, Tutor Panel

Dr Kevin Buchanan, Senior Lecturer in Psychology, University College, Northampton

Dr Richard Cains, Tutor Panel

Professor Stephen Clift, Tutor Panel

Linda Corlett, Associate Lecturer, Faculty of Social Sciences

Victoria Culpin, Tutor Panel

Dr Tim Dalgleish, Research Clinical Psychologist, Brain Sciences Unit, Cambridge

Dr Graham Edgar, Tutor Panel, Research Scientist, BAE SYSTEMS

Patricia Fisher, Equal Opportunities critical reader

David Goddard, Tutor Panel

Dr Dan Goodley, Lecturer in Inclusive Education, University of Sheffield

Victoria Green, Student Panel

Dr Mary Hanley, Senior Lecturer in Psychology, University College, Northampton

Dr Jarrod Hollis, Associate Lecturer, Faculty of Social Sciences

Rob Jarman, Tutor Panel

Dr Hélène Joffe, Lecturer in Psychology, University College London

Dr Helen Kaye, Associate Lecturer, Faculty of Social Sciences

Professor Matt Lambon-Ralph, Professor of Cognitive Neuroscience, University of Manchester

Rebecca Lawthom, Senior Lecturer in Psychology, Manchester Metropolitan University

Kim Lock, Student Panel

Patricia Matthews, Tutor Panel

Dr Elizabeth Ockleford, Tutor Panel

Penelope Quest, Student Panel

Susan Ram, Student Panel

Dr Alex Richardson, Senior Research Fellow in Psychology and Neuroscience, Imperial College of Medicine, London, also Research Affiliate, University Laboratory of Physiology, Oxford

Dr Carol Sweeney, Tutor Panel

Dr Annette Thomson, Associate Lecturer, Faculty of Social Sciences

Dr Stella Tickle, Tutor Panel

Carol Tindall, Senior Lecturer in Psychology, Manchester Metropolitan University

Jane Tobbell, Senior Lecturer in Psychology, Manchester Metropolitan University

Martin Treacy, Associate Lecturer, Faculty of Social Sciences

Professor Aldert Vrij, Professor in Applied Social Psychology, University of Portsmouth

External assessors

Professor Martin Conway, Professor of Psychology, Durham University

Professor Anne Woollet, Professor of Psychology, University of East London

Introduction

Troy Cooper and Ilona Roth

The challenges of Book 2

In Book 2, we present some of the most challenging topics in contemporary psychological research. The chapters range from discussions of development – as a capacity which continues throughout the lifespan (Chapter 1), and which may take different pathways in different individuals (Chapter 5) – to the nature of language (Chapter 2) and consciousness (Chapter 4), and the complex question of the factors which influence our emergence as men or women (Chapter 3). In discussing these topics, we build on perspectives, theories and themes which you have already encountered in the course. We introduce new ideas and frequently juxtapose approaches which challenge one another.

In Book 1, a key theme was the extent to which psychology can explain what makes us distinctive as individuals – as similar to, or different from other human beings. The topics of Book 2 were chosen with a related question in mind: are there aspects of our behaviour and experience in which we are essentially distinct from other animals? Each of the five chapters deals with an area of functioning which is either unique to humans or which, arguably, takes on a distinctive form in humans. Key dimensions of this human distinctiveness, such as the fundamental nature of language and consciousness, are considered. The chapters weave in the second and third key themes from Book 1. For example, Chapter 1 returns to the theme of fixity and change in a discussion of human development across the lifespan. We, like other animals, develop physically and in terms of behaviour and capability during our early lives – but does that early development then determine our behaviour and capability in later life to the large extent that it does for other animals? Or is there evidence that the development of advanced social and cognitive skills represents a degree of change which other animals do not have?

Several chapters in this book illustrate the third theme of 'nature-nurture' by evaluating the contributions of both biological and social influences to human distinctiveness. The discussion in Chapter 2 ranges from the evolutionary origins of language as a species-specific characteristic to the role of social interaction and context in determining meaning. Chapter 5 contrasts biological accounts of what causes dyslexia with sociocultural analyses of why this category is differentiated as a 'problem'. Chapter 3 addresses sex and gender, an area in which there is heated debate about the nature of attributes which mark humans out as qualitatively distinct from one another and from other animals.

You should already be familiar with the notion that different perspectives fit together in various ways. They may *conflict* (where the contrasting claims of different perspectives are mutually exclusive and cannot be resolved), or be *complementary* (where contrasting claims are mutually compatible and can be accommodated within a common explanatory framework). They may also *coexist* (when particular perspectives, even in the same topic area, have no real point of contact: they neither conflict nor complement one another). Book 1 introduced the shorthand notion of the 'three Cs' to refer to these relationships between theories. In Book 2 we highlight areas where these interrelationships take particularly challenging forms. For example in Chapter 2, the cognitive and social constructionist perspectives make conflicting assumptions about communication. The cognitive perspective embraces a view of language as the more or less successful transmission of meanings created by one individual to another individual. The social constructionist perspective views language as creating meaning *between* people as they negotiate their different goals and purposes. Similar conflicts will be apparent in Chapter 4 where psychologists and philosophers dispute whether a distinctive aspect of human consciousness exists at all, or is a 'trick' deriving from the way our language shapes our conceptual thinking.

Sometimes the question of how perspectives relate to each other in terms of the 'three Cs' is open to debate. This offers *you* opportunities to consider the ways in which different perspectives interrelate. For example, in Chapter 5, the sociocultural perspective suggests that historically and culturally produced norms and expectations for cognitive development are key reasons for defining dyslexia as a 'problem'. In contrast, biological and cognitive perspectives assume that there are identifiable causes of this 'problem' at the levels of individual biology and information processing. Are these perspectives fundamentally opposed or is it possible to resolve their contradictions within a complementary framework? Throughout this book it is important to think about whether particular perspectives can do no more than coexist because they make no shared assumptions about the phenomena under consideration.

One challenging issue which may occur to you is how such a diversity of perspectives can all fall within the subject area of psychology. This is perhaps most apparent in relation to the diversity of methods used by different perspectives. In Methods Booklet 1 you encountered both subjective and objective approaches to methodology, a discussion of the philosophical assumptions of each approach, and of the particular methods favoured. As you read about the very different types of research conducted from different perspectives, you might begin to wonder how such striking differences in what is accepted as a legitimate means of investigation and valid evidence can prevail within one subject area. For example, in Chapter 4, you will be introduced to a key perspective on consciousness from the discipline area of philosophy, and to methodologies that also originate in that discipline. These are quite different to the cognitive and neuropsychological perspectives that have been developed within mainstream psychology and to their methods of producing evidence. This diversity is a key feature of psychology in the twenty-first century as the boundaries of psychology shift and change to encompass new methods and perspectives. It is this dynamism that helps to make psychology a vibrant, exciting discipline. We hope that you enjoy learning about approaches which reflect this diversity as you work through this book.

Meeting the challenge

Below are summaries of key features of chapters in this book. The summaries focus on the perspectives with which you should already be familiar. You will encounter new approaches and concepts in this book which will build on those from Book 1. You may therefore wish to add your own notes and observations to these summaries.

Chapter 1
Lifespan development

Perspectives
- The evolutionary perspective informs the notion that development fulfils adaptive functions for the species.
- Cognitive and psychometric perspectives inform studies of intellectual functioning in later life.
- The psychoanalytic perspective underpins attachment theory.
- The humanistic perspective underpins Erickson's theory.
- The sociocultural perspective informs work on friendship and collaborative learning.

Themes
The chapter focuses on the theme of fixity and change, and the extent to which human beings are determined by their early developmental experiences, or have autonomy and the capacity for change. It also considers how, and in which areas, development continues over the lifespan, and what may be gained rather than lost in older age. The chapter explores the issue of the interaction in development between biology, cognition, the environment and physiology through experience and learning, and how the balance may shift throughout the human lifespan.

Chapter 2
Language and meaning

Perspectives
- The evolutionary perspective informs theories of the human species-specific development of language.
- The cognitive perspective underpins theories of how language is processed and understood by communicating individuals.
- The social constructionist perspective underpins discursive psychological theories of meaning as emerging from context and interaction.

Themes
The chapter looks at whether language is a specific form of communication that distinguishes human beings from other animals. It examines what form that distinctiveness takes and how it might have come about. Part of the discussion of that distinctiveness concerns the place of rules and operations within language, and whether what distinguishes language from other forms of animal communication is its ability to create highly developed social interaction. It also focuses on the place of language in relation to cognition, the creation of meaning, and the debate about the relationship between language as reflecting or creating our perception and understanding of the world.

Chapter 3
The psychology of sex and gender

Perspectives
- The biological perspective offers theories of the relationship between genetic and physiological aspects of sex, and their implications for gender.
- The evolutionary perspective underpins theories that sexual behaviour and sexual partner choice are determined by behaviours and dispositions that have been selected for in evolutionary history.
- The psychoanalytic perspective underpins theories that the earliest relationships with parents and other significant individuals determine progression through a series of psychosexual stages and consequent sex and pleasure seeking behaviours.
- The social constructionist perspective underpins theories that the construction of meaning through language and social practices has produced current gender-differentiated patterns of behaviour, cognition and emotional response.

Themes
The central debate of the chapter is around the terms 'sex' and 'gender': what the different perspectives construe those terms to mean and the differing priority they give to each term in explaining patterns of difference between men and women, boys and girls. Each perspective presents its own account with little evaluative comment or critique from other perspectives. The chapter raises issues and debates relevant to comparing and evaluating the four perspectives.

Chapter 4
Consciousness

Perspectives

- The cognitive perspective informs theories of the information processing role of consciousness in providing distinctive features of human experience.
- The biological perspective informs theories of the production of consciousness by the brain and brain processes.
- The philosophical perspective underpins theories about the nature of different dimensions of consciousness, and whether phenomenal consciousness exists at all.

Themes

A central theme of the chapter is about the 'slipperiness' of the more complex topics of psychology. The psychological study of consciousness is dominated by the issue of what exactly the phenomenon of consciousness is, and of how different perspectives articulate or interrelate in terms of the 'three Cs'. Crucial to this debate in relation to consciousness is the contribution of different levels of analysis to overall understanding.

Chapter 5
'Normal' development? The case of dyslexia

Perspectives
- The psychometric perspective underpins theories of how dyslexia is identified through measurement.
- The cognitive perspective underpins theories of what kinds of differences or difficulties in processing information might account for behavioural symptoms of dyslexia.
- The biological perspective underpins theories of difference in neuropsychological organization and response which are related to dyslexia.
- The sociocultural perspective highlights the theoretical importance of social, historical and cultural contexts.

Themes
The central theme of the chapter concerns different notions of normality, abnormality and disorder which psychology has helped to generate and sustain. The nature of dyslexia as a phenomenon is presented as a point of difference and debate between different perspectives, and one in which notions of abnormal/atypical functioning play a key role. Within this chapter as with the previous chapter on consciousness issues of the priority and importance of insider or outsider perspectives and of levels of analysis are an important part of the debate about dyslexia.

Some of these topics may have personal relevance to you as a student. In a study of Open University (OU) psychology graduates, many spoke of attaining long cherished goals for intellectual and personal development, of challenging expectations of them based on traditional sex roles or disabilities, or of achieving heightened consciousness of self and others as a result of acquiring the language and concepts of psychology (Barrett *et al.*, 1999). You will undoubtedly encounter material that challenges you to think about your own life history and the ways you view the world. We hope that it will enable you to reflect creatively on what you think, experience and do in your personal life. In bringing that reflection to bear in evaluating the academic subject matter of psychology, we hope that you will begin to formulate your own challenging psychological issues.

Reference

Barrett, C., Roth, I., Barnes, P. and Woodley, A. (1999) 'The aspirations and achievements of Open University psychology graduates and diplomates', Open University Working Paper.

Lifespan development

Clare Wood, Karen Littleton and John Oates

Contents

Aims

This chapter aims to:

- discuss the role of peer relations in social and cognitive development
- introduce the notion of 'attachment' as one explanatory device for understanding human relationships
- discuss evidence for psychological development throughout the lifespan
- describe and contrast different perspectives and theoretical approaches to human development.

1   Themes in lifespan development

Lifespan psychology, also referred to as developmental psychology, is concerned with the way our psychological characteristics change and develop throughout life, from conception to old age. This includes:

- how our personality develops
- how we learn to interact with others
- how our cognitive capacities change as we mature
- how changes in our biology can affect us psychologically, for example during puberty.

Developmental psychology encompasses a wide variety of the psychological perspectives that you have studied in the first course book (*Mapping Psychology*) and examines the way they interact. For example, as we mature biologically this can influence our cognitive and social development; our social development influences our cognitive and self-development, and so on. In other words, a developmental change in just one aspect of our psychology will have an impact on some or all of the others.

The idea that psychological changes occur during adulthood has not always been addressed by developmental psychology. For a long time it was primarily concerned with the changes that occur during childhood, with some theories suggesting (by omission) that adulthood was a time of psychological stability – the 'product' of developmental processes – until old age, when the trend turned towards psychological decline. Evidence now suggests that these ideas are not necessarily sound. This is why some psychologists prefer the term 'lifespan psychology', which indicates that we no longer accept such assumptions.

This chapter will introduce you to key ideas and research areas from within lifespan psychology. This first section will revisit the psychological perspectives that you encountered in the first course book and show how discussions of human development are influenced by a variety of perspectives. One theme that emerges from such discussions is the important influence that our relationships with others have on our psychological development. To illustrate this point, we have selected research and ideas relating to two important sources of interpersonal influence: our peers and our parents. Section 2 examines sibling and peer relationships and how they contribute to our development. Section 3 introduces you to the concept of 'attachment' and the way our early relationships with our parents may affect the way we interact as adults with others and with our own children. A second theme addressed by this chapter is that of change throughout the lifespan. This includes a re-evaluation of the idea that adulthood is the expression of all that we have acquired during childhood and that ageing in adulthood equals deterioration. In Section 4 we will present material that has begun to address the relative lack of research into adult development. The chapter concludes with an explanation of the historical development of lifespan psychology and how ideas from different perspectives have contributed to this area of psychology.

1.1 Thinking about perspectives

In the first course book you looked at various psychological perspectives to understand how different psychologists might answer key questions that occur in everyday contexts. The key perspectives in psychology identified in the first course book were:

- behaviourism
- biological psychology (including neuropsychology)
- cognitive psychology
- evolutionary psychology
- experimental social psychology
- humanistic psychology
- psychoanalytic psychology
- psychometrics
- social constructionism.

As you can see from this list, when we talk about psychological perspectives we are referring to different 'styles' of psychological explanation. They also tend to have a historical tradition that underpins their ideas and methods. It is easy to think of these perspectives as being in opposition to each other. Certainly there are some perspectives that do have some conflicting ideas, such as behaviourism and cognitive psychology. However ideas from different perspectives are often complementary, and can overlap. For example, both biological and cognitive psychologists try to explain memory processes. Their methods and explanations differ, but they often draw on research from each other's perspective in formulating their theories (see Chapter 8 in the first course book).

Developmental psychology is a good example of a psychological perspective that draws heavily on other psychological perspectives. This is because one of the key ideas in lifespan psychology is that human development is the result of *multiple influences* including individual psychological and physiological differences (**internal influences**), as well as historical and cultural factors (**external influences**). In order to acknowledge these multiple influences it is necessary to draw on a variety of psychological perspectives in our discussions of development throughout the lifespan. As you will see in Section 5, approaches to developmental psychology have been informed by evolutionary theory (Darwin in particular) as well as biological, psychodynamic, psychometric, social and cognitive perspectives.

Internal influences
Potential influences on development that are part of the individual, such as physical or psychological variables.

External influences
Potential influences on development that are not part of the individual, such as the immediate context, culture or history.

1.1 Revisiting the 'three Cs'

One of the things that you will notice about this course book is that it is impossible to give an account of the topics in each chapter without drawing on two or more psychological perspectives. The commentaries in the first course book highlighted the fact that when we consider two or more perspectives we need to reflect on the 'three Cs': whether they are *complementary, coexisting or conflicting*. Thi type of reflection will help you to develop your own critical awareness of psychology when you write your assignments. Whenever you start to learn about a new topic in psychology, or begin to write an assignment about that topic, do the following:

- explicitly acknowledge which perspectives have relevance to the topic area
- identify areas of commonality and compatibility between ideas, methods and findings relevant to that topic
- acknowledge any areas of conflict, and show that you understand why these conflicts are difficult to resolve
- offer an evaluation of which perspectives provide the most compelling explanations to you, as a student of psychology.

You can see that psychology does not present a neat, coherent picture in which all ideas from all perspectives are seen as valid and complementary. Accounts of psychology often highlight longstanding conflicts in areas of research and as a student it is important that you understand them, are aware of the research that the ideas are based on, and can begin to evaluate the nature of the evidence presented to you.

1.2 Thinking about relationships

We will now begin by reflecting in a very simple way on one of the themes of the chapter: the importance of relationships in human development. Modern developmental psychology embraces the idea that we are able to shape our own personal development, while acknowledging that development occurs within, and is therefore subject to the influence of different social and cultural contexts. Our relationships with others are an important social context for development.

Activity 1.1

Take a moment to consider the ways that a close friend and one of your parents have influenced your development. How do you think they influenced you? In which of the following aspects have you been most influenced?

- personality
- cognitive development
- social development
- biological development
- other

At first, you may find it difficult to say whether you have been influenced in any of these ways. Or you may find that there are some areas where your parents influenced you more than your friends. Similarly, you may feel that your friendships helped you to develop in ways that your relationship with your parents did not. However, how do you know that your parents and friends have influenced you? What evidence are you drawing on? How would you go about 'testing' such claims? These are exactly the questions that developmental psychologists working in this area are faced with. This chapter will take you through some theories that make claims about the influence of siblings, parents and friends on social and cognitive development, and describe some of the evidence that supports them.

1.3 Thinking about adulthood

The other theme of the chapter is a reflection on some of the assumptions that psychologists have made about adulthood. One assumption is that adulthood is the product of childhood – that, psychologically at least, we do not really change a great deal: our mental capabilities, our personalities, our interpersonal style, and so on are all 'fixed' by the time we are adults. The only scope for change in adulthood is assumed to be negative, such as the loss of memory.

Activity 1.2

Take a few moments to reflect on whether you agree with the types of claims made above. Thinking about yourself, to what extent would you say that the person you are today reflects the experiences that you had as a child? Can you think of any ways that you have developed, either positively or negatively, during your adult years?

Comment

Many people can think of connections between their experiences as a child and aspects of themselves as adults. This is a notion that has been popularized in Western cultures over the last 100 years or so, originally due to the ideas of Sigmund Freud. You will recall that Freud's theory suggests that the (psychosexual) experiences we have as children impact on the development of our adult personalities. However, you may have also been able to think of ways that you have developed during your adult years. You may have come up with quite a long list of ways that you have developed positively during adulthood, perhaps in response to major changes in circumstance, such as entering or leaving a committed relationship, parenthood, becoming a student, taking a new job or acquiring a new friendship. At the same time you may have noted that some of your adult attempts at learning seem quite effortful when compared to those of a child (e.g. learning about a computer!). You may also find it quite difficult to say for certain when adulthood really began for you, as often it is culturally, rather than chronologically, defined (e.g. when you get your first job or leave home).

While development in childhood is dramatic and significant, positive psychological change continues throughout our adult lives, although we know relatively little about the processes involved. The notion of when adulthood begins is a complex one. We will return to these issues in Section 4. We will begin by looking at research that has attempted to explain how our relationships with our siblings and peers can impact on our psychological development, both in childhood and in adulthood. We will consider some ideas relating to the influence of our parents in Section 3. As you read on, keep notes on what psychological perspectives are being reflected in the research described to you.

Summary Section 1

- Lifespan psychology acknowledges and draws on multiple psychological perspectives.
- Development during the lifespan is the result of many interacting influences, both internal and external.
- One important influence on our development throughout the lifespan is the relationships we have with others.
- For a long time the idea that we continue to develop psychologically during adulthood was neglected.

2   Sibling and peer relationships

In this section we focus on the importance of sibling and peer relationships for development across the lifespan. First however, it is helpful to understand the distinction that is often made between 'horizontal' and 'vertical' relationships.

2.1 Horizontal and vertical relationships

Horizontal relationship
A relationship between people of equal status and/or power.

Reciprocity
Refers to the principle of 'give and take' – that if one person 'gives' in some way, there will be a similar gesture made by the recipient at some point.

Vertical relationship
A relationship which involves one person who has more knowledge or power than the other person in the relationship.

A **horizontal relationship** is characterized by **reciprocity** and egalitarian interactions and expectations. This is because such relationships are formed between individuals with similar knowledge or social power. A typical example of a horizontal relationship would be a friendship between peers of the same age.

A **vertical relationship** involves an attachment to someone who has greater knowledge or social power – a typical example is a child's relationship with a parent or a teacher. The interactions on which a vertical relationship is based are characterized by the *complementarity* of roles such as a child asking for help and a teacher offering it. Whilst the roles of the people involved are inextricably interwoven, the behaviour patterns demonstrated by each one differ markedly.

The distinction between horizontal and vertical relationships is not an absolute one. As Schaffer (1996) notes, a relationship with an older sibling may contain both complementary and reciprocal elements. Occasionally there are also circumstances when a relationship with a peer or peers can assume some of the functions more typically associated with an adult–child relationship (Freud and Dann, 1951). However, the distinction between horizontal and vertical relationships is a useful one as it captures the essence of two different types of relationship, each of which contributes to the development of the individual. Vertical relationships provide the child with protection and security, and enable the child to gain knowledge and acquire skills (Schaffer, 1996). But horizontal relationships also represent important contexts for development and learning and their significance should not be underestimated. In the sub-sections that follow we will illustrate the significance of sibling and peer relationships by drawing on research which highlights their importance for the development of social and cultural understanding, and a sense of self. We will also consider the opportunities for learning afforded by working with a peer.

2.2 Living together, playing together

As Schaffer (1996) notes, siblings have a significant influence on each other, which should not be underestimated. They spend substantial amounts of time in each other's company, watching each other interacting with other people and sharing experiences. Moreover, as any parent will testify, their relationship with each other is often highly emotionally charged. Observational studies of siblings (e.g. Abramovitch, Corter, Pepler and Stanthorpe, 1986) have revealed that their interactions are diverse and multi-faceted. Whilst there is certainly evidence of 'sibling rivalry', there is more to sibling interactions than competition and conflict. In most cases their interactions can be characterized as being positive, with clear evidence of cooperation, sharing, support and assistance.

Observations such as these, which highlight the complexity of sibling interactions, emphasize the need to understand the developmental significance of sibling relationships. Sibling relationships are notably different from the parent–child relationship. Work focusing on children's conversations throws this into stark relief. Caretaking activities represent an important topic of conversation when the child is interacting with the mother. In contrast, when a sibling is the partner, humour and playfulness predominate. Furthermore, while mothers have a tendency to focus on the child's feelings during their interactions, siblings typically emphasise their own (Brown and Dunn, 1992). As Schaffer explains:

> *Each conversational partner ... fulfills a different function: in one case supporting the child's attempts to understand and come to terms with his or her own feelings; in the other drawing the child's attention to another individual's inner life.*
>
> *(Schaffer, 1996, p.265)*

Judy Dunn's work also emphasizes the distinctive developmental contribution made by sibling interactions. Her naturalistic observational studies revealed that issues of fairness and justice are paramount and are heatedly discussed, contested and debated between siblings (Dunn, 1988). It is also evident that joint play brings with it the need to construct shared meaning and establish collective goals in accordance with mutually negotiated rules. Schaffer summarises the distinctiveness of sibling relationships as follows:

> *What does distinguish sibling relationships in general is that they are characterized by a mixture of* complementary *and* reciprocal *features ... Complementary features are most evident in the parent-child relationship, where the older individual plays a role that is different from but interrelated with that of the younger one. Reciprocal features are found in peer interaction: both individuals play similar, matching parts. Among siblings there is a difference in knowledge and power, yet that difference is not so great that the two children cannot sometimes play and talk together on the same level. It is this combination of features that makes sibling relationships potentially so influential: on the one hand the older child can act as teacher, guide and model to the younger; on the other hand, however, both children share interest and competence to a sufficient degree to tackle jointly the task of social understanding.*
>
> *(Schaffer, 1996, pp. 266–7).*

The developmental significance of playfulness and play between children has been discussed by many psychologists, and we will turn to this next.

2.3 Pretend play and development

Activity 1.3

Pretend play
Refers to play that involves the use of imagination where a person 'pretends' to be someone or something else, or uses an object as something else for the purposes of play.

If you are able to, observe two or three young children engaged in **pretend play** together. Pay particular attention to what is said and how it is said. What strikes you about the children's talk and joint activity?

As adults we are often captivated by the richness and diversity of young children's social pretend play. However, we usually take the occurrence of such play for granted and do not consider its function in the development of social and cultural understanding. Neither do we fully appreciate the skill with which even very young children negotiate shared understanding and meaning while engaged in pretend play together.

Göncü (1999) argues that social pretend play is a complex activity that involves negotiating shared meaning on different planes simultaneously. Göncü maintains that children engage in social pretend play to share and explore emotionally significant experiences with their peers. Göncü notes that while successfully establishing a mutual pretend focus is necessary, it is not a sufficient condition for social pretend play:

> *It also must be communicated that a pretend message is to be interpreted as such, rather than a literal message. Bateson (1955) refers to such communication as metacommunication ... The metacommunication*

indicates the changing form of interaction from play to non-play, and provides ... an interpretative frame for the activity. Used effectively this metacommunication conveys a desire to have fun by playing with representations.

(Göncü, 1999, p.124)

To understand both the complexity of pretend play and what is meant by metacommunication consider the extract of a video transcript reproduced below. This is an edited sequence of young children in a London nursery playing 'doctors and patients'. Girl 1 is the 'doctor' and Girl 2 is the 'patient'.

(1) Girl 1: Here's a drink of water

(2) Girl 2: OK, there – drink it. I got lots of ... on my laster band [elastic band?]

(3)   [To third child]   Oh, don't do that to me

(4) Girl 1: Don't do it to the doctor. Go huh huh huh huh

(5) Girl 2: You're hurting its cold

(6) Girl 1: In your ears

(7) Girl 3: My baby's not very well

(8) Girl 2: OK

(9) Girl 3: Yeah, I think he's got spots. Know what? My baby's got spots

(10) Girl 1: Wait

(11) Girl 2: That's not for your tummy. Is that for your tummy?

(12) Girl 1: No what's it for?

(13) Girl 2: It's for going like this – this

(14) Girl 1: Yeah – and what do you have to do like that? And what do you have to do like that?

(15) Girl 2: Look like that

(16) Girl 1: No

(17) Girl 2: OK, like that, have that one, that's much better. What's that for?

(18) Girl 1: Snapping your tummy

(19) Girl 2: Snapping your tummy – ouch, it's hurting, that hurts

(20) Girl 1: And now, so you can breathe

(21) Girl 2: Not my mouth!

(22) Girl 1: What do you have to do then?

Source: Faulkner *et al.*, p.48

Göncü would argue that the girls in this extract are able to establish a joint theme based on past experience (and presumably past play), where both have implicit knowledge of appropriate roles and narratives. But more than this, they must also negotiate their non-play relationship as friends in a nursery, surrounded by other children and adults, within the framework of daily routines and expectations about what is and what is not acceptable behaviour. The extraordinary feature of pretend play is the capacity of very young children to switch apparently effortlessly from one level of representation and mode of communication to another.

At the start of the sequence, the two girls have already established a joint pretend focus and themes for their play (Line 1). There is a brief negotiation with a boy (also playing a doctor) (Line 3), and shortly afterwards Girl 3 tries to initiate an interaction within the play theme (Line 7). She offers an appropriate entry bid: 'My baby's not very well'. Girl 2 (the patient) acknowledges Girl 3's overture, saying 'OK' (Line 8), but neither Girl 1 nor Girl 2 encourages Girl 3 to join in. At line 11, there is a shift in the joint focus of the girls' attention from play to non-play signalled by the patient's comment: 'that's not for your tummy', referring to her friend's 'misuse' of a toy syringe. Between lines 11 and 16 the children are actually negotiating what a toy syringe is used for. This continues to line 17, where Girl 2 reverts to her 'patient' role.

In short, the children shift from playing out an asymmetrical relationship (dominant doctor/passive patient) to negotiating within their symmetrical friendship relationship (discussing how to use a syringe). It is important to note the subtlety of the metacommunicative signals between play and non-play. The shift (at 11) is most clearly signalled by the 'patient's' challenge to the 'doctor' – 'That's not for your tummy'. Perhaps her voice tone shifts a little along with her facial expression. But in circumstances like this it is often difficult for a researcher to pinpoint exactly which cues the children are using. This is in itself interesting, as it draws attention to the importance of taking account of the shared play history of play partners, both separately and as a pair – as a general rule, the more they share in common, the less they will need to make their metacommunication explicit.

Boundary markers of metacommunication in children's play are sometimes made much more explicit for example, at transition points, at the beginnings and ends of play, and especially if a child is no longer sure the game is fun. Note there is a hint of ambiguity when Girl 2 comments on the 'snapping' of the syringe on her skin 'ouch its hurting, that hurts' (19). Is she expressing pain within the communicative frame of 'play' or 'non-play'?

Such complex interactions in social pretend play can be seen in children as young as 18 months and it is through play that children begin to explore role relationships at a 'pretend' level. This enables them to acquire social skills, perspectives and cultural roles that are well in advance of their actual abilities:

In play a child always behaves beyond his average age, above his daily behaviour; in play it is as though he were a head taller than himself. As in the focus of a magnifying glass, play contains all developmental tendencies in a condensed form and is itself a major source of development.

(Vygotsky, 1978, p.102)

In most play situations, children are not bound by the normal rules of interaction, but they experiment with them. In their pretend world, the meanings of words, objects and actions are not strictly defined as they are in the 'real' world. Cardboard boxes can symbolise ships or cars, rugs can be islands and children can become adults or animals. Meanings, rituals and roles are more important than reality (Shotter, 1974). This illustrates how the capacity to function symbolically is important developmentally and we see how pretend play allows children to learn about roles and interaction by experimenting with them. What is done in a conscious, deliberate and exaggerated form in play is often taken for granted in real life.

A good example of this was given by Vygotsky. As reported by Damon (1983), Vygotsky observed two young sisters aged five and seven years who decided to play at being sisters. As they did so, their behaviour changed dramatically from their normal sisterly conduct. For example, it became stylised and self-conscious as they acted out stereotypes of sisterhood roles by dressing alike and always holding hands. Vygotsky commented that the 'vital difference in play is that the child in playing tried to be a sister' (Damon, 1983, p.107). According to Vygotsky, instead of behaving as real sisters they are intending to be sisters and are conscious of each other's aims:

In life the child behaves without thinking that she is her sister's sister ... except perhaps in those cases where her mother says 'Give in to her'. In the game of sisters playing at 'sisters', however, they are both concerned with displaying their sisterhood; the fact that the two sisters decided to play sisters makes them both acquire rules of behaviour ... only actions which will fit these rules are acceptable to the play situation.

(Vygotsky, 1933 quoted in Damon, 1983, p.107)

Vygotsky argues that play affords children unique opportunities to manipulate and test out rules of social interaction. He also makes the important point that in play, children are able to substitute symbols for the real world. When a box is used as a ship, it is a symbol for the ship. In the same way, the exaggerated sisterly behaviour is a symbol for real sisterly behaviour. Symbols are in fact representations of what is going on in the real world. It is only through the shared meanings of symbols that concepts about the self, personal roles and behaviour of others can develop. Language provides the most potent symbols, as we shall see in the next chapter.

2.4 'Others' and the development of self-concept

Through increasingly complex social relations children gain awareness of other people's points of view. They learn that these might be different to their own and must be taken into account in planning their own course of action. By imitating the role of adults during their pretend games, children acquire the ability to see objects, other people and themselves from a different perspective. Thus they become more socially aware and also begin to form and clarify their own self-concepts. So, pretend play is also one of the principle means through which children can explore their sense of self in relation to others. Play allows children to imagine themselves as another, thereby clarifying or consolidating aspects of the self which are either similar to or different from other people. It is through this process that children gain a sense of their own unique distinctive identity and develop a coherent sense of self (Fein, 1991). (You will remember that the topic of identities and diversity was discussed in detail in Chapter 1 of the first course book.)

Symbolic interactionism
A theoretical approach which emphasizes the significance of social interaction and the use of 'symbols' within these interactions.

The idea that self-concept develops through social experience and social interaction is a position broadly based on **symbolic interactionism**, which stresses the importance of social interaction in human life and of symbols or meanings that exist between people in their interactions. Symbolic interactionism views the development of the self as inextricably bound up with the development of the person as a social being.

According to the symbolic interactionists, the self-concept develops through the internalisation of interactions with parents, siblings, teachers and peers. So whilst peer interaction is not the only form of social interaction important for the development of the self, sibling and peer interactions nevertheless represent an important context for development. They are part of the rich and complex social world in which the child participates. To give you a flavour of the symbolic interactionist stance, the ideas of one of its key proponents, George Herbert Mead, are presented in Box 1.2.

I
A theoretical construct which refers to the conscious, decision-making part of a person's self-concept.

Me
A theoretical construct which refers to knowledge about oneself, and is suggested to be another part of the self-concept which can reflect the views of others.

1.2 Mead on 'Self'

George Herbert Mead (1934), following James (1892), saw the self as being divided into two parts: the '**I**' and the '**me**'. The 'me' consists of what can be known about the self, such as physical descriptions of ones own body, clothes, possessions, one's manner of thinking, moral and religious values, roles, social identity, reputation and behaviour ('self as object'). The importance placed on these aspects is influenced by other people's attitudes. Thus we can suggest that the influence of the social context upon the self-concept is felt mainly on the 'me' part of the self-concept.

The 'I' is the active process of experiencing. The 'I' represents the basic capacity for conscious awareness. This part of the self-concept enables individuals to be free from relying absolutely on other's views for their sense of self. Whilst the 'me' represents the perceived attitudes and perspectives of other people, the 'I' is free to reject or change these views. The 'I' is the 'self as subject', the part that acts and reacts to circumstances creatively and spontaneously.

Mead believed that we experience and reflect on ourselves in the same way that we experience and reflect on other people around us. In order to achieve this however, we have to be able to role-take, to put ourselves 'in the role of' the other person, to anticipate their responses, imagine how we appear to them and adjust our responses to come into line with theirs.

Taking the role of the other in interaction is not an easy task, and we gradually master it throughout life. People vary in their capacity to do this and some people never master it. In particular, many people with autism (see Chapter 5 in the third course book, *Applying Psychology*) seem unable to understand any point of view different from their own. Mead argued that it is not until we can gain an understanding of other's reactions to ourselves that we can reach an understanding of ourselves. He did not believe that chronological age was of paramount importance in determining the ability to take the role of other. Instead, Mead stressed that social meaning arose in *interactions with other people*. Thus a very young child who had experience in many varied interactions might show greater role-taking ability than an older but less experienced person.

Internalising the 'generalized other' into the 'me' of the self-concept allows children to participate competently in social interaction. This early development is called primary socialization. Mead also suggests that adults continue to adapt to new roles and new relationships as they encounter them throughout their lives in what he calls secondary socialisation. New perspectives on the self are encountered through relationships with other people and this changes the self by adding to and changing the 'me'. Thus the self is not fixed and continues to evolve and change throughout our adult lives as different reflections of and views on the self are encountered.

What counts as a developmental theory? Mead's approach offers a general theoretical perspective on the central function of social role-taking in the development of the self. But Mead's concept of what is meant by role-taking is abstract and ill-defined, and details of the processes by which such role-taking abilities might develop are unspecified. In practice, the social and cognitive skills implied by the capacity to take another person's point of view are exceedingly complex, and a 'developmental theory' which fails to address this complexity is, at best, incomplete. A possible consequence is that Mead's theory over-emphasizes the importance of role-taking as the main route to self-

development. As we shall see in a later chapter, children with autism have great difficulty in 'taking the role of another', and while this may mean that they have a different sense of self, it does not follow that they have none. In summary, Mead's theory has been useful to more recent researchers in developing ideas and theories which have then been investigated or explored through empirical research (see Selman, 1980) but it has not been itself the basis of empirical investigation. Its main value is as a broad conceptual framework, rather than as a set of specific claims about the developmental process.

We can summarize Mead's view on the related development of self and of perspective taking as follows:

- Through their use of language, their games and their play, young children begin to take the perspective of other persons towards themselves, and in doing so, become capable of reflecting on themselves.
- As a result of the process of taking the role of the other, the reactions of a 'generalized other' are internalised into the 'me' aspect of an individual's self-concept to allow him or her to make comparisons and judgements about how other people would react, even when no other people are actually present.

Another important result of the ability to take the role of the other is that individuals are able to find agreement between the meanings that they and others place on the various actions and events, in other words, they establish shared meanings. For Mead human society rests upon shared meanings between people, upon shared understandings about each others' intentions and upon being able to interpret each other's behaviour. To be a social being, we must therefore be capable of putting ourselves in the position of the other person. To understand their meanings we have to be able to imagine how they might react to us. We acquire a sense of self by being able to see ourselves from the perspective of another person. By being able to anticipate the interpretation that the other will place on something, the individual can adjust his or her behaviour to ensure that the intended meaning is conveyed, and that communication is effective. This is what Mead meant by symbolic dialogue, which is, in his view, the basis of both social interaction and personal identity.

2.5 Working together

So far we have talked about horizontal relationships as important contexts for *social development.* However, collaborative interaction between peers can also constitute an important context for cognitive development and learning.

The influential developmental psychologist Jean Piaget saw children as actively constructing their own understanding and identified peer interaction as being particularly important for progress (Piaget, 1932). According to Piaget, the young child cannot treat adults' ideas on their own merits because of the differences of status involved. However, disagreements with other children serve to highlight alternatives to the child's own point of view much more effectively. The alternatives can be considered 'on equal terms' and since the resulting conflicts of opinion demand resolution, the children involved are effectively prompted towards higher level solutions which incorporate the partial insights reflected in their varying initial positions.

Inspired by Piaget's ideas, Doise and Mugny (1984) and Perret-Clermont (1980) undertook studies which demonstrated that individual progress in understanding could be fostered by **socio-cognitive conflict**; that is, exposure to the conflicting ideas of peers during paired or small group problem solving. The typical design adopted in their studies involved individual pre-tests and post-tests, separated by a period of practice on a task undertaken either individually (the 'control' condition) or in pairs or groups (the 'experimental' condition). A recurrent finding was that children who had the chance to work on the task with others made greater individual progress at post-test than those who had not.

Socio-cognitive conflict
The experience of being aware of conflicting ideas held by peers, which forces a re-examination of one's own understanding of that idea.

Activity 1.4

Work by Doise and Mugny (1984) and Perret-Clermont (1988) suggests that exposure to conflicting perspectives is important for cognitive development. Can you think of any other explanations for why working with a peer might be beneficial?

Comment

In thinking about this you may well have remembered some of the work discussed as part of the socio-cultural perspective on learning in Chapter 3 of *Mapping Psychology*. That work suggested that there is a key role for collaborative as well as conflictive processes. The emphasis was on the negotiation of meaning and processes of joint construction of understanding. We saw how primary school children could work together jointly to construct understanding and knowledge. Moreover, we saw how, by exploring each other's ideas, the children in Mercer's study were able to create a new collective outcome, such that personal meanings and understandings were 'created, negotiated and enriched within interpersonal exchanges' (Crook, 1999, p.369). These exchanges were situated in the particular institutional context of the school. The group, rather than the individual, was the focus of analysis, and the emphasis was placed on the socially constructed properties of interaction, rather than, as here, on individual performance on pre- and post-tests.

Whilst there is compelling evidence to suggest that in some circumstances working with peers can be beneficial, there are a number of factors which impact on the productivity of interaction. These involve:

- the age of the learners
- the difficulty of the task
- personality of the learners
- the level of interpersonal acquaintance.

These factors are likely to interact in complex ways. Consider for example, the issue of friendship. To date there is little consistent evidence concerning the impact of friendship on the processes and outcomes of collaborative work. For example, Berndt, Perry and Miller (1988) found no difference in the cognitive gains made by friends and non-friends working together, while Azmitia and Montgomery (1993) did find benefits for 'friendship pairs' as compared with 'acquaintance pairs' on at least some of the scientific reasoning tasks they studied. Following a review of a number of studies addressing the issue of friendship, Azmitia concludes that the nature of the task is crucial and its 'difficulty may mediate differences in the processes and outcomes of the collaborations of friends and acquaintances' (Azmitia, 1996, p.151). In particular, she notes that those studies which appear to lend support for the cognitive benefit of working with a friend had employed particularly challenging tasks or tasks which drew heavily on so called 'meta-cognitive skills' involving activities such as planning, monitoring and evaluating evidence. Thus, peer interaction is not an educational panacea and careful thought needs to be given to how best to support effective group-work.

In addition to evidence suggesting that children can benefit from peer interaction, there is increasing evidence to suggest that adults also benefit from opportunities to work collaboratively on problems and learning tasks (see Joiner, Littleton, Faulkner and Miell, 2000) and there is much ongoing work considering how we can optimize and resource such collaborations.

1.3 The effect of revision materials on students' discussions

If you think back to Chapter 3 of the first course book, you will remember the idea that human cognitive activity is mediated by tools and artefacts. The implication is that the nature of the tools and artifacts provided impact on the ways in which learners engage with a task. A study by Crook (2000) provides a striking demonstration of this. Crook studied undergraduate students revising for a finals examination on a particular lecture course. These students were invited to form pairs in order to take part in some informal revision sessions and they were assigned to one of two different conditions. In the first condition the students engaged in discussion of their own personal notes from lectures. In the second, the students were provided with a set of cross-referenced web pages constructed from the lecturer's own notes for these sessions. The students clearly had the same purpose, which was to revise for the examination and were oriented to the same syllabus. They had similar resources available to them – textual notes on the lecture course. However, Crook found that the interactions that occurred in the two sessions were distinctively different. Those students who were asked to talk around their own notes engaged in more exploratory and creative talk in which they oriented towards key disciplinary themes. Talk around the web-notes was characterized by discussions of 'what was expected' and comparisons within the pair regarding what each of them knew. The web-notes seem to invite the learners to learn them, as they represent the lecturer's expectations. The personal notes, however, invite a more exploratory and open-ended form of use.

Crook did not go on to report how well these two groups did in the subsequent examination. Nevertheless, these sorts of findings highlight the crucial need to understand the role of tools and artefacts in shaping and supporting joint activity.

A note on culture and society

The account of horizontal and vertical relationships developed in this section has not addressed the issue of whether the nature and extent of sibling and peer relationships are influenced by the specific social and cultural contexts within which a child is developing. This is a significant omission as there is evidence to suggest that the time spent in the company of parents, siblings, peers, grandparents and friends, for example, varies from culture to culture (Schaffer, 1996). These observations remind us of the importance of not over-generalizing from patterns of relationship observed in a particular society at a particular historical moment in time, using particular methods. We must be careful not to turn descriptions of particular relationship patterns into prescriptions for healthy development. We need to develop an understanding of the processes of development that respects the plurality of psychologically adequate pathways from infancy to maturity.

One influential topic area that has developed within developmental psychology and illustrates the need for this kind of sensitivity is known as *attachment theory*. The theory offers an account of how our early relationships with our parents may impact on our relationships with others later in life. We will turn to this topic next and consider the contribution of a variety of perspectives to the theory, and evaluate the evidence it is based upon.

Summary Section 2

- Relationships with peers and siblings are important contexts for development and learning.
- Relationships with siblings and peers contribute to the development of social understanding and contribute to a developing sense of self.
- Opportunities for interaction with peers can promote learning.
- We must guard against turning descriptions of particular patterns of interactions into prescriptions for development.

3 Attachment and the development of the individual

A central issue in developmental psychology is whether our experiences during childhood – our vertical relationships with our parent figures (child–adult), in some way shape the patterns of our later, adult, horizontal relationships (adult–adult). It is perhaps easy to conclude from the research presented in Section 2 that children's peer relationships have some kind of primary importance in this respect. What role do parents play in influencing their children's development? Do they contribute at all? In *The Nurture Assumption*, Judith Rich Harris (1999) argues that parents do not influence their children in the way that has culturally been assumed and that it is peer groups that are the major influence in determining how children will grow up. This conclusion has been the source of much controversy. However, there are theories that suggest that vertical relationships during childhood have an equally significant impact on how we develop. In this section we will introduce you to **attachment theory** as an example of one such theory.

Attachment theory
Bowlby's theory that children have a drive to feel secure by forming an emotional bond with a primary care giver.

Continuities
Connections between experiences at one point in life and behaviour at some later time.

The study of human development seeks to explain influences on people as they develop in terms of 'internal' as well as 'external' factors. It also seeks to identify **continuities** – consistent connections between experiences at one point in life and behaviour at a later point. Given the complexity of such influences, it is unlikely that developmental psychology could ever be able to specify such continuities as absolute laws in the way some theories suggest, but rather that some connections will emerge as more valid and likely to occur than others.

What if it was possible to state with absolute certainty how early childhood experiences (with peers or adults) determine adult behaviour? What would this mean? Would it rule out the possibility of an individual making a difference to how their life turns out?

In some areas of psychological development it appears that there may be certain developmental pathways along which individuals are likely to travel. The key word here is 'likely'. Starting on a particular path does not absolutely guarantee that you will arrive at a particular destination, it just makes it more probable, and the further down a specific path you go, the greater this probability becomes. Such an approach is therefore not **deterministic** but rather, **probabilistic**.

Many lifespan psychologists find it helpful to think of development as a **transaction** between the individual and their environment, with each influencing the other and in turn affecting the developmental path followed. One only needs to think about how differently one might react to a crying and to a smiling baby to realise the power that a person has to affect what happens to them. This highlights the role that people can play in determining their own environments. This is one reason why the so-called nature–nurture distinction is a particularly problematic one in developmental psychology.

Deterministic
An approach that assumes that a particular outcome is fixed and inevitable.

Probabilistic
An approach that assumes that outcomes are more or less likely to occur.

Transaction
Refers to the idea that individuals affect their environments, that environments can affect individuals and that the combination of these influences affects development.

To make this point a little clearer consider the following example: babies vary in how responsive they are to external stimuli. In itself this is neither a desirable nor undesirable characteristic, and it is probably influenced by genetic factors. Yet the effect of this trait (responsiveness) on the baby's development depends in part on how it affects the baby's environment. First, imagine that a baby who is highly responsive to external stimuli is cared for by someone who interprets the baby's responsiveness as a sign of irritability or hypersensitivity. Next, imagine that the baby is cared for by someone who, in contrast, sees this responsiveness as a sign of engagement and liveliness. It is likely that each of these two carers will provide different environments, for example by controlling the level of exposure to external stimuli according to their belief about the cause of the baby's responsiveness. Thus, we can see in this example a genetic factor actually affecting the baby's environment, through (mediated by) the mother's reaction. Processes like this, which show how difficult it can be to talk about genes and environments as if they are separate, are usually called 'transactional' effects.

Intimate social relationships, such as mother–infant relations and romantic partnerships, are intrinsically bound up with how two people mutually affect each other. An increasingly important area of modern developmental psychology deals with issues surrounding the ways in which close relationships are formed and continue in early infancy along the way to adulthood and through the rest of the lifespan.

3.1 What is 'attachment'?

Attachment
A strong, ongoing emotional bond between two people.

Attachment is the concept used to describe relationships that are ongoing and involve emotional bonds. Attachment theory sets out to explore the nature of the different ways in which people can become attached to each other and the processes involved in the formation of these bonds. For most of us, the special relationships that we have with a small number of other people are very important to us. They may be with a partner, children, parents, close relations or friends. What singles out these special relationships is often a combination of a feeling that we mean something to these others and that they mean something to us. We usually think of these relationships as enduring over time. We expect them to continue even when we are not physically present, so that the relationship is ongoing. When we do meet again after an absence of a day, a week, or more, we expect to be able to 'pick up where we left off'. Indeed, we have many expectations of the particular others to whom we become attached; expectations of how they will behave towards us and how we will behave towards them. We tend to expect that their feelings towards us will stay much the same, as will our feelings for them. To use the language of psychology, these 'significant others' have become part of our mental life and contribute to our feelings of well-being and being valued. For many people, what they are is defined in a very real sense by their relationships with their significant others. But it is not just being able to think about 'the other' that is important for us; we also feel drawn to be with our significant others. In other words, we find it rewarding to spend time with them and we feel motivated to do so when we are apart. Using terms from attachment theory, we 'seek proximity' to them and can use them as a 'secure base'.

Of course, many people also have difficult relationships with others. It may be that we do not get on as well as we would like with our children or we feel that a friend has let us down in some way. Problems in relationships can trouble us and affect the way that we feel about ourselves. Often, when this happens, it can affect other aspects of our lives as well, for example our productivity at work. Perhaps the most frequent reason why people seek some form of psychological help, such as counselling or therapy, is that they are experiencing difficulties in their relationships with others. This shows that there is something which is central to our psychological well-being, that is to do with our ongoing connections with others. Attachment theory is an arena within which psychologists from a number of different backgrounds are seeking to explain this central aspect of human life and experience.

Attachment styles

There are two key assumptions in attachment research:

- individuals tend to have characteristic styles (or stances) in relationships that are reflected in the way they behave towards others
- these styles have their origins in peoples' previous relationships, most particularly in their first relationships, as infants with their caregivers.

Activity 1.5

The following is an adaptation of part of a 'love quiz' that was printed in the US newspaper *Rocky Mountain News* by two attachment researchers (Hazan and Shaver, 1987) to gather a large amount of data on people's attachment styles in romantic relationships:

These questions are concerned with your experiences in romantic love relationships. Take a moment to think about these experiences and answer the following questions with them in mind.

Read each of the three self-descriptions below (A, B, and C) and then place a checkmark next to the single alternative that best describes how you feel in romantic relationships, or is nearest to the way you feel. (Note: The terms 'close' and 'intimate' refer to psychological or emotional closeness, not necessarily to sexual intimacy.)

(A) I am somewhat uncomfortable being close to others; I find it difficult to trust them completely, difficult to allow myself to depend on them. I am nervous when anyone gets too close, and often, others want me to be more intimate than I feel comfortable being.

(B) I find it relatively easy to get close to others and am comfortable depending on them and having them depend on me. I don't worry about being abandoned or about someone getting too close to me.

(C) I find that others are reluctant to get as close as I would like. I often worry that my partner doesn't really love me or won't want to stay with me. I want to get very close to my partner, and this sometimes scares people away.

(Hazan and Shaver, 1987)

Comment

Although this is a very simple 'quiz' it illustrates what many attachment researchers believe to be characteristic of three different stances which people can take towards relationships with others. A distinction is made between 'secure' and 'insecure' styles, with style B called secure, and styles A and C called 'insecure'. Style A is described as an *anxious–avoidant* style, and C as an *anxious–ambivalent* style.

You may have found it difficult to characterize your own attachment style from these three options. For example, you might feel that there are ways in which two, or even all three, of the statements describe you to some extent, or that none of them really captures your 'style'. You might feel that sometimes you are closest to one option and at other times closer to others, or that you are different with different people. These possibilities highlight some potential problems with this approach. These issues are in part methodological, concerning aspects of the validity of the underlying concepts and problems with using such measures in research.

We can ask whether these three styles are:

- exhaustive (do they describe all possible styles of relating?)

- mutually exclusive (can people only fit one category at a time?)

- stable (do people shift from one to the other over time?)

- context-dependent (is 'style' affected by whom one is with, and the setting?)

- accurate (are people able to introspect in the way this approach assumes?)

- biased (do people give responses that they think will show them in a good light?)

Different approaches to describing attachment

Note that the approach mentioned above is a *categorical* one; it sets out to assign (classify) people to one of a number of *categories* (classes). In Chapter 5 of the first course book, you were introduced to a contrasting approach: *trait* theories of personality, in which a person can be located along one or more *dimensions* (e.g. extravert–introvert). Some attachment theorists have adopted a trait approach and they have suggested that adults' attachment styles can be described by using two dimensions: approach–avoidance and autonomy–dependence (Bartholomew, 1990).

Table 1.1   **Attachment styles using two dimensions**

		Model of self	
		Autonomy	Dependence
Model of other	Approach	Secure	Preoccupied
	Avoidance	Dismissing	Fearful

Activity 1.6

Try to find a match between trait and category descriptions of adult attachment by thinking about how each of the cells in Table 1.1 could be linked to one of the three attachment styles (A, B and C) introduced in Activity 1.5.

Comment

Clearly, the B classification fits the 'Secure' cell. The style A classification fits quite well with the 'Dismissing' cell. The C classification seems to fit both the 'Preoccupied' and 'Fearful' cells. The labels used for the theoretical constructs in attachment can evoke evaluative associations; the label 'secure' may evoke positive associations, while the labels 'insecure (anxious–avoidant)' and 'insecure (anxious-ambivalent)' may appear negative. The same dimension of positivity–negativity might be evoked by the four-way classification shown here. There is a risk that the concepts in attachment theory may seem to pathologise some styles of attachment while presenting others as 'normal' or even 'ideal'. Psychologists working in the attachment field argue strongly that these labels are not intended to be evaluative and you should certainly refrain from applying them in this way to yourself. For instance, the assumption that high dependency is problematic for an individual can be seen as a cultural value. Remember too that the attachment approach rests on the assumption that there *are* consistent attachment styles across different social situations and relationships. The arguments and evidence presented in this section indicate several ways in which this assumption needs to be questioned.

Correlates of attachment classifications

Hazan and Shaver received over 1,200 replies to the 'love quiz' after it was published. More than half of the respondents (56 per cent) classified themselves as 'B' (secure), 25 per cent classified themselves as 'A' (avoidant) and 19 per cent as 'C' (ambivalent). As well as the three questions on attachment style, the article also included numerous other questions on current and past relationships. The researchers were interested in finding out whether other aspects of people's relationships were correlated with their attachment style (as measured by the three-item set). 'B' respondents reported that their relationships with their partners had lasted twice as long as for the insecure respondents, but one of the highest correlations was found with how people described the quality of their relationships with their parents. The study was repeated with a sample of 108 college students and very similar results were found.

Activity 1.7

The 'love quiz' (see Activity 1.5) is a **self-report measure**. What are the limitations of self-report measures and what implications might they have for the results of Hazan and Shaver's study?

Self-report measure
A measure that relies on the participant in the research making judgements about him or herself.

Comment

Two things that may affect people's responses to self-report measures are:

i)   The tendency to give 'socially-desirable' responses. This could mean that people are less likely to report themselves as (for example) being uncomfortable with closeness.

ii) Such measures depend on people being sufficiently self-reflective to be able to give a good account of their feelings. This is not always the case!

3.2 The adult attachment interview

The way in which a person describes their previous and current relationships with their parents has turned out to be an important, core feature of their attachment style.

Mary Main, working in the US in the 1980's, developed a way of studying attachment in adults by conducting a standardized form of interview (Main, Kaplan and Cassidy, 1985). This follows a predetermined structure, with a set of questions exploring how adults describe their childhood experiences with their parents. Importantly, the focus of analysis of the tape recording of the interview is not on the content of what the person says, but on the way in which they talk about it. The person coding the interview looks particularly at the structure and amount of detail in the individual's account, its internal consistency (the extent to which it contains contradictory statements) and its coherence (the degree of linking between points in the narrative).

Main described three basic positions which people take in talking about their relationships during the interview:

i)   Insecure: dismissing

A *dismissing* narrative is one in which the person asserts that what happened in their childhood is not important. They may say for example, 'my father shut me up in the cellar when I was naughty, but I didn't really mind, and anyway, it's in the past now. No, I didn't get upset, it didn't bother me at all. In fact, I've forgotten about it'. The person gives the impression that personal relationships are not of much significance. The narrative is sparse, with little detail, and events and people are recalled in a rather bland, unemotive way, even where the content suggests that emotions would have been felt. The past is not described as having an influence on the self.

ii) Secure: autonomous/free to evaluate

An *autonomous* narrative is one in which the person acknowledges the importance of relationships to them, both in the present and during their childhood and talks freely and in some depth about past and present attachments. Richly described examples are given of both positive and negative experiences, and the person shows a capacity to integrate these. Insight is shown into the motives and feelings of others, and into influences on the self.

iii) Insecure: preoccupied/enmeshed

A *preoccupied* narrative is lengthy and without a clear structure. The link from one statement to another is often not apparent; points may be repeated. The person acknowledges the significance of past experiences, but does not seem to have resolved these and moved on from them. Past events are talked about with feeling; the person seems to re-experience the feelings in the interview. The person seems to be 'stuck' in unresolved issues from the past.

You will see the similarities between the adult attachment classifications described by Main and the style A, B and C classifications of Hazan and Shaver mentioned in Section 3.1.

Earned security

In relation to the secure, autonomous type, it has been found that this is not necessarily associated with a generally harmonious and happy childhood as described by the person. Some people appear to have had difficult childhoods, but have nevertheless come to terms with them and have moved on. Often, this is associated with strong and positive marital relationships (Rutter, Quinton, & Hill, 1990). This type of autonomous adult attachment has been called *earned secure* (Main and Goldwyn, 1984).

The 'earned secure' classification questions the idea that childhood attachment styles are enduring states that will inevitably *affect future relationships in designated ways. Clearly there are other factors that can influence the way we learn to interact with others. For example, the experience of good relationships in adolescence and adulthood seems to make a difference, and psychotherapy may also be able to bring about significant changes. By the same token, negative life experiences may have a detrimental effect on attachment style: arguably if there is an 'earned secure' style of attachment, there should also be special labels for styles which involve a move from secure to insecure status. In Section 3.5 we will look more specifically at the evidence of how other factors besides early relationships influence attachment style, and the extent to which attachment styles are stable or not over the lifespan.*

3.3 Internal working models and attachment theory

The evidence that there may be something which happens between parents and their children during childhood which has effects extending well into adulthood brings us to one of the central ideas of attachment theory: the concept of *internal working models*. The idea of 'internal objects' and the notion that one can usefully think of an 'internal world' with its own dynamics and elements, was first proposed by the psychoanalytical theorist, Melanie Klein (see Chapter 9 in Book 1, *Mapping Psychology*, for further discussion of her work).

John Bowlby, the key figure in the development of attachment theory, placed this concept centre-stage in attachment theory. He began his work on the theory in the 1940's. This was a time of quite exceptional creativity in psychodynamic theorizing, and indeed in psychology more generally. Bowlby read widely across many scientific disciplines and it was this eclecticism that made his theory so rich and productive. He drew on numerous sources, the main ones of which were:

- Psychoanalytic theory: Bowlby was himself psychoanalytically trained. Although Freud devoted little attention to early infancy, he did state that the relationship between infant and mother figure was effectively the prototype for all future love relationships. This is one of the central concepts that Bowlby took up and elaborated.

- Systems theory and cybernetics: showing ways of understanding how complex organisms and mechanisms could maintain stability in changing environments. In particular, Bowlby made use of the concepts of *feedback* and *homeostasis* from systems theory.

- Ethology: this was describing and explaining behavioural patterns in different animal species. From this field, Bowlby drew the ideas of *critical* and *sensitive periods* in development, and of *imprinting*, whereby the young chicks of some bird species become very strongly attached to the first moving object they see.

- Neuroscience: this was beginning to find out how networks of neurons in the brain could store complex information about the environment. From this field, attachment theory incorporated the notion of *mental representations* or *internal models* of things and events outside the person.

- Primate research: experimental studies with young monkeys were beginning to show that what motivates them to cling to their mothers is not only, or even primarily, the source of food, but rather their mothers' provision of comfort. From this, Bowlby drew the concept of *security* as a primary motive.

- Object relations theory: this was exploring the psychodynamics of early human infancy and explaining the processes by which an infant develops *internal objects* out of relations with their mother figure. Bowlby used this idea in his concept of *internal working model*.

- Developmental psychology: which was discovering that exploration and curiosity seem to be things that young children like to do, for their own sake. Bowlby added *exploratory behaviour* to *security* as another primary motive in human behaviour.

Bowlby's central idea was that human infants have a biological drive to achieve security through a particular form of relationship to what he called 'the mother figure' (since a person other than the biological mother could equally provide such a relationship, in Bowlby's view). This **primary attachment relationship** depends on the infant coming to represent the mother figure as a *secure base* from which exploration is possible, in the knowledge that the mother figure can be returned to if the demands of the environment become too great, and that the mother figure will reliably be *available* as a source of comfort and security. Bowlby saw this as happening through the infant building up an **internal working model** of herself and her mother figure, which is in the infant's mental world, even during times when the mother figure is not physically present. It is important to stress that this model is one of a *relationship* with three components: a model of self, a model of the mother figure and a model of the relationship between the two. Bowlby believed that the establishment of a 'healthy' internal working model is essential for later mental health, future relationships and socially responsible behaviour. He argued that this is a basic, biological process, much like imprinting in chicks, which happens during a critical period in early infancy. This, in essence, is the core of attachment theory.

Primary attachment relationship
An attachment to another person, normally a parent or other caregiver, formed by a child during early infancy. Is also used to refer to an older child's or adult's close relationship(s).

Internal working model
A set of expectations for how oneself and another person will relate to each other. According to attachment theory, this is established during childhood and affects later adult relationships.

Is the establishment of a 'healthy' internal working model during infancy essential for later mental health? As we have seen the existence of the earned secure *adult attachment type suggests that this is not necessarily the case. Moreover, as we shall see, what constitutes a 'healthy' internal working model is culturally defined.*

3.4 Mary Ainsworth and the 'Strange Situation'

Mary Ainsworth spent some years in the early 1950's working with Bowlby at the Tavistock Clinic in London, mainly researching the effects of 'maternal deprivation' (the lack of an adequate mother experience in infancy) on children's development. It was the results of this research that led Bowlby to believe he had found the main reason for juvenile delinquency: inadequate or non-existent 'mothering'.

In 1954 Ainsworth left for Africa and moved attachment theory forward through her observations of 28 mothers and their children in Uganda. She noted that although there were some important differences in how children behaved when they were separated from their mothers, it was during **reunions** after separations that differences between children's behaviour were most evident. She kept in touch with Bowlby and reported that she had identified three different types of attachment: secure, insecure and absent. She later moved to Baltimore, in the USA, and spent a long period closely observing and recording the behaviour of 15 infants and their mothers. It was during this time that she clarified her attachment categories by subdividing the insecure classification into two. She also developed a method for assessing attachment in infants aged around one year, the **Strange Situation**, which has become a standard experimental laboratory technique for attachment researchers (Ainsworth, Blehar, Waters and Wall, 1978).

Reunion
An episode in the Strange Situation when a child and mother (caregiver) are reunited after a brief separation.

Strange Situation
A standardized set of episodes involving a child, their mother and a stranger in a laboratory in a sequence of separations and reunions. A way of assessing attachment security.

1.4　The Strange Situation

This assessment is carried out in an observation laboratory, with video cameras strategically placed to record the behaviour of mothers and their infants.

- The laboratory contains two easy chairs, a play area, perhaps defined by a rug, and a set of toys.
- Once the mother and infant have settled, the mother sits reading a magazine and after about three minutes, a stranger enters and sits quietly on the free chair.
- After a minute or so, the stranger starts talking in a friendly way with the mother, and after another minute, moves to the floor and starts to play with the child.
- A minute later, the mother gets up and leaves the room, while the stranger stays with the child.
- After three minutes (or less if the infant becomes very distressed), the mother then enters the room and returns to her chair. The stranger leaves the room.
- After a further three minutes or so, the mother gets up and leaves the room, leaving the child alone.
- After three minutes (or less if the infant becomes very distressed), the stranger then enters, offers comfort to the child if necessary, and tries to play with the child again.
- Finally, the mother returns, the stranger leaves the room, and mother and child remain in the room for a few more minutes.

The video recording of the whole session is then coded by trained observers.

There have been three important criticisms of the Strange Situation procedure. First, the ethics of causing a child distress by separating them from their mother are questionable. Second, it has been argued that the test lacks 'ecological validity' in that it is indeed a 'strange situation', unlike other situations in a child's life. Finally, it has been argued that children's previous experiences of separation (e.g. if the mother works) will influence their reactions, making the test less reliable and valid. With regard to the first criticism, a researcher using the Strange Situation will typically follow an ethics protocol by which the mother or the researcher will respond rapidly if either feels that the infant is experiencing more distress than they can easily tolerate. With regard to the second criticism, a counter argument is that it is indeed the very 'strangeness' of the situation that evokes the infant's security-seeking behaviour, which is the focus of interest. Finally, it is indeed the case that an infant's previous experience of separation affects behaviour in the test, but it can be argued that this is because experiences of separation have an effect on attachment security, so the test is still a valid measure.

Infant attachment classification

Based on the behaviour observed in the Strange Situation, Ainsworth identified the three basic attachment types:

i)   Type A: insecure, anxious avoidant

This is when a child does not seek proximity on reunion and rejects the mother's attempts to calm or comfort.

ii) Type B: secure

This is when a child seeks proximity on reunion and allows the mother to comfort him or her.

iii) Type C: insecure, anxious ambivalent

This is when a child shows both avoidant and proximity-seeking behaviours, and may behave in apparently inconsistent ways towards the mother.

In current attachment research, each type is further subdivided.

Methodological criticisms notwithstanding, the infant attachment types mentioned above have been widely accepted as valid, sensitive measures of attachment. According to attachment theory, these types show the three main ways in which a child's internal working model can operate:

*   A child with a Type A (insecure, anxious avoidant) attachment is likely to show distress at the separation, suggesting that the mother's presence is important to her. But she seems to lack a firm belief that her mother will return, and fails to use her mother as a source of comfort at reunion. She is not easily able to comfort herself, nor does she seem to feel herself worthy of affection from her mother. She rejects the stranger's attempts to console

her. Her expectation seems to be a pessimistic one, that upset cannot be eased by another. Her relationship style is one of maintaining distance and avoiding closeness.

- A child with a Type B (secure) attachment has an image of her mother as a secure base, who is available for comfort. She also has an image of herself as worthy of her mother's attention and love, and can gain some comfort from this when separated, having confidence that her mother will return. Her reactions to separation do not show panic; she has some capacity to contain them in the knowledge of her mother's availability. She is able to use her mother and shows pleasure at reunion. She has an untroubled expectation of closeness and warmth between people and this is also shown in her being able to accept some contact with the stranger.

- A child with a Type C (insecure, anxious ambivalent) attachment shows more engagement with her mother, but of a rather troubled kind. She is upset at separation and not easily comforted on reunion, but she does get close to her mother. She shows some response to the stranger when alone with her in the room, but doesn't settle while her mother is away. She seems to be torn between anger at her mother for leaving her and pleasure at her return. She may show some aggression towards her mother or the stranger. She seems to expect the relationship to be difficult and she seems to lack a solid sense of herself as worthy of affection. She oscillates between closeness and distance.

It can be seen from the above three types that each is associated with a different internal working model of the self, the other and the relationship. Bowlby's view was that the particular working model a child had formed has a major effect on how children approaches subsequent relationships with other people. He argued that an individual's internal working model contains expectations about how others will behave and will thus mean that the individual will behave in ways consistent with these expectations. Someone with a Type B attachment for example, will approach a relationship with a degree of confidence that the other will respond positively, while someone with a Type C attachment will be hesitant and rather wary. How the relationship then develops will, of course, also depend on how the other person behaves and their attachment type. This is discussed again later in this section.

3.5 From infant attachment to adult attachment

According to attachment theory, if internal working models persist and continue to affect people's relationships after childhood, each type of infant attachment should be associated with a particular type of adult attachment.

Activity 1.8

Look at the following table. Work out which adult attachment type (secure; dismissing; preoccupied) you would expect to be associated with each of the infant attachment classifications, and write it in the appropriate cell.

Infant Attachment Type	Adult Attachment Type
A: Insecure, anxious avoidant	
B: Secure	
C: Insecure, anxious ambivalent	

Comment

A logical set of predictions would be that a Type B infant attachment would lead to a secure adult attachment type (AAT); that a Type A infant attachment would be associated with a dismissing AAT; and a Type C infant attachment would go with an enmeshed/preoccupied AAT.

A good way to test out these theoretical predictions would be to conduct longitudinal research lasting for at least 17 years or so. It would be necessary to carry out Strange Situation assessments with a selected sample of infants and to then assess their AAT classification when they reached young adulthood, say 16 years of age. Some longitudinal studies of this sort have indeed been carried out. The Bielefeld longitudinal study for example, has been tracking the development of children in 49 families in Germany (Zimmerman *et al.*, 2000). Forty-four children, whose attachment security was assessed when they were between 12 and 18 months of age, were later assessed for AAT classification at 16 years of age. Information was also systematically collected on the occurrence of various 'life events', such as divorce and death or illness of parents, in the intervening period between the two assessments. It was found that the Strange Situation type (SST) classification was not a good predictor of the adolescents' AAT; what emerged as a significant influence was, instead, the life events, particularly divorce and parental serious illness, which had happened during childhood. However, another study (Hamilton, 1994) of 30 adolescents in California, did find a strong correspondence between SST and AAT classification. This study also collected data on intervening events and experiences. A careful analysis of these data showed that the correspondence was largely found for children where their family circumstances had remained stable over the 16-year period between the SST and the AAT assessment. This was true for both secure and insecure type classifications on the two measures. Those children who changed from a secure to insecure classification (or vice-versa) were much more likely to have experienced major changes in their family circumstances.

Taking these two sets of results together suggests that there is some support for the link between infant and adult attachment status, but that life events are also a potent factor in influencing AAT. In a stable childhood, SST may be a predictor of AAT, but in a less stable developmental pathway through childhood, other events can have a major effect, both positively and negatively. Again, this illustrates the argument that no single factor can reliably account for developmental change, albeit in one narrowly defined area of psychology.

Adult attachment's influence on infant attachment

It has been much easier for researchers to look at the way that a mother's AAT might influence their infant's SST typing. A large number of studies have been carried out looking at how mothers with different AAT classifications behave towards their infants, and what types of attachment their infants show. Three consistent findings have emerged from these studies:

- Mothers' AAT is predictive of their infants' SST types, particularly for secure attachment. But the prediction is not 100 per cent accurate; for secure versus insecure classifications, it is around 75 per cent. For the two types of insecure attachment, it is weaker, at around 40 per cent.
- AAT is also predictive of how mothers behave towards their infants: secure mothers are more likely to behave sensitively towards their infants, responding to their bids for attention, comfort and communication. However, AAT is a rather inaccurate predictor of this, too. Only about 35 per cent of the variation in sensitivity is predicted by AAT.
- Maternal sensitivity does predict infant attachment, but it only explains about 33 per cent of variation.

These findings are drawn from a large-scale *meta-analysis* of attachment research (van IJzendoorn, 1995). The second of these findings is of particular interest, since they point to one route by which attachment security might be transmitted from mother to child. The so-called 'intergenerational transmission' of attachment has been a major concern of researchers for some years, in part because it has been felt that intervening in the process might be of major benefit to children who would otherwise suffer from the difficulties associated with insecure attachment.

1.5 **FEATURED METHOD**

Meta-analysis

This is a statistical technique of growing importance in psychology, especially in developmental psychology, where it is particularly difficult to set up large samples of participants. Meta-analysis is the analysis of analyses; it is a way of putting together the results from a number of different studies on the same topic. Through meta-analytic techniques, it is possible to gain a more reliable estimate of the true effects being investigated. Since studies vary in their sample sizes, adjustments are made for these and the analysis is based on the **effect sizes** found in the studies, which typically vary to some extent. These are measures of the strength of association(s) found between the variables being examined in each study. The end result of a meta-analysis is an estimate of the true effect size underlying the effects found in the different contributing studies.

Effect size
How strongly two variables are associated. Often assessed by a beta coefficient, which can range from -1 to 1.

3.6 Reflecting on attachment theory and relatedness

So how does Bowlby's theory stand up in relation to the various pieces of evidence discussed above? There is some support for parts of the theory: it does now seem that infant attachment is related to adult attachment in *certain conditions*. It also appears that adult attachment style may explain *some* of the differences in how mothers behave towards their infants. And research has also illuminated some of the processes by which attachment *type* may be transmitted. But it has also shown that this is only part of the picture; that life events may, in some cases, have an equal or greater effect. Generally, as in much psychological theorizing, Bowlby's seminal ideas have led to a great deal of fruitful research and some important modifications to his theory.

Relatedness and relationships

It appears that the concepts of attachment styles and their origins in early childhood do have some validity, along with the idea that there is not a permanently fixed style arising from these early experiences but rather that life events play a part as well. But it is worth reflecting on the factors that come into play when we enter into relationships with others. Clearly the specific form that the relationship takes is the outcome of the complex 'chemistry' between two people: we all know, for example, how one mistimed word or gesture can set off a whole chain of interpersonal negotiation. Given this, a person's attachment style is just a starting point for an interplay with the other's attachment style. You might find it helpful to think about what sorts of starting points various combinations of Type A (insecure, anxious avoidant), B (secure) and C (insecure, anxious avoidant) classifications might give. What would a Type A person be like with a Type C person, for example? Or, how might a Type C person's relationship with a Type B person begin and then develop so that Type C becomes 'earned secure'?

Relatedness
The capacities a person has to relate to another; the qualities of their approach to a relationship.

It is worth distinguishing **relatedness** (which is what our attachment style gives us as more likely ways of relating with another person) and *relationship* (which is what results from the interplay between the two people's attachment styles). Attachment theory can tell us which qualities of relatedness come easily to us and those that we find less easy to engage in. It also sheds some light on how we come to have these particular propensities, how they have origins in earlier relationships and how they may be perpetuated through later ones.

The two explicit assumptions highlighted within the introductory account of attachment theory in Section 3.1 were:

- *individuals have a specific style of approach to attachment which is a consistent characteristic of them as individuals*

- *these 'styles' have their origins in previous relationships, particularly those which infants have with their care-givers.*

However the arguments and evidence reviewed in this section has shown that:

- *attachment styles may not generalize across different situations nor across the different people with whom an individual has relationships*

- *attachment styles may be affected by positive or negative experiences across the lifespan as well as by the infant's earliest relationships with carers.*

In this section we have also noted a more implicit suggestion of attachment theory, that secure attachment is somehow a 'good thing' and a type B style is a desirable goal. But we have suggested that the traits or attachment styles characterized as 'secure' are not the only beneficial attachment styles, and that attachment theory makes subtle culturally-biased judgements about what constitutes 'good' relating and what does not. For example, some other cultures place much less value on 'closeness' than Western culture, and indeed there are many where even trance states and high levels of disengagement from others are highly valued. We should not forget that views about the desirability of 'secure' attachment are located within, and arose from historically specific social and economic conditions which allow this kind of attachment behaviour. For example, a century ago in Great Britain, working class mothers in industrial cities with young children would have found it much more difficult to provide the conditions in which secure attachment was fostered. Different forms of child-rearing have become valued during different historical periods in the West, and it is also worth reflecting on the great diversity of ways of relating that there are in different cultures and ethnic groups around the world.

Summary Section 3

- Attachment relationships can play an important part of our lives.
- Researchers have described adults' attachment styles using both categorical and trait approaches.
- Secure, insecure/avoidant and insecure/ambivalent classifications have been used to describe both infant and adult attachment.
- The concept of internal working models was developed by John Bowlby as a way of explaining how infants' relationships affect their adult attachment.
- There is some evidence that Bowlby's theory has some validity, but life events are also important.

4 Development in later life

So far you have been introduced to the idea that social relationships have an impact on our psychological development throughout life and this theme continues in this section, which deals exclusively with development in late adulthood. The idea that we continue to develop throughout adulthood was neglected until relatively recently, but is an important area in lifespan psychology. In this section we will consider the way psychologists have changed their characterization of adulthood and critically examine the question of whether later life really is a time of loss and decline.

4.1 Defining 'age'

You may have observed how frequently our concept of 'age' needs readjustment. Young children appear to engage in behaviours that we did not do 'when we were their age'. Similarly, our view of later life alters as some people live longer and enjoy better healthcare. Age can be characterized in a number of different ways (Hayslip and Panek, 1993):

- *Chronological age* is the length of time since birth and it forms the basis of many people's judgements of whether they are 'old' or 'young'.
- This can be contrasted with *biological age*, which is the physical age of one's body. If healthy diet and exercise habits are maintained, bodily organs and processes may appear to be those of a much younger person.
- *Social age* is defined by the habits, behaviour, interests and attitudes of a person. For example, people in their 60's may share the attitudes and interests of their children and identify with people who are aged 20 or 30 years. Generally society reinforces age appropriate behaviour, although these boundaries are changing all the time. There is an implicit emphasis on 'acting your age' and some behaviours are culturally or legally forbidden until an appropriate age has been reached (e.g. sexual relations).
- Finally, *psychological age* refers to our 'adaptive' behaviours (the way we cope with situations) such as problem solving and intelligence.

Trying to describe age is, in some ways, a subjective process. An attempt to arrive at some form of objective measure has resulted in the concept of *functional age*. Functional age is obtained by measuring performance on a range of measures or tasks that reflect the various social, biological and psychological aspects of ageing. Functional age may be a useful way of thinking about age as it defines individuals in terms of their actual ability rather than how long they have been alive. However, it also assumes that better ability is a feature of 'youth'. As you will see, this is not always the case.

Activity 1.9

Think about the characteristics and behaviours that you associate with both being young (e.g. under 20 years), and becoming older (e.g. over 65 years). Write them down in two lists, and carefully consider whether you regard each aspect to be positive or negative.

Based on your list, would you say that you have a broadly positive or negative view of ageing? Does this contrast with your characterization of being young? When you compiled your list of features associated with being young, it is unlikely that you included increased tendencies towards certain types of disease (yet for example you are more likely to contract meningitis when young). However, it is likely that you listed some health-based characteristics of growing old. It is useful to make a distinction between 'age related' and 'ageing related' conditions. That is, not all 'disorders' are an inevitable consequence of growing old (ageing-related); they are simply more prevalent in older populations (age related). How many of the features you compiled are genuinely features of growing old and how many are simply 'increased risks'?

The characterization of later life as a time of illness and decline has, until recently, even been apparent in psychological textbooks (Pennington, 1999). However, as we shall see, ageing is characterized by both growth *and* decline in ability, and the social context of ageing is an important influence on this.

While adulthood has been a neglected area in developmental psychology, this is not the case in other areas of psychology, where adult samples have been used to study cognitive, social and biological psychology to name but a few. However, what was lacking in these 'static' accounts was a sense of the developing adult. Moreover, it is only relatively recently that attempts have been made to consider the broader social, historical and cultural influences on such data.

4.2 Characterizing later life

We will now consider how psychologists have characterized late adulthood, it being a particularly stereotyped and under-represented area of developmental psychology. One attempt at describing psychological development in later life is that of Erik Erikson (see Chapter 1 in *Mapping Psychology*). He devised a theory of psychological development (from the psychoanalytic tradition), where each stage of a person's life is seen as requiring the resolution of an 'issue' as part of that person's ego development. The way each person resolves these issues will result in the acquisition of a 'virtue' – an ego 'strength' or special quality (see Table 1.2).

1.6 Summary of Erikson's (1950) eight stages of psychosocial development

Trust versus Mistrust (birth to one year of age)

The quality of parental care in meeting basic physical and psychological needs largely determines whether the child learns to view the world and people as safe and dependable.

Ego Strength: Hope

Autonomy versus Doubt (one to three years)

Parental responses to children's growing physical and mental abilities and their need to do things for themselves produce either a sense of self-government and self-sufficiency or self-doubt.

Ego Strength: Will

Initiative versus Guilt (three to six years)

Children given ample opportunity to initiate motor and intellectual activities learn to be self-starters, capable of planning and responsibility. Non-responsive and derisive parents foster guilt.

Ego Strength: Purpose

Industry versus Inferiority (six to eleven years)

Children who are encouraged to make, build, and do things and who are rewarded for their efforts develop skills as well as pride in accomplishment and become productive and achievement oriented. Lack of opportunity and support, as well as criticism, lead to feelings of inferiority.

Ego Strength: Competence

Identity versus Role Confusion (adolescence: the teenage years)

Adolescents must use newly developed cognitive abilities to develop a coherent sense of self that integrates past experiences with direction for further adult roles.

Ego Strength: Fidelity

Intimacy versus Isolation (young adulthood: 20s and 30s)

Young adults must develop the capacity to share with and care about others, without fear of losing their own identities. The alternative is to be alone.

Ego Strength: Love

Generativity versus Self-absorption (middle adulthood: 40 to 65 years)

Concern about future generations and the legacy one will leave behind us ushered in by a growing awareness of mortality at midlife. Those who fail at this task remain focused on their own needs and wants.

Ego Strength: Care

Integrity versus Despair (late adulthood to death)

Integrity refers to the ability to look back over one's life and see it as satisfying and meaningful. It also implies an acceptance of death. Those who despair see their lives as unsatisfying, have great regrets, feel that time precludes any attempts at change, and fear of death.

Ego Strength: Wisdom

Source: adapted from Lemme, 1995, p.46

Erikson's theory is an important one. For a long time it was one of the few which explicitly recognized that psychological development continued throughout life. It is also important because of its emphasis on the relationship between the individual and society in affecting personal development – something that is now a central idea in modern lifespan psychology. Note in particular the critical role that parents are seen to play during the early years. You will recall from Chapter 9 of the first course book that parents are seen as important early influences by psychoanalytic psychologists. This is also a central idea in attachment theory, which you will recall is the product of a variety of psychological perspectives, including psychoanalysis.

Activity 1.10

Look critically at Box 1.6 above. What difficulties do you see in the way Erikson has characterized later life?

Comment

Erikson characterizes later life in very narrow terms. Most developmental change is seen as occurring in early life with later life seen as a period of relative stability, where the primary concern is coming to terms with death and dying. As Peck argues, 'Ego-Integrity vs. Despair seems to be intended to represent in a global, non-specific way all of the psychological crises and crises solutions of the last forty or fifty years of life' (Peck, 1968, p.88). In an attempt to address this difficulty with Erikson's last two stages, Peck divided middle age and old age into additional sub-stages that attempt to characterize the crises in more detail. In doing this, Peck also characterized later life positively, as a time for growth (see Box 1.7).

1.7 Peck's characterization of later life

Middle age

The first crisis is *valuing wisdom versus valuing physical powers*. This describes the need to come to terms with a loss of physical strength and stamina, and in some cultures a loss of attractiveness. However, at the same time we experience gains in making informed judgements or 'wisdom'. Peck suggests that it is wrong for people to cling to physical ability as the main tool for coping with life's problems. This is followed by a crisis in personal relationships: *socialising versus sexualising*. Peck suggests that it is necessary in middle age to redefine individuals in terms of their personality and potential for companionship rather than viewing them as potential sexual partners. Another relationship crisis is *cathectic flexibility* (the ability to shift emotional attachments) *versus cathectic impoverishment*. This is seen as especially important in late middle age when children may be leaving home and the parent-child relationship is redefined. Individuals are often coping with the loss of their parents and friendships may also be affected by death. The ability to form new emotional bonds is therefore important. More positively, people at this stage have the opportunity for diversity in their personal relationships that may include friendship with both young and old. The fourth and final crisis of middle age is *mental flexibility versus mental rigidity*. Peck observed that a common criticism of middle age is that people become 'set in their ways' and closed to new ideas. Consequently, the ability to take stock of past experience while maintaining a flexible and open attitude to life is valued over rigid adherence to rules.

Old age

Ego differentiation versus work-role preoccupation relates to the crisis experienced on retirement from work. That is, some people may value their ability to do paid work (e.g. 'being the breadwinner'), but are unable to characterize themselves in other ways. Consequently there is a need for older people to engage in a range of valued activities to help redefine themselves.

The second crisis of old age relates to the increased vulnerability to illness and pain. *Body transcendence versus body preoccupation* refers to the need to cope psychologically with increased physical vulnerability and to learn to enjoy life through social relationships and mental activity, rather than becoming increasingly preoccupied with physical deterioration. The last crisis, *ego transcendence versus ego preoccupation*, relates to coming to terms with one's own death. The idea is that this crisis can be resolved by unselfishly contributing to one's own legacy through children, friendships and cultural contributions, so that one can die knowing that one's contribution to society will continue.

Activity 1.11

Think about Peck's characterization of later life. Does it seem valid based on your experience of and knowledge about growing old?

Comment

Culturally specific
Something that is relevant to one specific culture.

Peck's characterization seems appealing and accounts for many of the issues of later life and it emphasizes the role of social relationships in ageing. However, you may have noticed that it is **culturally specific** (as is Erikson's). For example, the need for cathectic (emotional) flexibility is based on assumptions about the age at which people typically have children and the age at which those children will leave home and gain independence. Both these factors will vary across cultures, and even across generations, and as a result this crisis may actually be encountered much earlier in life than Peck assumes. Work role differentiation is similarly based on the Western concept of paid employment and enforced retirement. While Peck acknowledges that some variation will occur as a result of gender differences and emphasizes the possibility that individual lives may influence the timing of these stages, little thought is paid to whether Peck's own cultural experience of ageing is 'universal'. He also assumes that people need to compensate for a decline in sexual activity. While there is evidence that sexual activity can decline with age, there is also evidence which suggests that sex continues to be fulfilling and plays an important role for people well into their 70s and beyond.

The issue of stereotypes of old age is not a trivial one as it has implications for the way society views the needs of older people. One example of this is the way that disability is seen as a 'natural' aspect of ageing. As a result of this, the opportunities for activity and independence that are presented to younger people with disabilities in residential care are not made available to many older people in sheltered accommodation (Walker and Walker, 1998). Such practices limit the opportunities available to older people to demonstrate that these stereotypes are misleading.

Losses and gains

Both Erikson's and Peck's models of later life are *person-centred* (see Chapter 9 in the first course book). Other psychologists have taken a *function-centred* approach that looks at just one type of behaviour (e.g. memory) and measures variation in it across the lifespan. This approach focuses on changes in ability with age.

'Successful' ageing is defined by Baltes *et al.* (1999) as maximizing gains while minimizing losses. It is suggested that we achieve this balance between loss and gain as we age by *selection, optimisation and compensation (SOC)*. They give the example of an 80-year-old concert pianist who was asked how he maintained such high levels of performance. He said that he played fewer pieces (selection), which he practised more often (optimization), and when he needed to play fast sections of music he would play the preceding section more slowly to make the next appear quicker (compensation). As we look at research into changes during adulthood, consider whether there is evidence of SOC taking place.

Memory

It has been suggested that episodic memory for older people obeys **Ribot's law** – that the past is remembered better than the present (Ribot, 1882).

Ribot's Law
The idea that older people remember past events better than recent ones.

Activity 1.12

Holland and Rabbitt (1991) asked two groups of people to generate as many memories as they could in ten minutes from each third of their life. Their results are shown in Figure 1.1. Which group do you think is older?

Figure 1.1   Results of Holland and Rabbitt (Source: adapted from Maylor, 1996, p.457)

Comment

Group B shows the recall of older people who were in residential care in the UK at the time of taking part. As you can see, their scores are consistent with Ribot's law. However, Group A also shows the recall from a group of older people of the same intellectual ability as the first group, but living in the community at the time of taking part. The results suggest that the need to rely on memory for day-to-day activities prevents the loss of recent episodic memories. Alternatively, the conversational activities and need to retain one's own identity that is especially important for people in residential care may lead to the rehearsal of older memories to do with family and friends. What this example illustrates is the effect of context and situation on cognitive development in later life. These differences in memory may reflect the effects of the different social contexts on SOC.

As the example from Activity 1.12 suggests, memory change in later life is not necessarily about decline, but about *qualitative changes* taking place. For example, Maylor (1994) contacted contestants from Mastermind (a formerly long-running quiz show on British television) and looked at their age and performance. She found that performance on the general knowledge questions (semantic memory) correlated with age – the older the contestant, the better they performed. In short, it appears that semantic memory improves with age.

These studies do not deny the biological fact that as we age, activity in our cerebral cortex, frontal lobe and hippocampus reduces: all areas that are involved in memory function. However, biological changes are affected by external influences. Kramer *et al.* (1999) have found that performance on cognitive measures such as speed of switching between two tasks can be improved by simple aerobic activity such as walking.

Twin studies show some genetic basis to memory functioning in later life, with short-term memory function showing the highest degree of *heritability* (Johansson *et al.*, 1999). However, the degree of heritability (see Chapter 5 in the first course book) is less for other types of memory and there is evidence from intervention studies that poor memory performance in later life can be improved by the tuition of specific memory strategies. For example, Noice *et al.* (1999) found that 65 to 82-year-olds who were taught to learn scripts by enacting the emotional states of characters in a study showed higher recall and recognition. Practising memory tasks also appears to result in improvement, regardless of age. Luszcz and Hinton (1993) asked two groups of participants (18 to 32 years old and 65 to 86 years old) to study a list of words. The list changed in each of four trials. They found that the repeated practice at the memory task particularly improved the performance of, and the strategies used by, the older group.

But while recall can increase after repeated exposure, studies of false memory suggest that this is not the whole story. McDermott (1996) found that, in general, adults remember twice as much correct information and half the number of false memories if they are tested on the same material five times, compared to just once. Kensinger and Schacter (1999) wanted to see whether older adults, who are more prone to false memories, also benefit from repeated exposure to stimuli (see Box 1.8).

1.8 Kensinger and Schacter's (1999) experiment

Kensinger and Schachter sampled two age groups: adults between 17 and 25 years, and between 60 and 75 years. The participants listened to a list of 45 words, which was constructed from three sets of 15 words. Each set of 15 words was semantically associated with a 'false' target word. After the list had been read out, the participants were invited to recall as many words from the list as possible. The same word list was then played a further four times and the participants were asked to recall the words from the list after each reading. The younger adults recalled more correct items than the older participants on the first trial and overall, and both groups correctly recalled more items in each successive trial. However, the younger group also recalled fewer false items in each successive trial. The performance of the older participants did not show this improvement.

You might conclude from this that older people have poorer memories than younger people. However, in this experiment it may be that older people were relying on using the gist of the information they were exposed to. This contrasts with younger adults who also learn details relating to the actual items as much as possible, rather than just relying on their overall impression of the stimuli. This successfully allows them to reduce false recall and recognition in experimental tasks of this kind. In other words, older people are simply relying on one strategy that is normally effective for day-to-day tasks – suggesting the operation of SOC once again.

Experimental studies of the kind described in this section are often problematic in their sampling of older participants. Many studies use a single group that covers a broad age range. The evidence presented in Section 4 so far shows that older people cannot be treated as a homogenous group (i.e. having similar characteristics):

> *… it is surprising that normative values for 'the elderly' are often based on mean performance data derived from populations with an age range from 60–100 years; no competent researcher would refer to 'the young', combining data from 10–50 years.*

> *(Richie, 1998, p.97)*

Intelligence

While it is a cliché that wisdom comes with age, it has been suggested that intelligence deteriorates with age. David Wechsler (1972) who devised the Wechsler Adult Intelligence Scale (WAIS) believed that just as we experience physical decline in later life, we also experience cognitive losses. However, this 'decline' depends upon the way intelligence is characterized and who is assessed.

Activity 1.13

Write down a definition of intelligence and ask some other people to do the same. How would you measure intelligence?

Comment

If you compare your definition to those of your friends you may find some variation in what is believed to be the most important feature of intelligence. This high degree of variation suggests that there are a number of components that underlie intelligent behaviour.

Sternberg (1985) has suggested that we demonstrate intelligence in the way we adapt to our environment. This suggests that the nature of intelligence varies across cultures and ages. However, he also argues that there is a set of cognitive components that underlie intelligent behaviour, such as how we allocate attention or acquire knowledge. He argues that intelligence is best assessed by giving someone a novel task or by observing the automatization of new skills, as being able to do a task 'automatically' frees up cognitive resources (see Chapter 6 in the first course book). Traditional IQ tests measure a variety of cognitive behaviours, including memory, cognitive speed, vocabulary and problem solving, but do not attempt to address cultural or context specific aspects of intelligence.

Older people are not required to do as well as a younger person in order to be given an IQ score of 100 (which indicates 'average' or typical performance for a given age group), because of an apparent decline in cognitive performance with age. However, some tasks show more of a decline with age than others. For example, verbal sub-tests such as general knowledge, comprehension, verbal memory and vocabulary show relatively little decline. However non-verbal tasks do show a marked decline in ability with age. Horn and Cattell (1967) found that older people do better than younger people on tasks that require experience, such as general knowledge, vocabulary and so on. This type of intelligence is referred to as **crystallized intelligence**. Younger people do better than older people on tasks that measure efficiency of brain functioning and processing speed, known collectively as measures of **fluid intelligence**. As fluid intelligence is associated with brain function it is more vulnerable to loss and damage with age than crystallized intelligence is. For example after a stroke many crystallized abilities can be regained with time and training. This division between (crystallized) intelligence as acquired 'cultural' knowledge and (fluid) intelligence as information processing has been reflected in many theories of intellectual development but is most closely mirrored by Baltes' *two-component model* (see Figure 1.2).

Crystallized intelligence
Abilities that are the product of experience (e.g. vocabulary, general knowledge).

Fluid intelligence
Abilities that reflect efficient information processing (e.g. speed of processing).

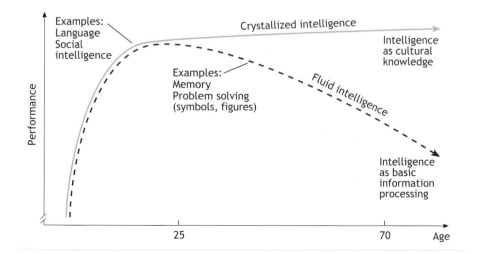

Figure 1.2   The lifespan trajectories of fluid and crystallized intelligence (Source: adapted from Baltes, 1987, p.615)

Cross-sectional design
A research design that
compares the
performance of different
age groups.

The data supporting the distinction between crystallized and fluid intelligence were taken from studies using a **cross-sectional design**, where different age groups are compared to each other. This approach can be problematic when the range of age groups is large. In 1953 Schaie (1988) tested people aged from 22 to 70 years. The scores were grouped into age categories according to the year of birth and the average score for each age group was calculated (a cross-sectional approach). These averages showed a clear decline in performance with age. However, he then re-tested as many participants as possible in 1963, 1970, 1977 and 1984. When these data were analysed longitudinally, (i.e. when the scores of individuals were charted across their life), no decline in performance was observed (see Figure 1.3).

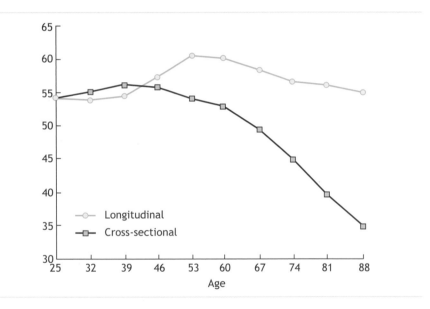

Figure 1.3   Lifespan trajectories for verbal meaning test scores analysed cross-sectionally and longitudinally (Source: adapted from Schaie and Willis, 1991, p.405)

Why would the data on the same people produce such different results? This is due to differences in ability across generations. That is, in many countries, each generation tends to differ from the one that preceded it, due to improvements in education, nutrition, healthcare and other historical factors known as **cohort differences**. Therefore, when a cross-sectional study presents data from participants aged 30, 40, 50 and so on, there will appear to be a decline because the younger people are slightly more advantaged than those in the older groups. However, if we look at the same person throughout their life, their mental abilities remain stable.

Cohort differences
Differences that occur
between different groups
because of changes in
external factors across
time (e.g. improvements
in state education).

Longitudinal data on people over the age of 70 years suggests that it is not simply the case that IQ will decline with age, but that other factors may differentiate between those whose IQ will drop and those for whom it will remain stable. Deary, MacLennan and Starr (1999) found that those with high verbal ability, high social class and better education are less likely to experience decline in verbal ability with age. Moreover, verbal intelligence is a good indicator of successful ageing as defined by living in the community without disability, with a good self-rating of health and a high score on a cognitive functioning test (Jorm *et al.*, 1998).

Instead of there being a decline in intelligence in later life, it appears that older people's reasoning is both socially and contextually orientated. For example, one study presented older people with a model meadow with a number of houses on it (Newman-Hornblum, Attig and Kramer, 1980, reported in Schaie and Willis 1991). The participants were asked if the arrangement of the houses would affect the amount of grass left to mow. Older participants did not get the answer right (the arrangement would make no difference), but their reasoning was perfectly logical. They explained that if there were a lot of narrow spaces it would affect the ease with which the grass could be mowed in some areas. In everyday settings older people are found to be especially efficient in their ability to handle complex social information and conflicting evidence. This sort of evidence supports theorists who have suggested that adult thought is characterized by *dialectical maturity* – the ability to live with and accept contradictory evidence.

Summary Section 4

- 'Age' can be defined in a number of ways, some of which are more objective then others.
- Holistic psychologists such as Erikson characterized later life in very narrow, undifferentiated ways. Peck elaborated on this period but presented a culturally-biased view of ageing.
- Function centred approaches focus on losses and gains in specific abilities during life. A balance can be achieved between loss and gain by selection, optimization and compensation of skills.
- Research suggests that there are qualitative changes in memory and intelligence with age (rather than loss). Overall, functioning in later life is affected by social contexts and adult thought is characterized by dialectical maturity.

5 Approaches to lifespan development

At the beginning of the chapter we talked about the contribution of multiple perspectives in psychology. Lifespan psychology reflects a wide variety of psychological perspectives that have each contributed to theories about how we develop with age. Attachment theory (see Section 3) is a good example of a developmental theory that has been influenced by the ideas of several perspectives. This final section is concerned with the historical development of lifespan psychology. The purpose is not just to explain the sources of contemporary lifespan psychology, but also to show that by drawing on multiple perspectives we can often achieve a more comprehensive account of a given topic area.

5.1 Darwin's influence on the study of development

One of the first major influences on developmental psychology was Charles Darwin. His theory of evolution (see Chapter 2 in *Mapping Psychology*) prompted a re-examination of the way people thought about human development. The first idea that developmental psychology inherited from Darwin's theory was a functionalist perspective. **Functionalism** means that explanations about why behaviours change are based on the idea that the change will serve a new and adaptive purpose (i.e. the behaviour has a function to serve). This idea directly derives from Darwin's theory, which argues that behaviours which increase the organism's chances for survival are selectively retained through evolutionary processes.

Functionalism
The idea that changes occur in people and their behaviour because they serve a new and adaptive function.

Prior to Darwin, the study of human development focused on describing the differences between adults and children. However, Darwin's work highlighted that there is considerable continuity and similarity between adults and children within any one species, as well as degrees of difference. This is reflected in his diary account of his son's first year of life. In it, Darwin observes that some of the behaviours his new-born son was exhibiting, such as sneezing, were as 'perfect' as those of an older child, while others were clumsy and still in the process of being learned. From this he suggested that some actions must be innate reflexes rather than learned behaviours. At any one moment in time an individual is the result of a gradual sequence of prior changes, both in a broad evolutionary sense and within that individual's own lifetime and further development and change lies ahead. This emphasis on gradual and continual change forms the basis of modern lifespan psychology.

The theories presented to you in this chapter reflect the influence of Darwin's ideas. For example, the account offered in Section 2 implies that social relationships are functional, as they promote both social and cognitive development in various ways. There is an implicit idea in attachment theory that attachment is functional because, it is argued, the bond between parent and child needs to be strong if the child is to become socially confident. The work presented in Section 4 proposes that change during later life is also adaptive in many respects.

5.2 Organismic approaches

At the beginning of the twentieth century, developmental psychologists were particularly concerned with charting the ages at which certain changes in behaviour 'normally' occur (e.g. when does a child talk for the first time). This developed into an approach to studying human development that is known as the *organismic* approach. That is, the individual (or 'organism') is its main focus.

The organismic approach assumes that human development has an end point or goal that is predetermined. Changes in behaviour throughout life are typically presented as a natural sequence of changes that occur one at a time, in a fixed order to bring the organism closer to the goal of development (referred to as a **stage theory**). For example, in the first stage of learning to walk the child is unable to support itself. As its muscles develop it becomes able to sit up unaided, perhaps crawl and finally take its first steps. As this example implies, one of the assumptions of an organismic stage theory is that environmental influences, while important, can only affect the speed of development. They may slow development down, or accelerate it, or even stop it, but they cannot alter the nature of the stages themselves, the sequence in which they occur or the end point they are designed to reach.

Stage theory
A theory that proposes that development occurs in a sequence of fixed order stages.

An early influential example of an organismic approach to human development was that proposed by Sigmund Freud (see Chapter 9 in the first course book) who claimed that children pass through a sequence of psychosexual stages. If a crisis occurred during any developmental stage, then it would be reflected in that person's personality. Consequently, Freud is credited with introducing the idea that the experiences we have as children will affect our personalities as adults. This theory, like many other organismic theories, assumes that adulthood is the 'product' of childhood – an end point rather than a time for change in its own right.

A more recent figure who adopted an organismic approach is Jean Piaget (1896–1980). Originally a biologist, Piaget became interested in children's intellectual development after working on the development of what became the Stanford-Binet intelligence test. Piaget noticed that when children made mistakes on the test, their errors often appeared to be systematic in nature. Piaget suggested that these systematic errors might hold the key to understanding how children's reasoning abilities develop with age. The idea that errors can be used to study mental processes is now commonly used in cognitive psychology. Cognitive processes are not directly observable, and have to be inferred from the way people respond to stimuli.

Still drawing heavily on the influence of Darwin's theory and influenced by his own biological training, Piaget began to study the development of intelligence as a form of adaptation to the environment. Piaget coined the term **genetic epistemology** to describe this area of study. Epistemology means 'the study of knowledge' and the term *genetic*, derived from 'genesis', refers to the origins of that knowledge. Like Darwin, Piaget observed his own children to formulate his ideas about cognitive development in childhood. From these observations, supported by work with larger samples of children Piaget suggested four main stages of cognitive development (see Box 1.10).

Genetic epistemology
Coined by Piaget, this phrase refers to the study of intelligence as a form of adaptation to one's environment.

1.10 An introduction to Piaget's theory of cognitive development

Sensory motor stage (approximately 0 to two years)

Children are born with innate behavioural patterns such as sucking and gripping, which are their first means of making sense of their world. They are able to take in new knowledge and experiences as far as they are consistent with their existing behaviours. Eventually children begin to generate new behaviours in response to their environment. As contact with the environment increases, they develop more elaborate routines or patterns of behaviour. This stage ends when children are able to represent their behaviours internally, through mental imagery or language.

Pre-operational stage (approximately two to six years)

Piaget saw the ability to build an internal representation of the world (a kind of mental model of how the world 'works') as a fundamental feature of cognitive development. At this stage children begin to use combinations or sequences of actions that can be carried out symbolically. For example, putting two objects together can be represented symbolically as an abstract mathematical principle (addition). However, at this stage children are only able to perform them as actions in the real world rather than representing them symbolically.

Concrete operations (approximately six to twelve years)

During this stage children are mastering the ability to act appropriately on their environment by using the sequences of actions they acquired in the pre-operational stage. They develop the ability to generate 'rules' based on their own experiences (e.g. noticing that adding something to a group of objects always 'makes more'). The children can now manipulate their environment symbolically too. They are still only able to understand the rules that they have had direct experience of, but they can begin some mental manipulation of these concepts. What they are unable to do at this stage is use rules to anticipate something that could happen, but that they have not yet experienced.

Formal operations (approximately over twelve years)

This is the stage at which children are able to reason in a purely abstract way, without reference to concrete experience. They can tackle problems in a systematic and scientific manner and become able to generate hypotheses about the world based on their accumulated knowledge of general rules of how it works. Piaget suggested that by the age of 14 or 15 years children achieve a stage where, having tried and rejected a number of personal theories about the way the world works, they finally devise a model of the world that is able to account for nearly all their experiences.

Although Freud and Piaget both adopted an organismic approach, their research methods and psychological traditions are very different. Freud, you will recall, was a proponent of psychoanalysis, whereas Piaget had a varied background that was informed by biological, evolutionary and psychometric perspectives.

Piaget's theory implies that adults demonstrate intellectual maturity as characterized by formal operational thought, and that there are no changes in the way we reason once we reach adolescence. As an adult student, your own experience of learning may tell you something rather different. We have already encountered evidence in Section 4 that intellectual development does continue into adulthood and context or personal experience are important influences on what we are able to achieve.

Piaget has also been criticized for the unproblematic way that he constructs intelligence. That is, 'formal' thought (rational, logical and deductive) is presented as the intellectual ideal. Kincheloe and Steinberg (1993) have argued that this is based on white, middle-class standards of 'intelligence' and as a result it devalues different forms of understanding that might be the product of other cultural experiences. They refer to other types of subjective reasoning which they call *post-formal thought.* They suggest that these are equally valid and characterized by an awareness of:

- what constitutes knowledge and how it is produced, including personal reflection on, and understanding of, one's own thought processes

- the hidden patterns and relationships that affect our experience of the world
- new ways of reading the world and attempting to make sense of oneself and society
- an appreciation that knowledge can never 'stand alone' from the context which it occurs within.

> *Cognitive development, then, is not a static, innate dimension of human beings, it is always interactive with the environment, always in the process of being reshaped and reformed. We are not simply victims of genetically determined, cognitive predispositions.*
>
> *(Kincheloe and Steinberg, 1993, p.300)*

Organismic stage theories continue to be appealing in their simplicity, but it is this same simplicity that is so often misleading and problematic. This chapter has presented you with two important ideas in developmental psychology: that development is influenced by interpersonal contexts and that development is lifelong. Organismic accounts underestimate the potential of the first idea and fail to acknowledge the second. The organismic accounts also assume the existence of an idealized end point to development, be it 'formal operations' in the case of Piaget, or an 'appropriate' mature personality resulting from successful negotiation of psychosexual development in the case of Freud. Attachment theory, having its roots in the psychodynamic perspective, also suggests an idealized outcome in the form of 'secure attachment', although there is awareness that this is culturally specific.

Contemporary approaches to developmental psychology attempt to acknowledge the full context of the individual and thereby offer a more fully informed account of influences on development. This approach is referred to as **developmental contextualism**.

Developmental contexualism
An approach to studying development by examining the interactions between the person and their environmental and historical contexts.

5.3 Development in context – developmental contextualism

Despite its name, the idea behind developmental contextualism is simple: *development does not occur in isolation, it is affected by the context of a person's life.* It is suggested that internal influences on development like an individual's biology and psychology interact with external influences such as their cultural context and interpersonal relationships. It is this interaction between influences that results in human development.

Activity 1.14

Think of something that you are good at, perhaps a sport or hobby. Try to think of all the things that influenced your development in this area. Think about them in terms of internal influences (biological or psychological tendencies) and external influences (friends, culture, prior life experiences).

Comment

Take the example of a woman who is good at tennis. She may be good because of repeated practice at tennis, because she is tall and physically fit (physical characteristics), because she received good tuition or because she is determined (personality). Practice, physiology, tuition and personality will all vary across individuals – in other words they can be thought of as *variables*. Come up with names that summarize the variables you identified as an influence on the development of your own 'skill'. Group your variables together into broad categories (e.g. interpersonal influences, cultural influences, cognitive factors). Each of these broad categories is referred to by psychologists as a *level of explanation* for why you are good at your chosen activity. Can you say that only one of your variables fully explains why you are so good? This is unlikely to be the case. This is the argument behind developmental contextualism: that even within just *one level of explanation* there are likely to be a number of variables that, in combination with each other, can explain development.

Another feature of this approach is that if just one of the variables influencing development changes, this can cause changes in other variables at the same or a different level of explanation. These changes will cause further changes of their own, and so on. This relationship between different variables and levels is referred to as **dynamic interactionism**. Some approaches might study human development at just one level of explanation, while acknowledging that other levels exist. Some theorists more dramatically suggest that just one level of explanation (e.g. biology) can account for changes that occur in all the other levels. However the idea of dynamic interactionism suggests that it is not possible to separate biology from the context of a person, an argument you may recall from the first course book, *Mapping Psychology*.

Dynamic interactionism
Used to describe the multiple interactions that can occur between different variables and different levels of explanation.

Physical environment

Figure 1.4 (overleaf) illustrates how internal influences are 'fused' into broader environmental contexts in a multidirectional way. The way human development is intertwined with a variety of contexts is referred to as **embeddedness**.

One person whose work illustrates such an approach is Urie Bronfenbrenner, who has proposed an 'ecological' theory of development, which attempts to acknowledge the full environmental and interpersonal context of development, and cognitive development in particular (see Box 1.11).

Embeddedness
Refers to the way development is 'rooted' in multiple contexts.

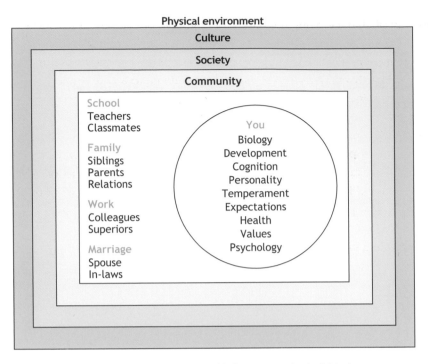

Figure 1.4   An illustration of contextual influences on the individual
(Source: adapted from Ford and Lerner, 1992)

1.11   An 'ecological' theory of development

Microsystem
The social, symbolic and physical characteristics of a person's immediate environment.

Mesosystem
Two or more environmental microsystems inhabited by the same person.

Exosystem
The links that occur between two or more environmental settings, where at least one of these settings is inhabited by the developing individual in question.

Macrosystem
The patterns of environmental systems that characterize any given culture or society.

According to Bronfenbrenner (1993), development is proposed to be the result of a person interacting with his or her environment. The term **microsystem** is used to refer to the social, symbolic and physical nature of an immediate environment: the social relationships present, the language used, and the physical resources available. But of course, environmental influences are much broader than any immediate setting. The term **mesosystem** is used to refer to two or more microsystems that are inhabited by the same person (e.g. a family setting and an OU tutor group) and how this combination of settings can jointly influence development. Perhaps you can think of ways that the combination of your home life and your activities in your tutor group have interacted to jointly promote your understanding of something. **Exosystem** is used to describe the links that take place between two or more settings, where at least one setting is inhabited by the developing person. This acknowledges the indirect, local influences on development such as the effect of a partner's job on a person's social development. Finally, the term **macrosystem** is used to refer to the patterns of microsystem, mesosystem and exosystem that characterize any given culture or social structure. All these levels of the environment are proposed to impact on the development of a given person in some way. Bronfenbrenner (1993) therefore urges developmental psychologists to build into their research an appraisal of the impact of culture on individual development.

This way of characterizing the nature of cognitive development contrasts with that of Piaget, although you will notice that it is consistent with the socio-cultural approaches to learning presented in Chapter 3 of the first course book. Piaget primarily explains development by reference to a child's microsystem, but does not include reference to broader environmental influences on development.

Box 1.12 summarizes the main assumptions of contextual approaches. As you can see, this approach suggests that people are able to act to promote their own development, rather than simply being subject to (and the product of) a variety of external and internal influences. If you re-read Section 2 you will notice that a contextual approach is reflected in much of the contemporary research presented there. Notice too how this approach contrasts with the ideas presented in attachment theory.

1.12 The guiding assumptions of developmental contextualism

(1) Variables from many distinct levels of explanation are involved in human life and development. The person and his/her internal psychology and biology must therefore be understood as embedded in the context of different levels of explanation.

(2) Individuals' development results from dynamic interaction within and between variables at different levels.

(3) Humans differ from one another in their genetic endowment and every human differs in the environments in which he or she is embedded during life. The dynamic interactions that occur between these two factors will also be unique for each person.

(4) Human development shows relative plasticity, so there is no single or ideal developmental pathway for any person.

(5) Individuals influence their own development through the decisions they make, their social networks, their effect on their environment, their environment's effect on them and their unique experience of the world.

(6) Individuals try to establish and maintain a correspondence between their personal characteristics and the contexts they are in, as well as trying to establish and maintain their own effective internal organization.

Source: adapted from Ford and Lerner, 1992, pp.88–90

What do the approaches covered in Section 5 have to say about development during adulthood? Organismic approaches like those adopted by Freud and Piaget seem to assume that there is little development after adolescence and adult cognition is portrayed as the product of psychological development rather than providing opportunities for continued development. Developmental contextualism explicitly acknowledges adulthood as a time for development and recognizes that the environment and biological factors and the interactions between them will result in a unique pattern of development for each of us. Psychologists are increasingly recognizing adulthood as a period of significant psychological change.

Summary Section 5

- The psychological development of an individual is subject to a number of influences.
- Organismic approaches to development emphasize the genetically and biologically predetermined outcomes of 'normal' development.
- Developmental contextualism emphasizes the multiple levels of influence on human development, including biological and environmental factors, and suggests that development is a lifelong process characterized by both losses and increases in ability.
- Psychological development is increasingly recognized as occurring during adulthood as well as childhood and adolescence.

6   Concluding remarks: factors affecting development

So what can we conclude about the development of the individual throughout life? Baltes (1987) provides a good summary of what we have learned from this chapter (see Box 1.3).

1.13 A characterization of lifespan development

- Development continues throughout life.
- Development is varied and complex: it occurs at different rates and is affected by a variety of internal and external factors.
- Development is characterized by both growth and decline in abilities at all stages of life.
- Development is characterized by the plasticity of individuals, whose developmental course is influenced by personal environment and experience
- Development is embedded within societies, cultures and histories.

- Development can be seen as the outcome of interactions between age-related factors (e.g. biological maturation, social events such as attending school), historical factors (e.g. evolution, the occurrence of war), and 'random' biological and environmental occurrences that only relate to one individual. This approach to lifespan development is known as 'contextualism'.
- Development is integrated, not just in the psychological perspectives it encompasses, but also the academic disciplines it draws upon, such as neuroscience, sociology and anthropology.

Source: adapted from Baltes, 1987, p.613

It is also worth reflecting on the breadth of methodological techniques that you have encountered in this introduction to developmental psychology. The reason why there are so many methods used to study human development is because of the way that lifespan psychology has sought to integrate ideas from a variety of psychological perspectives.

Revisit your answers to Activity 1.1 in the light of all you have read in this chapter. Would you change or expand your answers to this activity given the ideas that have been presented to you? Think about whether your answers 'fit' with the theories and research that we have presented to you in Sections 2 to 5.

Hopefully you now have a flavour of the complexity of human development, the need to consider multiple sources of influence that contribute to who we are today and the need to integrate multiple psychological perspectives to gain insight into them. The message of lifespan psychology is primarily a positive one:

> *Life is full of a smooth flow of events as well as unpredictable, fortuitous occurrences. Some people see and seize the opportunities that come to them and some do not. Some suffer from many more constraints on their possibilities than do others. Some suffer major life disruptions and create a reorganised life that is fulfilling in new ways, whereas others go through transformations that restrict rather than elaborate their lives. But the basic process is the same for all of us. The initial conditions of life do not determine one's life course.*

(Ford and Lerner, 1992, p.205)

Further reading

Crain, W. (2000) *Theories of Development: Concepts and Applications*, (4th edn), New Jersey, Prentice Hall.

This text is very readable and expands on the work of Ainsworth, Bowlby, Darwin, Erikson, Freud and Piaget. It also gives an account of the developmental significance of other psychologists that you will cover in the course, as well other figures whose work is of interest to lifespan psychologists.

References

Abramovitch, R., Corter, C., Pepler, D.J. and Stanthorpe, I. (1986) 'Sibling and peer interaction: a final follow up and a comparison', *Child Development*, vol.57, pp.217–29.

Ainsworth, M.S., Blehar, M.C., Waters, E. and Wall, S. (1978) *Patterns of Attachment: A Psychological Study of the Strange Situation*, Hillsdale, NJ, Erlbaum.

Azmitia, M. and Montgomery, R. (1993) 'Friendship, transactive dialogues and the development of scientific reasoning', *Social Development*, vol.2, pp.202–21.

Azmitia, M. (1996) 'Peer interactive minds', in Baltes, P. and Staudinger, U. (eds) *Interactive Minds: Lifespan Perspectives on the Social Foundation of Cognition*, Cambridge, Cambridge University Press.

Baltes, P.B. (1987) 'Theoretical propositions on lifespan developmental psychology: on the dynamics between growth and decline', *Developmental Psychology*, no.23, pp.611–26.

Baltes, P.B., Staudinger, U.M. and Lindenberger, U. (1999) 'Lifespan psychology: theory and application to intellectual function', *Annual Review of Psychology*, no.50, pp.471–507.

Bartholomew, K. (1990) 'Avoidance of intimacy: an attachment perspective', *Journal of Social and Personal Relationships*, vol.7, no.2, pp.147–78.

Bateson, G. (1955) 'A theory of play and fantasy', *Psychiatric Research Reports*, no.2, pp.39–51.

Berndt, T., Perry, T. and Miller, K. (1988) 'Friends' and classmates' interactions on academic tasks', *Journal of Educational Psychology*, vol.80, pp.506–13.

Bronfenbrenner, U. (1993) 'The ecology of cognitive development', in Wozniak, R.H. and Fischer, K.W. (eds) *Development in Context: Acting and Thinking in Specific Environments*, Hinsdale, NJ, Erlbaum.

Brown, J.R. and Dunn, J. (1992) 'Talk with your mother or your sibling? Developmental change in early family conversations about feelings', *Child Development*, vol.63, pp.336–49.

Crook, C. (1999) 'The uses and significance of electronic media during development', in Messer, D. and Miller, S. (eds) *Exploring Developmental Psychology from Infancy to Adolescence*, London, Arnold.

Crook, C. (2000) 'Motivation and the ecology of collaborative learning', in Joiner, R., Littleton, K., Faulkner, D. and Miell, D. (eds).

Damon, W. (1983) *Social and Personality Development*, New York, W.W.Norton.

Deary, I.J., MacLennan, W.J. and Starr, J.M. (1999) 'Is age kinder to the initially more able? Differential ageing of a verbal ability in the healthy old people in Edinburgh study', *Intelligence*, vol.26, pp.357–75.

Doise, W. and Mugny, G. (1984) *The Social Development of the Intellect*, Oxford, Pergamon Press.

Dunn, J. (1988) *The Beginnings of Social Understanding*, Oxford, Blackwell.

Dunn, J. (1993) *Young Children's Close Relationships*, Newbury Park, CA, Sage.

Faulkner, D., Ding, S., Woodhead, M., Littleton, K., Pretzlik, U. and Rowbotham, I. (2001) *ED840 Child Development in Families, Schools and Society, Project Guide, Audiovisual Notes and Video Transcript*, Milton Keynes, The Open University.

Fein, G. (1991) 'The self-building potential of pretend play or 'I got a fish, all by myself'', in Woodhead, M., Carr, R. and Light, P. (eds) *Becoming a Person*, London, Routledge.

Ford, D.H. and Lerner, R.M. (1992) *Developmental Systems Theory: An Integrative Approach*, Newbury Park, CA, Sage.

Freud, A. and Dann, S. (1951) 'An experiment in group upbringing', *Psychoanalytic Study of the Child*, vol.6, pp.127–68.

Göncü, A. (1999) 'Development of intersubjectivity in social pretend play', in Woodhead, M., Faulkner, D. and Littleton, K. (eds) *Cultural Worlds of Early Childhood*, London, Routledge.

Hamilton, C.E. (1994) 'Continuity and discontinuity of attachment from infancy through adolescence', *Dissertation Abstracts International Section A: Humanities and Social Sciences*, vol. 55, (2–A), p.217.

Harris, J.R. (1999) *The Nurture Assumption*, London, Bloomsbury.

Hayslip, B. and Panek, P.E. (1993) *Adult Development and Ageing* (2nd edn), New York, HarperCollins.

Hazan, C. and Shaver, P. (1987) 'Romantic love conceptualized as an attachment process', *Journal of Personality and Social Psychology*, vol.52, no.3, pp.511–24.

Holland, C.A. and Rabbitt, P.M.A. (1991) 'Ageing memory: use versus impairment', *British Journal of Psychology*, vol.82, pp.29–38.

Horn, J.L. and Cattell, R.B. (1967) 'Age differences in fluid and crystallized intelligence, *Acta Psychologica*, vol.26, pp.107–29.

James, W. (1892/1961) *Psychology: The Briefer Course*, New York, Harper Torch Books.

Johansson, B., Whitfield, K., Pedersen, N.L., Hofer, S.M., Ahern, F. and McClearn, G.E. (1999) 'Origins of individual differences in episodic memory in the oldest-old: a population-based study of identical and same-sex fraternal twins aged 80 and older', *Journals of Gerontology: Series B: Psychological Sciences and Social Sciences,* vol.54B, pp.173–9.

Joiner, R., Littleton, K., Faulkner, D. and Miell, D. (eds) (2000) *Rethinking Collaborative Learning*, London, Free Association Books.

Jorm, A.F., Christensen, H., Henderson, A.S., Jacomb, P.A., Korten, A.E. and Mackinnon, A. (1998) 'Factors associated with successful ageing', *Australasian Journal of Ageing*, vol.17, no.1, pp.33–7.

Kensinger, E.A. and Schacter, D.L. (1999) 'When true memories suppress false memories: effects of ageing', *Cognitive Neuropsychology*, vol.16, pp.399–415.

Kincheloe, J.L. and Steinberg, S.R. (1993) 'A tentative description of post-formal thinking: the critical confrontation with cognitive theory', *Harvard Educational Review,* vol.63, pp.296–320.

Kramer, A.F., Hahn, S., Cohen, N.J., Banich, M.T., McAuley, E., Harrison, C.R., Chason, J., Vakil, E., Bardell, L., Boileau, R.A. and Colcombe, A. (1999) 'Ageing, fitness and neurocognitive function', *Nature,* vol.400, pp.418–9.

Lemme, B.H. (1995) *Development in Adulthood*, Boston, Allyn and Bacon.

Luszcz, M. and Hinton, M. (1993) 'Try, try again: improving older adults' memory through practice', *Australian Journal on Ageing*, vol.12, pp.6–10.

McDermott, K.B. (1996) 'The persistence of false memories in list recall', *Journal of Memory and Language,* vol.35, pp.212–30.

Main, M. and Goldwyn, R. (1984) 'Predicting rejection of her infant from mother's representation of her own experience: implications for the abused-abusing intergenerational cycle', *Child Abuse and Neglect*, vol.8, no.2, pp.203–17.

Main, M., Kaplan, N. and Cassidy, J. (1985) 'Security in infancy, childhood, and adulthood: a move to the level of representation', *Monographs of the Society for Research in Child Development,* vol.50, pp.66–104.

Maylor, E.A. (1996) 'Ageing and the retrieval of specialized and general knowledge: performance of Masterminds', *British Journal of Psychology,* vol.85, pp.105–14.

Mead, G.H. (1934) *Mind, Self and Society*, Chicago, University of Chicago Press.

Noice, H., Noice, T., Perrig-Chiello, P. and Perrig, W. (1999) 'Improving memory in older adults by instructing them in professional actors' learning strategies', *Applied Cognitive Psychology,* vol.13, pp.315–28.

Peck, R. (1968) 'Psychological developments in the second half of life', in Neugarten, B. (ed.) *Middle Age and Ageing*, Chicago, University of Chicago Press.

Pennington, H. (1999) 'Cognitive aspects of ageing as portrayed in introductory texts', *New Zealand Journal of Psychology*, vol.28, pp.48–50.

Perret-Clermont, A.N. (1980) *Social Interaction and Cognitive Development in Children*, London, Academic Press.

Piaget, J. (1932) *The Moral Judgement of the Child*, London, Routledge.

Ribot, T. (1882) *Diseases of Memory*, New York, Appleton.

Richie, K. (1998) 'Establishing the limits of normal cerebral ageing and senile dementias', *British Journal of Psychiatry*, vol.173, pp.97–101.

Rutter, M., Quinton, D. and Hill, J. (1990) 'Adult outcome of institution-reared children: males and females compared', in Robins, L.N. and Rutter, M. (eds) *Straight and Devious Pathways from Childhood to Adulthood*, Cambridge, Cambridge University Press.

Schaffer, R. (1996) *Social Development*, Oxford, Blackwells.

Schaie, K.W. (1988) 'Variability in cognitive function in the elderly: implications for societal participation', in Woodhead, A., Bender, M. and Leonard, R. (eds) *Phenotypic Variation in Populations: Relevance to Risk Management*, New York, Plenum.

Schaie, K.W. and Wills, S.L. (1991) *Adult Development and Ageing*, New York, Harper Collins.

Selman, R. (1980) *The Growth of Interpersonal Understandings*, New York, Academic Press.

Shotter, J. (1974) 'The development of personal powers', in Richards, M.P.M. (ed.) *The Integration of a Child into a Social World*, Cambridge, Cambridge University Press.

Sternberg, R.J. (1985) 'Cognitive approaches to intelligence', in Wolman, B.B. (ed.) *Handbook of Human Intelligence: Theories, Measurements and Applications*, New York, Wiley Interscience.

van Ijzendoorn, M. (1995) 'Adult attachment representations, parental responsiveness, and infant attachment: a meta-analysis on the predictive validity of the Adult Attachment Interview', *Psychological Bulletin*, vol.117, no.3, pp.387–403.

Vygotsky, L.S. (1978) *Mind in Society: The Development of Higher Psychological Processes*, Cambridge, MA, Harvard University Press.

Walker, A. and Walker, C. (1998) 'Normalisation and 'normal' ageing: the social construction of dependency among older people with learning difficulties', *Disability and Society*, vol.13, pp.125–42.

Wechsler, D. (1972) '"Hold" and "don't hold" tests', in Chown, S.M. (ed.) *Human Ageing*, New York, Penguin.

Zimmerman, P., Becker-Stoll, F., Grossman, K., Grossman, K.E., Scheuerer-Englisch, H. and Wartner, U. (2000) 'Longitudinal attachment development from infancy through adolescence', *Psychologie in Erziehung und Unterricht*, vol.47, no.2, pp.99–117.

Acknowledgement

The authors would like to acknowledge the use and adaptation of the following material in the preparation of Sections 2.3 and 2.4 of this chapter:
Dorothy Faulkner and Martin Woodhead for material from ED840, *Child Development in Families, Schools and Society*, Study Guide.

Dorothy Faulkner, Sharon Ding, Martin Woodhead, Karen Littleton, Ursula Pretzlik and Iris Rowbotham for material from ED840, *Child Development in Families, Schools and Society*, Project Guide, Audiovisual Notes and Video Transcript.

Dorothy Miell for material from DSE202, *Introduction to Psychology, Volume 1*, Chapter 2, 'The self and the social world'.

CHAPTER **2**

Language and meaning

Troy Cooper and Helen Kaye

Contents

Aims:

This chapter aims to:

- evaluate debates about whether language is a distinctively human characteristic that distinguishes us from other animals
- consider evidence concerning how listeners and readers use the context of language to understand its meaning
- outline how computers can be used to model language understanding
- outline how the usage of language in everyday talk has been studied
- evaluate the differences between perspectives in terms of the relationship between language and thought, and language and the world
- consider the differences between perspectives in terms of what they take 'meaning' to be, and where the meaning is made

1   Introduction

Language is the main medium for communication between human beings and where we express, explore and pursue those goals that mean most to us: love and sex, friendship, intellectual thought and problem-solving, planning... the list is endless. This importance is reflected in the number of academic disciplines devoted to studying language, for example, how to use its current forms (modern language studies), its use for self-expression (literary theory), how different modern languages are related structurally and historically (linguistics), how the same language is used differently by various social and cultural groupings (sociolinguistics), and how language is used to communicate and create meaning (psychology).

As social beings, constantly interacting with others, we all spend a lot of time thinking about how to use language well to serve our needs. This is because language is one of the most important aspects of being human, our most distinctive and interesting characteristics as a species. But why is that? What is so distinctive about human language in comparison to animal communication? As we shall discuss in more detail in the first part of Section 2, it is clear that animals can communicate, from bees doing their 'waggle' dance in order to give the directions to nectar, to higher primates who have learned a system of signs to communicate with humans. However, do these forms of communication have enough in common with human language to indicate an essential similarity, with only a difference in degree of sophistication? Or is there a *qualitative* difference? If there is evidence of a qualitative difference, then we shall need to explore how that difference came about and why.

Activity 2.1

Most people who have had a pet like a cat or dog, believe that their pet comes to understand what they say to some extent. Do you think this could be true and, if it is, what do you think pets might understand when their owners talk to them?

While language undoubtedly does convey information, that is not all it does. The owner who speaks to their pet like a child or a companion is being affectionate and playful, and the animal can respond to this by recognizing the purpose and value of the communication, without necessarily understanding any of the word–meaning content of speech. This prompts the thought that if most animal communication functions to convey information of set kinds, perhaps the qualitative difference between language and other animal communication is that language conveys the specific meanings of the separate noises generated.

Later on in Section 2, we will see how language can be used creatively, to say things that have never been said before, to build relationships and convey affection, to enable us to think about and try to represent the world to ourselves.

Having considered the defining characteristics of language and how it may have evolved, we shall spend the rest of the chapter considering how language is actually used. Sections 3 and 4 describe the development of two different psychological perspectives on language: cognitive and social approaches. These approaches take their evidence from very different bodies of research each with a different focus.

Section 3 explores the cognitive focus on how human beings understand language: how they process what they hear or read in order to extract meaning. People are very efficient at understanding language and this has led cognitive psychologists to use experiments in which the processes involved can be manipulated and measured. Computer models are also used to investigate how the various processes can fit together. The cognitive approach proposes that incoming linguistic information is combined with stored knowledge to construct a mental representation of the meaning of a piece of text or speech. In order to do this we need to look at the meanings of individual words and sentences as well as aspects of social and contextual knowledge about the communication. Have you ever come in half way through a conversation and made a contribution that you subsequently realise is foolish or mistaken once the speakers have told you what the topic actually is? Communication is often ambiguous and we will look at how people make sense of what they hear and read.

There is a distinction to be made between 'knowing' a language and 'using' or doing things with it. Using the distinction very broadly, cognitive approaches to language are concerned with what an individual must know about a language, and the context in which it is used, in order to be able to understand it. By contrast, in Section 4, the social psychological perspective proposes that our human world is created through language, and that this is one of its most powerful and important characteristics. This approach to language emphasises that individuals use language to take action and accomplish goals, and that understanding language and creating meaning in it is about using language to do things. This has produced a particular social psychological approach to language called discursive psychology, which has its own particular methods grounded in analysing talk and text from everyday activities. Discursive psychology proposes a model of how meaning is created in language that would, if accepted, entail a radical revision to how psychological theories are made and research is done.

From this brief outline you may appreciate that there are many points of debate about how to characterise the psychology of language. As you work through the chapter, keep thinking about whether the different approaches you are introduced to conflict, co-exist or complement each other. This is one of the main topics of debate currently within the psychology of language, and we shall discuss it in more detail in Section 5 at the end of the chapter.

The issues discussed in this chapter are very important questions that psychologists, together with those in other academic disciplines, are currently grappling with. We do not expect you to be able to provide answers to them by the end of the chapter, but we do hope that you will have a grasp on some of the evidence and terms of the debates that rage around them.

2 Origins of language

This section will consider the claim that language is a uniquely human ability. We will look at whether naturally occurring animal communication is similar to human language, and review one of many attempts to teach a human-like language to an ape. We will then look at differences between animals and humans and finally consider two ways in which human language may have evolved.

2.1 Communication and non-human animals

Animals can undoubtedly communicate in quite complex ways and we will briefly illustrate this fact using two very different species: honeybees and vervet monkeys.

Honeybees are social insects that live in hives. Individual bees have specialized roles, for example, worker bees are sterile females responsible for finding food for the community. Every day a number of worker bees leave the hive and forage for pollen and nectar. On finding food they return to the hive and 'tell' the other workers, who then go to collect more of it. Karl Von-Frisch (1950) carried out extensive investigation into just how this 'telling' is accomplished. If the source of food that has been located is within 50 meters of the hive, then the finder will perform a *round* dance. The bees near the dancer crowd around her, apparently observing her movement, and then fly off to the food location. If the food is more remote then a *waggle* dance is performed, which transmits information about the distance and direction to be flown. In a set of ingenious experiments Kirschner and Towne (1994) used miniature robot bees to discover that the sound of the finder bee's wings flapping was necessary for these dances to be effective. The finder also needed to distribute samples of the food that she had brought back with her. So it seems honeybees use various modalities – visual, auditory and chemical – to transmit and receive quite complex messages.

Vervet monkeys also live in social groups and communicate with their group members. Vervet monkeys give alarm calls when they spot a predator, and the kind of call varies depending on the predator. Seyfarth *et al.* (1980) report that if an adult monkey spots an eagle, then its call causes the other members of the group to look to the sky. A monkey call upon sighting a leopard in contrast elicits immediate fleeing to the safety of the trees, while the call upon sighting a snake causes the group members to look downwards.

Activity 2.1

What do you think are the differences between these examples of communication and the language that people use? Compare the range of events that the communication can refer to and how much flexibility there is in how the message is conveyed.

There are many other examples of natural communication systems used by a variety of species: birds use song to attract mates and warn off rivals, and the postures adopted by domestic cats and dogs signal aggression or submissiveness. So, animals communicate with each other in varied ways.

2.2 Criteria for language

The next questions we will ask are: can we say that these are instances of the same kind of communicative ability that humans have? Can we compare human language with animal communication? To answer these questions we need to decide what defines a language. Harley describes human language as involving 'associating a finite number of words with particular meanings or concepts, and using a finite number of rules to combine those words into a potentially infinite number of sentences' (Harley, 1995, p.11). Many researchers have proposed a set of **language design features** or general properties that characterise human language and could act as criteria for deciding how far animal communication qualifies as language. Hockett (1960) identified 13 such design features, Aitchison (1983) later refined these to 10 and proposed that four were unique to humans. Let's briefly consider these four criteria and the evidence that some animal communication might satisfy them.

The first two criteria Aitchison considered definitive of human language, **semanticity** and **displacement**, can be considered with evidence of the animal communication systems already described in this section.

- *Semanticity*: in a human language each word has at least one specific meaning. Animals learn to respond to particular signs, for example, a vervet monkey will flee when one of their group gives a call indicating that a leopard is approaching. However, it is not clear that the monkey knows what the call means (a semantic representation), it could just be that it simply knows how to respond to the call, i.e. stimulus-response learning. The call could act as a signal for 'run away' rather than convey the meaningful message 'there is a leopard close by'. However, if you review Chapter 3, Section 2 of Book 1, you will see that there is evidence that animals do not simply *learn* stimulus-response relationships, but form internal representations. This means they are capable of representing and using knowledge about the world and that some kind of representation of meaning *may* be used in some animal communication.

- *Displacement*: people can talk about anything regardless of its displacement in time or space, whether it is true or not. People talk about the past and the future, about hypothetical situations, 'what would happen if ...', about ideas and even, as we are asking you to do in the activities of this book, use language to reflect on the use of language. However, no clear evidence has been found that animals do these things: as Harley puts it, 'Bees will never dance a book on the psychology of the bee dance' (1995, p.10). The strongest argument for such a possibility comes from the studies of communication in higher primates, which we shall review in Section 2.3.

The evidence concerning whether animal communication can satisfy the remaining two criteria has come largely from studies of higher primates who have been reared in captivity by researchers who have attempted to teach them a human-like language. The criteria are:

- Structure dependence. Language is characterized by a series of symbols that are abstract – they do not resemble in any way the object to which they refer. This means that the word 'dog' is a sound with no inherent 'dogginess', it is just a sound that happens to be attached to the concept of dog. In

Language design features
Properties that characterise language.

Semanticity
A design feature of language relating to how a word reflects aspects of the world.

Displacement
The ability to refer to events and items that are not currently perceived.

English, words can be put together into units of meaning in which their place in a sentence or a clause is important to the meaning generated. 'Dog bites man' has a very different meaning to 'Man bites dog', and these different meanings are related to the structural placing of the two words 'dog' and 'man'. The set of rules that governs how words can be combined and modified to make sense is called *grammar* or **syntax**.

- Creativity. Language can be used to produce utterances that have never been expressed before. It allows a great deal of flexibility in communication, people can produce an almost infinite number of sentences each conveying a different meaning.

The studies described so far in this section have adopted the methods of **ethology** pioneered by Konrad Lorenz (1952). These involve observing naturally occurring behaviour within the environment in which it normally occurs. Where there is experimental manipulation, such as the introduction of 'robot bees' great care is taken in ensuring that the situation remains as 'natural' as possible. We will now look at studies where the environment is considerably more controlled and artificial.

Syntax
The analysis of sentence structure.

Ethology
The study of behaviour in its natural setting.

2.3 Teaching human languages to apes

There have been many attempts to teach apes using sign languages and artificial languages that involve manipulating plastic tokens (classic accounts are by Gardner and Gardner, 1969; Premack, 1971; Terrace, 1979). Most of the studies have shown some degree of success in enabling communication between the trainer and the ape, but there are a number of problems in interpreting the results. We will consider the nature of these problems of interpretation in relation to one of the most successful cases of communication development, the training of Kanzi, a Bonobo or Pygmy Chimpanzee, to use a sign language by Sue Savage-Rumbaugh, a comparative psychologist at Georgia State University in America. Kanzi's achievements have been detailed and analysed by Savage-Rumbaugh and colleagues (Savage-Rumbaugh and Lewin, 1994; Savage-Rumbaugh *et al.*, 1998).

2.1 **Case-study: Bonobo use of sign language (Savage-Rumbaugh and Lewin, 1994; Savage-Rumbaugh et al., 1998)**

Kanzi's adoptive mother, Matata was trained to use a computer keyboard with symbols on the keys, and was rewarded for pressing the correct symbols in response to her trainer's questions. In common with the other studies, Matata received intensive training from an individual trainer. When Kanzi was small, Matata would not be parted from him and so he accompanied her to those 'lessons'. The trainers noticed that Kanzi spontaneously began using the keyboard. Subsequently Kanzi was encouraged to interact with people in everyday activities. At age 9 years, Kanzi's keyboard contained 256 symbols and he had also adopted gestures, which were interpreted as having specific meanings. Kanzi used these symbols in strings of 2 or 3 to make requests, to which the trainers responded appropriately. On one occasion Kanzi had played with a garden hose and later apparently requested another game by pressing the symbols for 'water' and 'chase', there being no symbol for 'hose'. Kanzi's ability to understand spoken language was tested by giving him a set of instructions, such as 'Hide the toy gorilla'; 'Pour the Coke in the lemonade' (Savage-Rumbaugh *et al.*, 1998, p.69). Kanzi responded correctly to about 72 per cent of such instructions.

A bonobo using a computer keyboard to communicate

Although Kanzi has undoubtedly learned a good deal, there are difficulties in determining exactly the nature of his learning. Kanzi's ability to respond appropriately to verbal commands is impressive and is consistent with Savage-Rumbaugh's assertion that he understands what is said. However, it is equally possible that Kanzi had learned to respond appropriately to the sounds of speech (i.e. in a stimulus-response way), a similar argument to that made when considering whether the calls of the Vervet monkeys demonstrate semanticity.

This is an appropriate time to consider what exactly is meant by meaning or semanticity. According to Pearce (1987) 'a signal has meaning if it excites a representation of the event to which it relates' (pg. 266).

Meaning, as Pearce defines it, is equivalent to an individual's own representation. If we can infer that an animal, or indeed a person, forms a specific representation corresponding to a particular word, then we can say that they understand the meaning of that word (note, however, that this is only one particular definition of the term meaning). As we signalled in the introduction we will consider different conceptions of 'meaning' as we progress through the chapter.

Kanzi's behaviour does suggest that he forms specific representations in response to the words he hears. For example, if Kanzi is asked to fetch an object, such as 'an apple from upstairs', he will ignore other apples that are visible to him and go upstairs to retrieve the requested apple. Similarly, Premack (1971) reports that one of his chimpanzees, Sarah, was able to select a brown object when her only training with the word 'brown' was being told that it was the colour of chocolate. It seems reasonable to explain her behaviour by assuming that for Sarah the word 'chocolate' excited a specific representation. In other words she had coded specific information about chocolate and linked it to the word 'chocolate', including the colour of it. However, not all approaches to language would accept this is a full description of 'meaning' as humans deal with meaning, and we shall return to the issue of meaning later in the chapter. However, there does remain the possibility that the apparent 'understanding' by animals of language is actually a set of conditioned responses.

Activity 2.2

Can you think of a way in which Sarah could select the brown object by using generalisation of a conditioned response she had already acquired? You might find it helpful to re-read the first part of Chapter 2 of Book 1 to remind yourself of these terms.

It is conceivable that the association Sarah had learned between the symbols for 'chocolate' and 'brown' led to a generalisation between 'brown' and the object most perceptually similar to chocolate. This possibility is the main reason why those investigating this area have turned to an animal's *production* of language as a more important test of its linguistic abilities than its *reaction* to language from someone else. Very early on it was noted that apes, unlike children, do not naturally mimic the speech sounds they hear. This, coupled with a vocal tract anatomy that would make production of some speech sounds impossible, meant that most studies have used non-vocal languages. Kanzi could have been taught sign language, as apes in other trials have been, but the muscles in a chimp's hand do not allow the same degree of flexibility as our own and so signing has been shown to be quite difficult for them. So Kanzi was given a keyboard with pictorial symbols that corresponded to particular events and objects with which he became familiar during his upbringing. Kanzi rapidly learned to press these symbols to communicate with his trainers. The drawback to this system is that his vocabulary was limited to 256 words, the number of keys that could be fitted on to a portable keyboard. That limitation is a considerable constraint for him to operate under if he is to show he is capable of using language.

As Kanzi produces communications that are quite restricted in length – arguably because of the constraints of the choice and type available on the keyboard – this means we do not have clear evidence either for or against his ability to understand structural dependence, or his ability to be creative with language. So the evidence for Kanzi's ability to produce language is not 'cut and dried' but has to be assessed within the context of these possible constraints.

Within this context then it seems that Kanzi can order the symbols consistently, but as with animals' 'understanding' of language spoken to them, we simply cannot determine whether this ordering reflects actions he has been rewarded for previously or a knowledge of syntax. Savage-Rumbaugh has argued strongly that Kanzi's utterances are very like those of a 2½ year old human being, and the simplest conclusion we can draw is that this reflects similar levels of linguistic competence and understanding. Therefore, Kanzi's achievements show that non-human animals have the capability for language, and rather than being qualitatively distinct from other animals, we are on one end of a continuum with them.

There are, however, psychologists who disagree with Savage-Rumbaugh's conclusion, arguing that a 2½ year old child is still developing linguistic competence, and that the inevitability of progression makes a great difference. Within a few years a child's vocabulary expands to adult size, and sentence length and complexity increase steadily to resemble adult speech. There is no clear evidence from any of the now long-standing and continuing research programmes in this area that any ape trained to use symbols to communicate undergoes a similar process of progress, despite increasing age and training. This has led some researchers, such as Pinker (1994), to conclude that language is a uniquely human ability.

There are many similarities between animal communication and human language. Both use symbols to represent events in the world and both rely on the sender and receiver of the message sharing a similar representation. Studies with captive primates suggest that they can learn the meanings of arbitrary symbols for communication. However, there are important differences too. Studies of animal communication have not provided evidence that animals can communicate about events other than the 'here and now'. Intensive attempts to teach human-like languages to primates have at best produced individuals with the linguistic abilities of a small child. These studies are continuing, but the evidence at present suggests that while there are many similarities between animal communication and human language, there may be important qualitative differences separating the two.

2.4 Natural selection of language

In Chapter 2 of Book 1, you were introduced to evolutionary theory and the concept of natural selection. Other species have very different lifestyles to our own and have been subjected to very different selection pressures in comparison to humans within their evolutionary history. We will turn to this theory now to develop an account of the historical emergence of communication systems in animal species. We will then consider whether we can identify particular factors or pressures within evolutionary history that suggest the possibility of *divergence* between human and other species modes and uses of communication. Finally, we will look at the idea that language may have arisen as a by-product of other aspects of human evolutionary development.

Within any species there is a certain amount of variation among individuals with regard to what form a characteristic (that is a behaviour or bodily feature) takes. Sometimes a characteristic helps the members of the species who have it to gain food, or mates, or to survive predation within their particular environment. This means that those individuals who possess that characteristic may live longer and may be more likely to produce greater numbers of offspring that survive to breed than those who do not possess it. Any characteristic that confers this advantage is called adaptive, because it adapts the individual to fare better (and reproduce successfully) in a particular environment than other members of the species that do not have the characteristic. These adaptive characteristics may have a genetic basis and be passed on to the offspring who will also tend to be more successful. This is, in essence, a consequence of natural selection: individuals with advantageous characteristics that enable them to survive and breed more effectively in their environment will leave more descendants than individuals without those advantageous characteristics. Subsequently, over time the proportion of individuals with advantageous characteristics will increase in a population, as individuals without that characteristic become less common. The population as a whole will have changed, and evolutionary change can be said to have occurred.

If you are having difficulty remembering what is meant by natural selection, go back now and review Chapter 2 of Book 1, Evolutionary Psychology.

Let's examine natural selection in the two examples of animal communication we began the section with. Within a beehive all of the individual bees are closely related and hence tend to share characteristics. Imagine the situation where the bees in only some hives are able to communicate the whereabouts of food to each other. Suppose that the workers from these hives have an advantage in producing food over worker bees from other hives that do not have this ability. The hive may well expand faster because more food is available and more larvae are produced and reared. Queen larvae eventually leave the hive to go and found other hives. If more queen larvae are produced and reared, then the 'communicative' bees may establish more new hives that in turn will repeat the cycle of success. In time the total bee population will gradually consist of more hives where the individuals can communicate with each other. Communication will have evolved by natural selection.

However, most adaptive characteristics have costs as well as benefits – for example, the dance that bees use to communicate about the location of food uses energy. The environment is crucial in determining the balance between costs and benefits, which constitutes adaptive value. If, for example, pollen and nectar were invariably found directly south of a hive, there would be no advantage to hives of bees with the abilities to communicate with each other about direction. Hence there would be no impetus for this ability to spread through the bee population, and the cost associated with it would make it likely not to spread.

Similarly, for vervet monkeys living in an area where there was only one type of predator, or where the optimal response was the same for all of the predators that were present, there would be no advantage to producing different calls. Conversely, if the environment changed so that there was an advantage in communicating more information rather than less, then a group containing individuals who were able to do this would be more successful. So a particular characteristic is adaptive for an individual if, in the current environment (called the environmental niche), it increases the individual's chances of successful breeding.

Perhaps then it is not so peculiar that human beings have developed language where Chimpanzees have not. As Pinker (1994) explains, we share DNA with modern apes, but the evolutionary lines leading to humans and to non-human primates split some 5–8 million years ago. However, other hominid species, for example, *Homo habilis* and *Homo erectus*, with whom archaeological evidence suggests we shared the evolved capacity for more highly developed language, have all become extinct. This has left us with our nearest DNA related species as apes, who did not evolve language because of their quite different evolutionary history after the split in primate lines. So perhaps the difference in communication abilities between humans and other species is an indication that the evolution of language conferred greater adaptational benefit only upon hominids in their particular environmental niche. Note that an environmental niche relates not only to the physical environment, but also to the interaction of individuals in their social groupings.

2.5 The adaptational costs and benefits of human language

If the theory of language as an evolved characteristic is to have validity we need evidence for it. In particular we should be able to find physical differences between humans and other animals that would have been produced by natural selection, and that can be directly linked to our propensity for using language. We also need some idea of what language does, or what we can do with it, that makes it adaptive. In looking for this kind of evidence we are adopting a reverse engineering approach, which is described in Chapter 3 of Book 1. Briefly this involves looking at a characteristic that exists now and deducing the conditions that led to its evolution.

Humans have a throat anatomy that is unique among mammals. The larynx (which houses the vocal cords) is positioned low down in the throat allowing a large amount of freedom of movement for the tongue. This allows us to articulate vowel sounds. However, it also means that, when we eat, food passes across the trachea (windpipe) bringing a risk of choking. This arrangement also compromises our breathing and chewing. Other mammals have a larynx positioned so that air can pass directly from nose to lungs avoiding these hazards. (Incidentally, newborn human babies have the typical mammalian throat anatomy and the larynx descends to the lower position only during infancy.) So, the physical ability to speak involves a cost, but to have evolved it must have conferred a greater benefit. We explore the nature of this benefit in the next section.

Planum temporale
Area of cortex involved in language.

The structure of the brain is also different in humans in comparison to other primates. A particular area of the cortex (the **planum temporale**) is larger, in most people, in the left cerebral hemisphere than in the right (this area is implicated in dyslexia, see Chapter 5 of this book). There is archaeological evidence of similar asymmetry in extinct hominids. This is not found in other primates and if parts of this area are damaged, by brain injury or stroke, a high proportion of patients exhibit language disorders. A neurologist named Carl Wernicke, working at the end of the 18th century, noted that damage to a particular area of cortex (**Wernicke's area**, situated within the planum temporale) often results in the inability to understand language, combined with the ability to produce fluent speech, which has normal intonation but which is meaningless. This has been termed **fluent aphasia**. A few years previously Paul Broca (another neurologist) had identified a more anterior cortical region that appears to play a role in language. This is known as **Broca's area** and when it is damaged a patient typically has difficulty in producing coherent

Wernicke's and Broca's area
Areas of cortex involved in language.

Fluent aphasia
An inability to produce meaningful speech despite being coherent.

speech, but instead generates disconnected words, a condition termed
non-fluent aphasia.

The area corresponding to Broca's in non-human primates has similar
anatomical features but is involved in the control of non-linguistic arm and
mouth movements. Broca's area has retained this function in humans but has
added to it a role in language (Preuss, 2000). There are difficulties, however, in
distinguishing between Broca's and Wernicke's aphasia and their anatomical
correlates, and brain imaging techniques suggest a good deal of individual
variability exists in terms of the areas of the cortex that are involved in
language. Strong evidence that parts of our anatomy, which continue in
structure and function to be similar to those of other primates, have also
changed specifically to support the additional needs of language.

We now need to consider what is it about language that could make it
such an adaptive characteristic.

> **Non-fluent aphasia**
> An inability to produce
> connected, coherent
> speech.

Activity 2.3

Look back at the beginning of this section on the differences between animal
communication and human language, try to list activities that those differences of
semanticity, displacement, structural dependence and creativity can be specifically used for.

Language and the evolution of social ability

It seems plausible that the ability to use a language may have given those
individuals who possessed it some advantage in procuring food, perhaps
via some enhanced representation of likely places to forage, or by enabling
cooperative hunting behaviour. Human languages allow flexible
communication about features of specific situations rather than the stereotypic
signals used by vervet monkeys, for example. This advantage alone might lead
to greater reproductive success, thus allowing language to spread. But human
behaviour is more complex than this, and in Activity 2.3 above you may have
identified social activities, like competition between individuals, forming
alliances or social manipulation, that are greatly enhanced by language.
Language allows knowledge and values to be transmitted so that, as well as
working with others, individuals can benefit from others' experiences and
perspectives. Language allows people to agree on plans and goals, and to work
collaboratively, thereby enabling achievements beyond the grasp of
individuals. So features that we have identified as distinguishing language from
animal communication systems (whether qualitatively or quantitatively) can
also support a very powerful (and possibly unique) set of abilities and activities
that could confer distinctive adaptational advantage.

To summarise then: language may have evolved because it conferred an advantage that allowed humans to prosper within their physical environment and indeed, as we'll discuss in Section 4, enabled them to create and manage their own social environment. The ability to use language was accompanied by anatomical changes in the throat and brain, and the costs incurred by this were outweighed by the benefits of the ability. Pinker (2000) provides an interesting review of work that has produced computer models of how aspects of language may have evolved by natural selection.

However, there are alternative accounts of how language may have arisen. Some researchers have proposed that language began evolving once humans had developed specific mental abilities. In other words rather than language *making* humans different from animals, language is seen as a *consequence* of humans being different from animals. The next section will introduce one such account.

Language and the evolution of thought

According to the philosopher and anthropologist Dan Sperber (2000) there are aspects of the ability to model what others are thinking that confer a very special adaptational advantage. In Chapter 2 of Book 1, you were introduced to the concept of theory of mind and Premack's evidence that Sarah (the chimpanzee) could understand the *intentions* of a human actor. Theory of mind is part of a set of abilities that Sperber refers to as **metarepresentations**, which essentially allow us to reflect on our own and others' mental processes. A teacher can say 'I think that some students may believe that their dog understands English'. This is a representation of a student's representation of their dog's representation – a metarepresentation. This ability doesn't necessarily require language – a footballer may use his body to try to fool the goal keeper when taking a penalty kick, and the goal keeper may likewise interpret the other's body movements as bluffs for his real intentions! The ability to reflect on the mental processes of other people could confer a large advantage: if we can predict what someone else is likely to do in a situation then social interaction of all kinds will be greatly facilitated.

Metarepresentation
An individuals representation of another person's representation, or of their own process of reflection.

Activity 2.4

Can you think of a situation where you respond to what you perceive as other people's intentions rather than their actions?

Sperber suggests that the ability to use metarepresentation conferred a huge evolutionary advantage so that this, as a characteristic in its own right, was selected for and this then *led* to the development of language. The reason that this led to language development according to Sperber is because language allowed human beings to formulate the difference between the meanings of 'I think', 'I think she thinks', and 'I think she thinks he thinks' and communicate these differences to others. It also allows us to lie to others. When we use language we seek to communicate something about our mental representations and understand those of other people. This ability lies outside of the 'concrete' nature of animal communication and requires the qualities of semanticity, displacement and structural dependence that seem to be the hallmarks of language. Thus 'metarepresentation ... . creates a favourable environment for the evolution of a new adaptation, a linguistic ability' (Sperber, 2000). The fact that apes that show limited metarepresentational abilities acquire only a limited linguistic ability is consistent with this.

So here are two possible accounts of how language could have developed through evolution, and each has very different implications for how we view its importance and the role it plays in the social and intellectual functioning that seem to distinguish humans from other species. One account claims that the facility for language development and use appeared at some point in history and delivered an adaptational advantage to those who had it. The mechanism of natural selection led to this facility for language becoming widespread in our species. What's more this suggests that greater and greater language capability would have been selected for as it conferred even greater fitness, and so language formed the foundation of development of our other cognitive capacities. A second account suggests a rather different process: that it was the development of abilities for metarepresentation, reasoning and information processing that were selected for. In this view language arose as a by-product of other cognitive capacities. So far we have presented this as an alternative to natural selection acting directly on language, but perhaps the two processes feed off each other. So while the ability to metarepresent might enable language to begin to develop, language development might in turn facilitate metarepresentational and other cognitive skills. In effect a 'ratchet' mechanism could operate, making language and other cognitive abilities interdependent.

Summary Section 2

- Animal communication is widespread, but is qualitatively different from human language.
- Attempts to teach language to apes have resulted in a few individuals achieving levels of competence arguably similar to a two to three year-old human child.
- Humans appear to have special anatomical features related to language.
- Language may have evolved through natural selection, perhaps in conjunction with other cognitive abilities.

3   Understanding language

In this section, we will explore from a cognitive perspective how people understand language. If you have ever tried to learn a new language as an adult you will probably agree that the first and most obvious difficulty is the lack of a large vocabulary, simply not knowing what words mean. In fact, when you listen to people conversing in a foreign language, it is not always easy even to identify individual words. Speech seems to be continuous. However, as you learn the language, the words stand out as discrete items and we can begin to understand their meanings. The starting point of this section will be to look at how we recognise words. However in addition, to make sense of the conversation, we need to know something of how words relate to each other. In everyday speech sentences rarely exist in isolation and the context they are set in is important to meaning too. The way we say a particular sentence can alter its meaning. The piece of text a sentence is set in influences its meaning and frequently in conversation the speaker will rely on the knowledge that they assume the listener already has. So to use and understand language effectively in communication we need access to several different sorts of knowledge. This section will look at how these three different levels of context – the word, the sentence or clause, and the larger textual context – have been theorized and investigated in terms of their contribution to understanding language.

A major concern of psychologists working from a cognitive perspective has been to investigate how this knowledge is represented and what processes are used to enable meaning to be communicated between people. As Pinker (1999) puts it 'the speaker has a thought, makes a sound and counts on the listener to hear the sound and recover that thought' (p.3). Cognitive psychologists are interested in the properties of the sound and the processes of recovery. Of course not all language is spoken and we will also look at a recent modeling of the processes involved in identifying written words, called computational modeling.

If you want to remind yourself about the characteristics of the cognitive perspective, look back at the commentary sections of Book 1, Chapters 3, 6 and 8.

3.1 Recognizing words

If you have ever looked at a piece of text written in an unfamiliar alphabet it most likely looked like nothing more than squiggles. When you look at something written in your own language though, words jump out of the page at you. The

Stroop effect, on which you work in your experimental project, (a test in which, for instance, participants try to respond 'blue' to the word 'red' written in blue ink) is a good example of how over-ridingly important semantic meaning can be when you see a word you can read. Similarly, if you hear someone speaking an unfamiliar language it can sound like a continuous stream of noise. Contrast this with your ability to pick out words in your own language even when heard on a badly tuned radio or noisy telephone line. How is it that we are able to pick out familiar words so readily? One factor that has been identified is context. Mayer and Schvaneveldt (1971) investigated the effects of semantic **priming** on a task in which participants had to decide whether or not a letter string that was flashed briefly on the screen formed a word. This task, termed a lexical decision task, was found to be much quicker when the target letter string was preceded by a word that was semantically related, that is of similar meaning. So people were quicker to judge that the letter string 'nurse' was a word if it was preceded by the word 'doctor' than if it was preceded by an unrelated word such as 'bread'. The finding that one word facilitates the recognition of another does not necessarily mean they are semantically related. Moss and Gaskell (1998) report evidence that words that frequently occur together can also facilitate the recognition of each other, for example, the word 'pillar' primes 'society', and 'elbow' primes 'grease'. This is termed *associative priming*.

> **Priming**
> A method of investigating the effect on recognition of a target word by preceding it with a different word: the priming stimulus. In semantic priming the two words are related in meaning. In associative priming they are typically words that occur close together in text or speech.

The effects of context can also be demonstrated for individual letters and sounds. Warren (1970) played tapes of sentences to participants in which a letter sound in some words was replaced with a meaningless noise. Several such sentences were used and two examples were: 1) The *eel was on the axle and 2) The *eel was on the shoe, where * represents the meaningless noise. Participants presented with the first sentence reported hearing the word 'wheel', whereas those who were presented with the second sentence heard 'heel'. Again a similar phenomenon has been reported with written text. Reicher (1969) performed an experiment in which a string of letters was very briefly shown to participants who had to identify, say, the middle letter. He found that if the letter string formed a meaningful word then the target letter was more easily identified. This is termed the **word superiority effect**. Interestingly there is also a pseudo-word superiority effect in which a letter is recognized more easily when it is presented in a letter string that could be a word but is not. For example, 'tife' could conceivably be an English word, whereas 'tfei' could not.

> **Word superiority effect**
> The finding that a letter is detected more readily when it is embedded in a word then when it is not.

Activity 2.5

Look at the two pairs of letter strings below. If you were asked to name the third letter from the left in each, which of each pair would be easiest to recognise if there was a word superiority effect and a pseudo-word superiority effect?

Pair 1) Fold or Fdlo.

Pair 2) Flod or Dfol.

Note: in an experiment the letter strings would be presented for a very brief period (20ms) and then you would be asked to identify the letter in a particular position.

McClelland and Rumelhart (1981) proposed what has proved to be an extremely influential model of visual word recognition. The model was designed to account for the word superiority effect, and uses general principles of information processing that have subsequently been the basis of a particular kind of model used widely in cognitive psychology to simulate other aspects of cognition. This type of model is often referred to as a **connectionist model**, although you may come across the terms 'parallel distributed processing' (PDP) and 'neural networks', which are sometimes used as near synonyms in some textbooks.

We will look quite closely at the way this model works to give you a basic understanding of what is involved in this kind of approach within the cognitive perspective on language (and indeed other aspects of cognition). We will then briefly outline how connectionist models of language are currently developing.

The connectionist model of language processes proposes that processing of a word occurs at three levels, and that all these levels can interact with each other. So if we take the process of recognising the word 'TIME', when we first see it, processing will occur at the level of features, letters and words. At the level of features, it is proposed that there are detector units in our information processing system that respond to the features of letters like curves to the left or right, circles, vertical and horizontal lines and so on. On seeing the first letter T of 'TIME' the feature detectors for a horizontal and a vertical line will respond strongly. This in turn will send a charge of energy to all the letters at the letter level of processing that incorporate, as part of their features, horizontal and vertical bars – letters like L, Z and T. But the amount of energy will be proportional to how much the letter exactly matches only the features that have been charged up by the stimulus letter, so most energy will go to the letter T.

The letter T will in turn pass on energy to the word level, to all those words that have the letter T in first place in the word, and so among the many words energised will be the word TIME. The energisation of the word TIME feeds back to the letter level, sending energy to letters I, M and E, so that when the second letter, I, is seen as the word is read, those letters already possess some energy and this is increased by actually seeing the features of the letter I. So the I is more easily recognised as the next letter of the word, and this feeds even more energy to the word level for the word TIME, and this in turn feeds back to energise the letter detectors for M and E. This makes M and E even more easy to recognise and so on. Many different types of this model have been developed, but the core principles remain those we have described. One of the earliest formal models was the Interactive Activation with Competition Model, shown in Box 2.2 below.

Connectionist model
A type of computer model that contains simple units that are connected to each other in a network structure.

2.2   The Interactive Activation with Competition (IAC) model (McClelland and Rumelhart, 1981)

This model is designed to show how two sorts of information can interact to allow a word with four letters to be recognized. The two sorts of information are first that coming in from the sense organs (bottom-up processing), and second a stored representation of the word (top-down processing). The main features of the model are set out below:

- The basic framework or architecture involves a large set of units arranged in three levels, a feature level comprising 14 units, a letter level of 26 units and a word level of 1179 units. Figure 2.1 shows a simplified illustration of this with considerably fewer units.

- The model analyses each letter separately so four copies of the letter and feature units are needed, one for each letter position.

- When a feature is detected the matching feature unit becomes excited.

- Each feature unit can pass excitation to the units for each letter that contains that feature. This is an example of bottom-up processing.

- Each letter unit can pass excitation to the units for each word that contains that letter in the appropriate position. This too is an example of bottom-up processing.

- Each word unit can also send excitation down to its constituent letter units. This is top-down processing.

- When a letter or word unit reaches a critical level of excitation it is recognized.

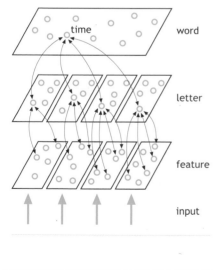

word

letter

feature   **Figure 2.1**   A simplified sketch of the IAC network (McClelland, 1985)

input   *The input is T I M E. Each of the four boards at feature and letter level refers to a particular letter position.*

As well as these excitatory links the model incorporates *inhibitory connections*. These are shown in Figure 2.2, which is a more detailed picture of what happens during the detection of a letter in the initial position of the word. Inhibition is represented by lines ending in small circles rather than arrows.

The rules governing inhibition are as follows (McClelland and Rumelhart, 1981):

- For a particular letter position when a unit at the letter level is excited it passes inhibition to every other letter unit.
- When a unit at the word level is excited it passes inhibition to every other word unit.
- Between levels excitation in a letter unit sends inhibition to words that do not have that letter in the appropriate position.
- A feature unit likewise sends inhibition to every letter unit corresponding to a letter that does not posses that feature.

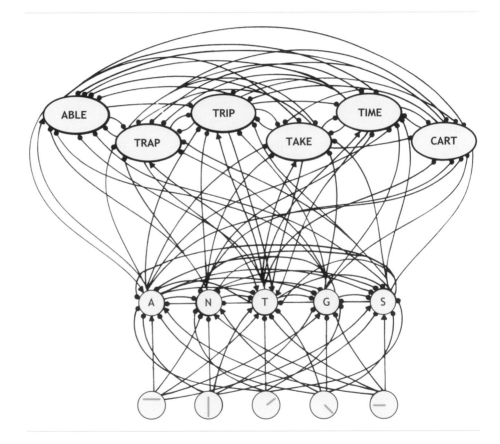

Figure 2.2 The microstructure of the IAC network showing inhibitory (●) and excitatory (▲) connections for the first letter position only (after McClelland and Rumelhart, 1981)

So, looking now at Figure 2.2, when the letter 'T' unit is excited it sends inhibition to all other letter units, this means that it becomes more difficult for those letters to be perceived in first letter position. Similarly, when the 'TIME' unit is excited it sends inhibition to all other word units. 'TRIP' and 'TRAP', which receive <u>excitation</u> from 'T', will also receive <u>inhibition</u> from 'TIME'. When the second letter 'I' is detected more excitation will be sent to 'TIME' but inhibition will be sent to 'TRIP' and 'TRAP'. 'TIME' will thus receive most excitation. The model is interactive in the sense that perception is occurring at all three levels: when a word is activated it excites the units corresponding to its constituent letters, which as we have noted are also excited by the feature units. The 'competition' in the name of the model refers to units receiving excitation and inhibition from different sources, and those that receive the highest net 'energy' determine what is perceived. One very important feature of this model is that the different processes occur in parallel with each other, so letter and word identification occur at the same time as feature detection. This enables very rapid word identification, corresponding to human abilities.

Activity 2.6

Looking at Figure 2.2 if 'A' is detected in position two which word units would be energised? (Answer at the end of Section 3.)

This model can account for what are termed the word superiority and pseudo-word superiority effects. Look at the example in Activity 2.5. When the word 'FOLD' is presented excitation from the letter units F, O & D will excite the unit that represents 'FOLD' and this in turn will transmit excitation to 'L' thus reducing the amount of energy it needs from the visual input. With FDLO very little excitation will occur at the word unit level and hence the 'L' letter unit will need to gain more excitation from the visual input in order to be recognized. The pseudo-word effect reflects the overlap with actual English word patterns. So the stimulus 'FLOD' (which is a pseudo-word) will produce some excitation in, for example, 'FLOW' and this will raise the excitation of the 'O' unit, so it will require less 'bottom-up' excitation to be recognized.

The original model does have a number of limitations (perhaps the most obvious of which is that it can only recognise a limited number of words and these must all be composed of four capital letters!). However, since 1981 computational models using these basic principles of a continuous interaction between stored and sensory information have been successfully applied to explain some of the range of linguistic processing phenomena discovered experimentally. For example, Moss and Gaskell (1998) discuss how semantic and associative priming effects can be modelled using this approach.

3.2 Understanding sentences

When we have recognized a word how do we know what it means? Most current models of language postulate a **lexicon** or 'mental dictionary'. The lexical entry for a word contains everything we know about that word, how to pronounce it (phonology), spell it (orthography) its definition (semantics) and

Lexicon
A mental dictionary that contains information about individual words.

what role it can play in a sentence (syntactic information). With this information we can start to build a representation of the meaning of a sentence. The issues involved in understanding sentences are somewhat different from those involved in recognizing words. Pickering (1999) has identified three differences. First, we *recognise* words, but the sentences we typically encounter are novel. For example, you are presumably familiar with each individual word in the sentence you have just read but have probably never heard or read that particular sentence before. Therefore, a representation has to be *formed* rather than *retrieved*. A second point is that sentences are sequential, the words are encountered in a particular order and this raises the question of when we begin building the representation. Do we wait until the sentence is complete or begin building as the words are being perceived? Finally a sentence contains two types of information – the meanings of the individual words and the syntactical structure. To illustrate these consider the two possible utterances below:

1   Colourless green ideas sleep furiously.

2   Skid crash hospital

The first sentence is perhaps the most famous sentence that the linguist Noam Chomsky ever wrote. He used it to demonstrate a grammatically correct though totally meaningless sentence. The second (from Scott and Spencer, 1998) is agrammatical and yet we know what it might mean, it conveys semantic information. How then do we combine these two sorts of information?

One problem with experimentally investigating how we understand sentences is that we are extremely quick and accurate in doing so. This makes measurement of the time it takes to read and to understand quite difficult. So psychologists have used sentences that are unusual and take longer to understand in order to investigate the processes we use to form representations of these and, by extrapolation, more usual sentences. For example, **garden-path sentences** are often used, so called because they initially trick the reader into a wrong conceptualisation – taking the reader (as the saying goes) up the garden path.

Garden path sentences
Ambiguous sentences in which the structure that is usually selected first is incorrect.

Activity 2.7

Read the following sentences.

1   As Jay always jogs a mile seems a short distance.

2   The old man the boats.

3   As the women edited the magazine amused all the reporters.

Did the sentences seem odd? And were you aware of having to puzzle over any particular word or words? See below for a discussion of why these sentences are difficult to understand.

In an experiment similar to Activity 2.7 above, Frazier and Rayner (1982) found that readers presented with the first sentence took longer to read the sentence than did those who received an identical version but with the word 'this' placed between the words 'mile' and 'seems'. They also looked at eye movements and found that, in reading the sentence, readers looked back at the first part of the sentence immediately after reading 'seems'. Reading the sentence with 'this' in did not produce this backtracking. This suggests that people do begin to process a sentence before it is completed. The next question to consider then is how we process an entire sentence. At the beginning of the section it was mentioned that the entry in the lexicon or 'mental dictionary' for a word includes information about the syntactical role or roles they can take in a sentence. So, for the second sentence (taken from Greene and Coulson, 1995, p.75) the word 'old' can be either an adjective (as in 'old man') or a noun (as in 'a home for the old'). Similarly, 'man' can be a noun or a verb. In processing the sentence then, we have the option to choose one of two syntactic structures and follow it through. So in the second sentence we might assign 'old' to an adjective and 'man' to a noun, which works fine until we encounter 'the boats' and realise that the words don't make sense. We would then need to backtrack and reassign words: this fits with other evidence that we move our eyes back to the words that need to be reanalysed.

Of course there is another source of evidence that will help us to make sense of the syntax of a sentence: semantic knowledge. Pickering and Traxler (1998) investigated another version of the third sentence, above. In that other version, the word 'sailed' was substituted for 'edited'. Both verbs can either take an object, so it makes sense to say 'edited a book' or 'sailed a boat', or not take an object, with just 'Jane sailed' or 'Jane edited' as acceptable. In their experimental study, Pickering and Traxler found that the 'sailed' version of the third sentence did not lead participants up the garden path, although the 'edited' version did. One interpretation of this finding is that the semantic information stored in the lexical representation of a word helps determine the syntactic role it is assigned.

An alternative way to consider how semantic knowledge could be used to make sense of 'The old man the boats' is to look at the context in which it occurs. If this sentence was encountered immediately after the phrase 'when the young leave the fishing village', then 'old' would be more likely to be identified as a noun.

This idea that semantic and syntactic knowledge are used in an integrated way to understand a sentence is still a topic of debate. The philosopher Jerry Fodor claims that sentence understanding happens too quickly for us to be able to bring all of our semantic knowledge to bear on every word. He suggests instead that syntactic knowledge is encapsulated in a module that analyses sentence structure, and it is only once this is done that semantic knowledge is used to understand the meaning of the sentence (Fodor, 1983). Steven Pinker suggests that the reason why some sentences lead us 'up the garden path' could be because certain words are associated in a non-semantic way with each other (Pinker 1994). So the reason why the word 'edited' induces a garden path effect, whereas 'sailed' does not in Activity 2.7, is because when the words 'edited' and 'magazine' have previously been encountered close together, then 'edited' has taken an object. If the syntax module can use statistical information such as this, then it is more likely that a correct syntactical category will be selected for an ambiguous word. The statistically most probable category is usually the correct one, so garden path sentences are deliberately chosen to trick the reader. This debate over whether linguistic analysis is accomplished by independent modules or by the integration of different knowledge sources has yet to be concluded.

3.3 Understanding stories

Discourse
In cognitive psychology, a piece of text or speech consisting of related sentences.

Effort after meaning
The attempt by listeners and readers to understand the meaning of discourse.

We now move to the level of how people understand written text and speech, or pieces of **discourse**. So far we have implied that people listen to individual words then put them together to try to decode the meaning of each sentence. But, except when carrying out a grammatical exercise, people are usually trying to grasp the meaning of the whole story. We continually make assumptions about events in the real world in a process referred to as **effort after meaning** (see Chapter 8 of Book 1).

Activity 2.8

Read the following passage and judge how easy it is to understand:

> If the balloons popped the sound wouldn't be able to carry since everything would be too far away from the correct floor. A closed window would also prevent the sound from carrying, since most buildings tend to be well insulated. Since the whole operation depends upon a steady flow of electricity, a break in the middle of the wire would also cause problems. Of course, the fellow could shout, but the human voice is not loud enough to carry that far.

> Taken from Bransford and Johnson, 1973, p.289–90

Bransford and Johnson found that participants rated the story in Activity 2.8 as incomprehensible unless they were shown the picture in Figure 2.3 (shown at the end of Section 3.3) before reading it. Now look at the figure and re-read the text in Activity 2.8. Another way that allowed participants to make sense of similar pieces of discourse was to provide a meaningful title before it was read. Bransford and Johnson concluded that, in order to make sense of a discourse, we must know the context in which it is set. In other words, we need a framework for organizing information.

One good example of such a framework is Schank and Abelson's representation of every day knowledge that is needed for understanding stories. The authors use the term **script** to describe events in normal situations. (A script is a kind of schema – see Chapter 6 of Book 1). According to this model, people build a representation of what has typically happened in the past, and use this to build an expectation of what will happen when that situation is encountered again. If we have this kind of information then we can supply the knowledge to make sense of a piece of text in which all of the details are not spelled out. For example, to understand an utterance such as *'If you try that new restaurant make sure you have plenty of time, and money'* you need to draw heavily on stored knowledge about restaurants, such as that you have to wait to be served and pay money for the meal. Scripts could be said to contain encyclopaedic information about particular situations that we have encountered in the past, and we can use that information to make inferences such as the money will be needed to pay for the meal. As we already noted, language also contains a good deal of bottom-up information and a number of models of understanding discourse have been proposed that take some of the principles of schema-based knowledge (i.e. top-down knowledge) and incorporate them with bottom-up processes.

Gernsbacher and Foertsh (1999) have presented three models with this kind of integration, but we will take one of these as an example: that of Kintsch (1988, 1994). This model takes the **proposition** as the basic unit. Propositions are the smallest unit of meaning that can be taken from a sentence or clause. For example, the sentence 'The black bat is in the barn' contains two propositions, the bat is black and the bat is in the barn. Propositions can be thought of as the simplest string of words that can be either true or false.

As you read the text, 'The black bat is in the barn', word meanings in the text are accessed and these produce propositions. Kintsch proposes that each proposition is represented by a unit that is similar to the units in the IAC model you encountered in Section 3.1. When a proposition is encountered the unit that represents it becomes energised. The unit passes energy at the same time to any other units that represent propositions about the barn that have previously been encountered. For example, the proposition 'the bat is in the barn' may energise propositions such as 'the ball is in the barn' and 'the barn is very dark'. The next proposition is then analysed and energises other stored units. In this way a huge number of units are activated and these form a propositional network or web composed of those in the text and those retrieved from long-term memory. This network is *constructed* of propositional units with varying levels of energy, as some of the stored units

Script
A schema that represents a typical event.

Proposition
A statement consisting of a single idea or unit of meaning.

Figure 2.3   Picture for Activity 2.8

will receive energy from other incoming propositions. So, for example, if another proposition, 'bats roost', was read then 'bats roost' will excite propositions that relate to roosting places and bats as animals, so it will also energise 'the barn is very dark'. It is the most highly excited units that will be *integrated* to form a stable representation of the text as a whole, a *mental model* of the meaning of the communication. Those units that are only weakly excited will not be part of the network that, because it has become strongly linked together, represents what the meaning is.

Kintsch has also incorporated a learning mechanism into his model that allows the excitatory links between units to be strengthened whenever they are activated in quick succession. So when two propositions are read sequentially the energy link between the units representing them is strengthened. Then, whenever one of them is subsequently activated again, excitation will be transmitted to the other related unit. This kind of system can be used to explain the ways in which past experience or knowledge is used. Kintsch called this a *construction-integration* model and in contrast to Schank and Abelson's scripts it is *driven* by information taken from the text. So, for example, the propositions formed from 'the bat is in the barn' may activate propositions in long-term memory that involve cricket and flying mammals. As subsequent clarifying propositions are read, they in turn will activate either units concerning 'cricket' propositions or different units concerning 'mammal' propositions so that, by the system of strengthening energy links described above, the correct sense of the proposition will gradually become apparent and the incorrect sense will be ignored.

3.4 Conversation and pragmatics

So far then we have looked at how cognitive psychologists suggest people understand well-constructed monologues. Experiments typically present participants with a written piece of prose to read, or a recording of an individual reading, often in a monotone, from a scripted piece of text. But our everyday language is more often *dialogue* – we hold conversations with each other. We may use rhythm and stress in our voice to clarify a sentence. For example, the utterance 'It was you' can be a statement or a question depending on the way we utter it. This intonation is termed **prosody**.

Prosody
Aspects of the sound of speech, such as stress and rhythm, that function to clarify or reinforce the meaning of a sentence.

Activity 2.9

Try saying 'The waiter gave Jim a drink then he gave him some money' in different ways, so that 'he' refers first to the waiter and then to Jim.

Prosody is another source of information that enables us to build a representation of meaning. It can be thought of as analogous to punctuation in written language. To indicate that 'It was you' is a question in written text we add a question mark. In speech we raise the pitch of our voice on the final word. Similarly, we could use a comma to clarify the written sentence in Activity 2.9, but we vary the stress on the words when we say them.

Conversations by their nature are social ventures so, as well as using linguistic information and our own knowledge, we also need to consider the knowledge of our conversational partner. Grice (1975) proposed that, in order to converse successfully, both parties need to cooperate and obey a number of maxims or principles on which to base their interaction. According to Sperber and Wilson (1986), the most important of these maxims or principles is the maxim of relevance. The sender and receiver of information enter into a kind of contract, such that the recipient of any information expects it to relate to the representation he or she already has. So the person sending or making the communication tailors it to fit the expectations and knowledge of the receiver. The proposal is that this kind of contract for communication allows ambiguities in conversation to be resolved, so individuals take turns to be speakers and to work on making their communication effective within the context of the knowledge and expectations of their listener. This fits with Sperber's later ideas, discussed in Section 2, of the importance of metarepresentation to the evolution of language in *humans*.

This use of metarepresentation in making communication means that our utterances are not simply composed to convey information. They are designed to carry meanings that are not contained within the syntactic and semantic content of the words alone. The statement 'It is nine o'clock' is a literal statement of the time, but the actual purpose of the statement may be to suggest that it is getting too late for something or that a particular event has occurred that was scheduled for nine o'clock. The statement 'you are standing on my foot' is generally intended and understood as a request for action rather than a simple communication of fact. These other factors contributing to the meaning of a particular communication, are called **pragmatics** – the knowledge of the contingent particulars of circumstances in which a communication is made, and of the knowledge, desires and intentions of the people involved in the communication.

Pragmatics
The way that the intended rather than the literal meaning of language is inferred.

So, in order to 'recover the thought' that someone is trying to communicate, cognitive psychologists working on language argue that we need to take account of many different types of information. We need to recognise words, we need to know how these words fit together, we need to select relevant information we already possess to interpret the new material, and we need to know about our expectations and those of the communicator. Cognitive psychologists characterise meaning in different ways. In the context of the connectionist models we have mentioned, meaning refers to the patterns of connections between units. In Kintsch's model outlined above, the meaning of a proposition in a piece of text depends on which other propositions are related to it. Cognitive psychologists have also investigated how the meaning of any particular word or string of words depends upon the context in which they are perceived. Finally, in conversation, meaning depends on perceptions of what a communicator meant to communicate, and on the hearer's metarepresentation as well as the speakers representation. In Section 4, we shall see how social psychologists studying language have taken up the issues of pragmatics; namely that meaning does not reside simply in the words and sentences of language, and that the purpose of communication may encompass more than recovering the thoughts of others.

Summary Section 3

- In order to understand a piece of text or an utterance people use a number of different kinds of information.
- Lexical, semantic and syntactic information, and also knowledge of what typically happens in our world, are all important for understanding. In order to engage successfully in a conversation, participants need knowledge of each other's representations and intentions.
- Cognitive psychologists are interested in how people integrate these different kinds of information to build representations of text meaning.
- Connectionist models have been developed that can explain how top-down and bottom-up processing might interact to produce various language phenomena.

Answer to Activity 2.6

The answer to the question posed in Activity 2.6 is: 'TAKE' and 'CART'.

4   Using language, creating meaning

In the previous section, you were introduced to the cognitive psychological perspective on language that focuses on how an individual understands language. Section 3 described how the recipient of a communication might successfully reconstruct the communicator's application of syntactic rules and semantics, and use their knowledge of the working of scripts and script events, and the social context of the communication.

4.1   Introduction

In this section, we turn our attention to social psychological approaches to language, which focus on understanding language and its meanings as first and foremost a social process. In this approach, it is crucial that language always takes place between at least two people. Language is seen as inherently social because it involves something taking place *among* a number of people, and it is in this social interaction that the meaning of language is made.

Activity 2.10

Below is a piece of dialogue that illustrates the importance of the social nature of language production. Read the dialogue and try to answer the questions that follow it.

Man: Right you can go back a little further, maybe a foot, then you'll have room to straighten up as you go forward.

Woman: Could you just let me do it on my own – I'll only learn by doing it myself.

Man: You could just go back and I can tell you when to stop – I'm taller than you are so I can see the car behind better

Woman: I wouldn't need you to tell me if I learnt to do it myself.

Man: I'm only trying to help, don't go off the deep end!

Woman: You're always trying to help me; I feel like I can't do anything without you offering advice.

Man: You trot out this kind of rubbish whenever I try to help you, no matter how gentle I am about it. If that's the way you feel, fine; I won't offer any help at all in future.

- Look at the first utterance to 'go back a little further' – how many different contexts can you think of where that instruction might be given?

- At what point did you realise that the context concerned parking a car – was it before the car itself was mentioned in the third communication - how did you infer this?

- What do you think the relationship is between the man and woman: are they friends, family members, driving instructor and pupil?

- How do you know? What kinds of knowledge are you drawing on?

- What is the argument about that is taking place in this dialogue – is there one topic of argument or several, and do the speakers agree about what they are arguing about?

A social psychologist would propose that there is much more to understanding the meaning of the conversation in Activity 2.10 than the knowledge of syntax, semantics, pragmatics and script sequences – no matter how much these are modelled as interactive within a cognitive language processing system. Consideration of this piece of 'real-life' dialogue presents us with an example of how meaning *emerges* during a whole episode of communication. It demonstrates that the argument taking place is not so much about informational content (i.e. how to park the car), as about what each proposes the other accomplishes by their contribution. The meaning that the man intends for his first utterance – giving advice – is interpreted by the woman as being domineering or exercising control. As the conversation continues the argument develops not about who can see better to park, but about the intentions of the speakers involved and what they seek to achieve. In other words the argument does not occur because the woman has failed to understand the words that the man says about his intention when giving advice. She is arguing with him instead about whether these really 'were' his intentions, since the effect of what he said seems to fit with another intention (to make her feel dependent).

Contested
The process by which an individual challenges the meanings being constructed, or actions accomplished, by another speaker.

Meanings here are constructed and **contested** between speakers as the interaction proceeds. It is clear in this context that there are meanings, and disagreements over meanings, that relate to an entire history of the relationship between the man and the woman. Most western readers of this exchange will have used their cultural knowledge of intimate, personal relationships between men and women to infer that these two people are probably husband and wife or living in some close relationship to each other. They will know that control and autonomy is currently a common area of contention in this kind of relationship. This knowledge is a crucial part of how meanings are dynamically constructed here; it is not simply additional context that is necessary to successfully reconstruct the meanings that each speaker intended to give their utterances.

There is a second further point to be made about the exchange above that reflects a contrast between the focus of social psychological and cognitive approaches to language. In social psychological approaches the purpose of language is not to reflect individuals' internal perceptions, cognitions or feelings and convey them neutrally to another. Instead it is proposed that when we communicate it is always because we want to <u>do</u> something: there is an action to be accomplished. In the conversation above, giving information about how to park is not a neutral act of describing the world. Would the man have given his advice if he thought the woman was capable of parking on her own, and could judge the distance and space adequately? Almost certainly not, so that is the apparent purpose in giving advice. The argument that then ensued was about whether the apparent purpose was the real one, or whether there were other intentions underlying the giving of advice and its results. The woman felt positioned by the man as 'inadequate' and 'dependent', while the man positioned himself as 'helpful' and 'caring'. It is a central theme of social psychological approaches to language then, that the meaning of any actual communication episode does not lie in the rules of syntax and semantics, or the application of pragmatic knowledge about scripts and schemas. Meaning lies in the goals, purposes and use of any communication, and in the interpretation of particular meaning by those (with their own goals and purposes) for whom the communication is intended. In the social psychological approach, this process of construction of meaning applies equally to solitary thinking or reading, where the use of language is in a dialogue with the self.

In this section, we shall explore the idea of meaning making as a dynamic social activity. We shall look at how individuals use language not only to interpret and understand their world but to become active agents within it, and use language to achieve their goals and purposes. We shall also examine the more general thesis of the social constructionist perspective on language, namely that language is the medium though which our selves, our actions and our knowledge of the world are constructed. In particular, this approach proposes that all knowledge about what people think, experience or do – all psychological knowledge – should be grounded in the study of how language creates that thought, experience and behaviour, not only at the level of the individual but at the level of groups and society.

4.2 Language and the social world

The focus on language as an arena of social activity, where people use language to pursue the goals and purposes of everyday life, came initially from a group of sociologists who began to study language in qualitative ways. They wished to move away from the assumptions of quantitative analysis, which they saw as excessively dominating work on language and social interaction. One sociologist, Harold Garfinkel (1967), developed a method called **ethnomethodology** – literally the study of how people(s) do things. The method in ethnomethodology meant that the researcher lived with the particular people or social group they were interested in, as one of them. By living their life, doing things the way they did them and listening above all to what was said (as this constitutes the most important medium for action), researchers were to analyse how things were done. They were to formulate

Ethnomethodology
A study of the socially shared knowledge of rules, roles and conduct, that individuals draw upon to analyse, understand and act in everyday life.

descriptions of frameworks, procedures and rules that represented a complete description of how things were done in everyday life.

A classic study by Wieder (1974, cited in Potter and Wetherell, 1987) is a good example of this method. Weider was a sociologist who went to stay in a half-way hostel for newly released prisoners that aimed to help them find their feet once out of prison and keep them away from drugs. He took part in all the routines, observed the running and business of the hostel, slept and ate and talked with the residents. It is part of accepted sociological knowledge that in most institutions there is an informal set of rules that guide the behaviour of those who live there, quite separate from the formal rules of the institution. Wieder identified such a set of rules for the hostel that he called 'The Code'. He claimed that 'The Code' gave the rules of conduct by which the residents lived.

The Code (taken from Potter and Wetherell, 1987, p.20)

There are eight basic maxims to 'The Code'

1   Above all, do not snitch.
2   Do not cop out.
3   Do not take advantage of other resident
4   Share what you have.
5   Help other residents.
6   Do not mess with other residents' interests.
7   Do not trust staff – staff is heat.
8   Show your loyalty to other residents.

But The Code itself was not seen by Wieder as the *explanation* for behaviour, as the set of rules that caused residents to behave the way they did. Instead, it was the *resource* that residents used to actively interpret their world and construct what they and others did. For example, Wieder noticed that quite often when he was chatting amicably to a resident he (the resident) would close the conversation with a comment that he did not wish to talk any further because he was not a 'snitch' (which is one of the very strong rules of The Code). Weider thought about the regularity with which this occurred and concluded that talking to him could be constructed as a risky thing to do – making the community vulnerable by giving information about them to an outsider. Wieder concludes that, by finishing the conversation in this way, the resident was not passively 'acting out' The Code, but using it to actively define the boundaries of his action – talking but not 'snitching' – and to use the rule that they don't snitch to control the extent of talk and risk being taken.

This sociological approach to language as a resource, actively used by speakers to construct their social world and take action within it, led some social psychologists to begin rethinking psychological approaches to language. They began to develop an approach that proposed that the personal and apparently individual world of experience, cognition and emotion was also constructed and enacted through language.

Discursive psychology: how meaning is constructed.

In Chapter 1 of Book 1 the notion of discourse, in terms of the construction of identity, was explained as 'ways of thinking and talking about issues currently available to our culture … the processes by which people construct meaning' (see Section 5.2 of Chapter 1, Book 1). Discursive psychology focuses on the proposal that the meaning created through discourses conditions our thinking about and understanding of the external world and of ourselves within it.

Parker (1992) describes a **discourse** as 'a system of statements which defines an object' (p.5). By this he means that discourses are sets of symbolic meanings created through the use of language (in talk, story-telling, novels, magazines, advertising, television, radio and so on) to construct a particular version of events or represent a particular thing in a particular way (note that discursive psychology uses 'discourse' in a different way to that of cognitive psychology). For example, in Chapter 1 of Book 1, you were given the example of the difference between calling Nelson Mandela a terrorist (as he was called by the apartheid supporting government of pre-1989) or a freedom fighter (by the apartheid opposed African National Congress movement of the same era).

Discourse (Social Psychology)
In discursive psychology discourse is the spoken or written matter by which a particular object is constructed.

Activity 2.11

Think about the description 'terrorist'. What thoughts come to mind? Think wide-rangingly and freely. How does a terrorist view their country, the value of human life, the issues of democracy and of morality? Think a bit more widely. Is a terrorist a socially integrated person, likely to give priority to friends and family in their lives? Are their interests going to be wide-ranging or narrow; will they be liberal minded or authoritarian? Now answer exactly the same for 'freedom-fighter'. Where do you think you have got this kind of awareness of what these two types of people are like?

You will probably have read books, films, newspapers, heard radio and TV news and so on, and so have a whole history of exposure to a wide variety of representations about these words, apparently descriptive of only one aspect of behaviour, but actually about a whole person and what they are like. This 'system of statements' defines the object under discussion – terrorist or freedom fighter – in quite complex and broad ways. They do much more than simply relate to the reason why an individual is engaged in acts of aggression against the powers of the state. These two words represent two different discourses that can then be used for the same man and construct him in two entirely different and complex ways, giving two different accounts of 'reality'.

Discursive psychology is not proposing that the representations and descriptions developed through discourse create an account that is imposed upon reality. After all, how can we establish whether Nelson Mandela was *really* a terrorist or a freedom fighter? Rather, discursive psychology proposes that discourses create what we think of as the reality of the world, and that is why Parker said that discourses *define* objects. The descriptions of Nelson Mandela as either terrorist or freedom fighter were not simply a difference of opinion about the nature of his activities, but constructions of reality that constituted or defined Mandela as a particular type of person (or 'object'). This in turn constructs or defines how all that he did and said is understood and given meaning.

Discursive psychology proposes that discourses are 'designed' to accomplish particular constructions of reality, in that discourses are chosen or created by individuals or groups to construct a reality that best serves their interests or needs. An important feature of language then, as hinted at in the Nelson Mandela example above, is that in any one situation there will often be a number of *competing* discourses being used by different people or groups with different interests. This competition is about which construction of reality will prevail; that is which will be accepted and acted upon by the larger community or those with power. Discourse psychologists propose, therefore, that an understanding of the interests and investments involved in the use of discourse, the goal or purpose of gaining or maintaining power at any level large or small, is an important part of understanding language use.

Given this view of language, discourse psychologists have found two areas of research important to pursue. One is to look at the actual content of particular discourses: how are people who use a given discourse constructing the world? You were given a flavour of this kind of research when we looked at the words 'terrorist' and 'freedom-fighter' in Activity 2.11. Discourse analysis of the content of the discourses of 'terrorist' and 'freedom-fighter' would look systematically at instances of talk or text that used these terms in order to establish how they are constructed in relation to each other and other objects of social, political, cultural and personal life. The second area focuses on one obvious consequence of the notion of many competing discourses being available to individuals or groups. This is that individuals are continually involved in choosing which discourses to use in order to construct and act within their world, and quite often they will need to be creative in finding a discourse that does what they want. They may even choose two or more discourses to construct parts of their world that are in conflict with each other. In that case, they will need to find some way of reconciling that conflict.

At the time of writing this chapter, one of the authors (Cooper) is a mother of two young children, and working full-time for the Open University: if I want to construct myself as a good mother I will have to draw on the dominant cultural discourse of traditional motherhood, which positions good mothers as loving, nurturing and self-sacrificing to their children. However as a woman working full-time, I am not constantly available to my children, and I have not sacrificed my career or economic independence to be with my children full-time. In constructing my identity as a good mother, I can resist seeing my involvement in paid work as selfish by drawing on a more recent discourse of motherhood, which includes in the notion of good mothering ensuring that one's children are provided for materially. Paid work is positioned as selfish in one discourse but not so in another.

There are many other discourses about being a good mother that I could bring in to use within my account of myself as a good mother. This act of creating an identity for myself as a good mother in relation to all these discourses is called the creation of a **subject position** (in that I have created my identity by positioning myself as the subject of particular discourses in particular ways). As we saw in Chapter 1 of Book 1, the construction of identity is an important and continuous part of an individual's life. Discursive psychology proposes that individuals are continually building and adjusting identities through the creation of subject positions in all kinds of discourse or set of discourses. Of course they are also positioning other people, by creating subject positions for them also.

I have created my subject position as 'good mother' using a very active process. I was drawing on some elements of different discourses of motherhood and rejecting others. The knowledge that I had of available discourses about what constitutes being a good mother, and the strategies I used to reposition behaviour that the traditional discourse might construct as bad mothering, is called my **interpretative repertoire**. Discourse psychologists use a method called discourse analysis to explore and establish the types of discourse that are available for people to use, and the way these are employed in particular interpretative repertoires.

> **Subject position**
> The place or character an individual can construct for themselves using discourses and particular recognized positions like 'the good mother'.

> **Interpretative repertoire**
> The sum of different discourses, and the ways that they can be combined or mixed together, which the individual has at their disposal to construct subject positions.

2.4 FEATURED METHOD

Discourse Analysis

Because of their emphasis upon the active construction of accounts, discourse analysts interested in the identification of interpretative repertoires (they sometimes refer to themselves as 'discourse psychologists') very often use transcripts or interviews and 'natural' conversations as their material for analysis (e.g. McKinlay and Potter, 1987, pp.443–63; Potter and Wetherell, 1989; Marshall and Raabe, 1993; Gill 1993). However, other kinds of material are occasionally used, such as newspaper reports (Edwards and Potter, 1992), television programmes (Potter et al., 1991) and child-care manuals (Marshall, 1991).

Interpretative repertoires ... are seen as linguistic resources or tool-kits available to speakers in the construction of their accounts. They are seen as analogous to the moves of a ballet dancer: finite in number and available to all ballet dancers for the design of a variety of dances suitable to a variety of occasions. If you went to enough ballet performances, you would eventually begin to recognise the repertoire of moves that the dancers have available to them. The idea of a repertoire, therefore, involved the idea of flexibility of use; the moves can be put together in different ways to suit the occasion (a feature not present in the idea of discourses as coherent, organized sets of statements.)

Researchers in the 'interpretative repertoires' field look for the metaphors, grammatical constructions, figures of speech and so on that people use in constructing their accounts. By examining the talk of different people when they are, say, interviewed about a topic, it is possible to monitor the way that some figures of speech, metaphors and so on keep turning up in the talk of different people. By abstracting such usages across different interviews on the same topic, it is claimed that the researcher can identify such repetitions or 'moves' as a repertoire. Therefore, both variability and repetition are features which such analysts are looking for in their material. Variability can be expected within a single interview, because respondents can be expected to make use of different repertoires to suit their current purposes. Repetition across different interviews can be expected because the same repertoires will be used by different people.

Burr, 1999, p.176–7

4.3 The implications of discursive psychology for doing psychology

Because of their position that language constructs thought and action rather than reflecting it, discourse psychologists have challenged many of the assumptions made within other perspectives in psychology. One of these is that language is a process that reflects 'underlying' cognitive processes taking place in an individual's mind. To illustrate how this challenge can be supported let us take as an example attribution theory.

At the end of Section 3, Chapter 7 of Book 1, there was a critique of the findings of actor/observer difference, and the fundamental attribution error and the theory used to explain them. The critique was based on two key points. The first is that a model of the individual as scientist trying to find causal explanations of behaviour is not a very plausible one because it disregards the issue of when people might look for the causes of social behaviour. We do not do it for all episodes of social behaviour (that would probably be impossible to do since it would take up so much time and attention): we only tend to do it when we need an explanation for that behaviour. It seems most likely that we need to do it when things go wrong in a particular situation ('why was that shop assistant rude to me?'), and when we need to attribute responsibility or social accountability for a particular action ('why has that person pushed in front of me in the queue?'). The second point is that, in terms of looking for who is accountable or responsible for actions, we may be looking at our own actions, not just the actions of others. In that situation we will have interests to protect as well as goals and aims to pursue.

These two aspects of the rationale for causal attributions for behaviour show that they are required by particular needs – to accomplish certain ends. When things go wrong in a social situation, or when we attribute responsibility, we may well want to find out if there are actions we could take that would make the situations go better for us. The discursive psychology perspective argues further that attribution takes place in the kinds of circumstances outlined above because speakers need to be able to construct an account, to create a subject position within their interpretative repertoire, which enables them to manage the responsibility or accountability in ways that are best for them.

To show how this is done, Derek Edwards and Jonathan Potter (1992) re-examined some of the data from a published study (Burleson 1986) that had used traditional attribution theory from the cognitive perspective to investigate the discussion about a failing student between two junior teaching assistants in an American college. The student is in the class of one of the teaching assistants (Don), and has just failed a test. She has also failed other tests that she was given on this course. In Box 2.5 is part of the transcript of interview material that Burleson used to illustrate how attributional information would be sought, by applying principles like consistency and consensus. (See Section 3, Chapter 7 of Book 1.)

2.5 Transcript of interview material (Burleson, 1986)

Don: She has – I gave quizzes which, you know, cover the material. So she's got copies of the quizzes which led up to the midterm, and some of the questions on that midterm are just lifted off the quizzes. Just exactly the same as those quizzes.

Bob: and you did go over those quizzes, right?

Don: oh yes, yes I did. And she was still missin' those that are exact copies of the ones on quizzes that she's got copies of.

Don: (Pause) I just don't see that I can do anything for her. I just have – I know the day has passed for dropping the course, but I gotta –

Bob: – Does she know she failed it?

Don: No.

Bob: Oh.... I don't envy you man. What are you gonna say to her?

Don: I'm just gonna say 'you failed it again. This is the last straw. I'm gonna get you out of this class'. I don't know how I'm gonna do it.

Traditional attribution theory would interpret the exchange in Box 2.5 as evidence that Bob and Don are weighing and considering information relating to the cause of the student's failure. Bob is looking for evidence of consistency and asks Don whether the student still fails the tests when she has been given quizzes that cover the material to be tested (quizzes with questions exactly the same as those in the test). Evidence of consensus is that this student has failed, but the others in the class have passed. But Edwards and Potter propose that in this exchange what seems to preoccupy these teaching assistants is not causal inference about the reasons for the student's failure, but their own accountability for it. As university teaching assistants they are held responsible for a variety of duties in teaching students and with providing adequate support for students to be able to pass their tests. Their work will be under scrutiny on these grounds, not only by their students but also by their university supervisors. This conversation takes place in the context of being in a teaching post in which students' pass results are important both to positive evaluation from colleagues and superiors, and to permission to continue in the post. The effect of this conversation is to create two subject positions through the use of particular interpretative repertoires concerning 'responsible teaching' and 'good studentship'.

Activity 2.12

Look at the transcript of the conversation between Bob and Don and make some notes about the following. What do Bob's questions tell you about his interpretative repertoire for 'responsible teacher'? What do Don's responses tell you about his interpretative repertoire for 'good student'? Finally make some notes about how the subject positions that are created justify the proposal for taking a particular course of action at the end of the exchange.

Don is located firmly within the discourse of responsible teacher, and the student within the discourse of 'inadequate student'. The entire exchange could be described as the creation of subject positions that will serve to justify Don in expelling her from his group. This working of the account by Don in creating these subject positions is where the play of power comes in. Specifically he achieves a representation of the world that best serves his interests by placing responsibility for the situation with the student.

4.4 Conclusion

Discourse psychologists regard much of the traditional research in cognitive psychology as mistaken in assuming that processes such as attribution and remembering can be transparently reported. They believe that language does not simply *represent* cognition, because the act of formulating thoughts into words *changes* them. Discourse psychologists also argue that, because words always have a particular function within the context in which they are spoken, it is necessary to rethink the basis of psychological methods that rely on language to produce evidence.

This challenge to established psychological methods can be illustrated in the work of discourse psychologists on memory. In the cognitive analysis of memory, as we saw in Chapter 8 of Book 1, concern is focused on how memories are represented, encoded and stored. This has been reflected, for example, in a long tradition of research involving memorizing of nonsense syllables within a laboratory. In this experimental paradigm, the issue has been how accurate an individual's recall of a list is. However, discourse psychologists would argue that, in ordinary life, recall is used for purposes other than simply an accurate representation of what was. They would argue that what people recall is always done to answer a purpose or need – for example, the need to attribute responsibility for a particular outcome (which is how Don was using his remembering in the example above). The meaning attached to Don's recall of his treatment of his student is not about accurately and objectively representing the details of his actions, but about presenting the evidence for a moral judgement as to his responsibility for a particular outcome. His recall is organized around interpreting his responsibility. In fact, in Chapter 8 of Book 1, the section on autobiographical memory shows how the meaning of memories, the reason why recall is occurring, may influence how people *go about* remembering past events in their lives. What is remembered will vary with factors like audience, with time of life and proximity to the event, relationship to other meaningful events, and so on.

Discourse psychologists contend that, just as there is no sense in looking for the 'truth' of whether Nelson Mandela is a terrorist or a freedom fighter, so, for most memories, there is equally little sense in asking how accurate or 'truthful' a representation is about what actually happened. There is certainly an individual cognitive process of representing, coding and storing a memory and there are questions about those processes and how they work. But access to memory in recall is through language, and is not a case of 'retrieving' a stored memory which is then reported transparently, but of re-presenting and reconstructing whatever is stored through the medium of language. Furthermore, if language is used to construct the world in line with the interests or purposes of the individual, so the language used within an act of remembering – the expression of memory – will be directly connected to the socially realized purpose of remembering (Edwards *et al.*, 1992).

For all these reasons discourse psychologists propose that their perspective represents a new way of understanding the place of language in psychological research and theory.

> It [language] exists as a domain of social action, of communication and culture, whose relations to the external world of event, and to the internal world of cognitions, are a function of the social and communicative actions talk is designed to do.
>
> Edwards *et al., 1992, p.442*

Summary Section 4

- Meaning is not created by the individual who speaks, but is produced jointly by the speaker and by those who receive and respond to a communication.
- Meaning is often contested between those involved in communication and may change dynamically as communication proceeds.
- Language is a resource used by individuals to construct objects within the world, and take action within it.
- The constructive function of language means that it cannot be assumed that it transparently represents cognitive processes in psychological research that uses verbal report.

5 Conclusion

You have been introduced to several different perspectives on language, each of which has different theories and methods associated with it. A central question that must be addressed is how to compare these perspectives, and on what grounds they can be found to be complementary, contradictory or independently co-existing. The evolutionary perspective looks at the similarities and differences that exist between communication used by humans and other species of animal. This approach argues for the adaptational advantage that might have been conferred by the development of language. The cognitive perspective focuses on what happens in the mind when language is heard or read. Traditionally a computational metaphor has been employed that portrays humans as sophisticated information processors. The emphasis is on how representations are constructed by integrating information from the input, from stored knowledge and from the wider social context within which language is encountered. In order to specify exactly what information must be extracted and how different sorts of information might be combined, most cognitive study of language has been done in experimental settings. The social constructionist perspective on language is linked to traditions that began in the sociological study of language. These look at the actual use of language in particular social episodes to examine how speakers use language as a resource to interpret and construct the world. The social constructionist perspective is based on the analysis of everyday conversations within the social world, outside laboratories or formal settings of study, and in open-ended interviews.

These different perspectives offer different understandings of language based on their level of analysis. The evolutionary perspective sees language as an adaptive acquired characteristic at *species level*, characterized by the ability to create meanings quite different to those of other species' systems of communication. The social constructionist perspectives see language as the vehicle for the socially produced and sustained meaning that operates *between individuals, in groups and society*: here language is the means by which individuals construct their world, interact with others and act to achieve their goals. The cognitive perspective sees language as the part of the information processing system that resides in the *individual* brain. Meaning is generated by the individual as they hear others speak or need to speak to others. To this degree, all the perspectives might be seen as complementary to each other.

These different levels of analysis are reflected in the methods and analysis used by each perspective to investigate language. The evolutionary perspective uses evidence about other animals' systems of communication to create hypotheses regarding the kinds of adaptational pressures that could have produced the species-specific characteristics of human language. This entails using the principle of reverse engineering and cross-species comparison. The social constructionist perspective looks at evidence from actual language use in day-to-day life. It uses discourse analysis to describe how language users organise their talk, using particular strategies like the creation of subject positions or constructions of the world, to achieve particular ends. The cognitive perspective collects evidence from the experimental setting about the kinds of response or output the cognitive language system would have to make to particular and controlled input. In addition it uses computational models to hypothesise the general parameters and operations of the language system.

These different understandings of what language is and how to investigate it entail different understandings of what meaning is and where it is made.

According to the cognitive perspective, meaning precedes language and is transmitted by language. The social constructionist perspective proposes that the meaning of language arises out of negotiation and construction with others, and so language creates meaning. The evolutionary perspective presents a view of meaning as created by evolutionary forces acting to produce linguistic ability and its capacity for creating meaning. These perspectives' different understandings of meaning can be broadly differentiated in terms of where they locate the creation of meaning to take place. For example, in this context the evolutionary and social constructionist perspectives could be said to be co-existing in terms of locating the creation of meaning in processes outside the individual.

Table I   Differences between where and how perspectives on meaning is made

Evolutionary view of meaning	Cognitive view of meaning	Discursive view of meaning
In section 2 on comparative models and the evolution of language, human language was distinguished from other forms of communication by the ability to use hypothetical constructs and abstractions, and to be originally creative. It was suggested that these characteristics allowed the creation of meaning that is distinctive to language, for example, through metarepresentation. Meaning is, therefore, a property of the development of particular characteristics of the language that humans use.	In section 3 meaning was defined in terms of the parameters of the individual's linguistic information processing system based in the brain. This system involves the parallel processing of a variety of types of syntactic, semantic, contextual and social information which creates meaning for what is to be said, or extracts it from what is heard. Meaning is, therefore, created by these information processing systems, and how they work to produce or understand language.	In section 4 meaning was suggested to be created not by individual cognition and understanding, but the inherently social process of language. Speakers use language in order to pursue particular goals, desires or needs, and adopt particular language strategies to help them. Meaning is continually negotiated, contested and actively constructed between speakers. Here meaning is created between individuals who use language to accomplish certain goals and purposes.

Finally, one of the interesting problems with research and development of theories of language is the problem of **methodological reflexivity**: we must use language itself as the medium by which we investigate language. This problem is at the heart of a dispute between cognitive and social perspectives on language: to what extent (if any) does the very necessity of responding in language predetermine what is said? From the cognitive perspective has come a tradition that assumes that there are separate cognitive processes that language can represent in communication to others, or in dialogue with the self. That representation will be more or less accurate depending on how closely language can map the cognition behind it. In studying what people say, cognitive psychologists believe that the thought processes underlying language can be studied more or less successfully. The critique produced by discursive psychology is that, when individuals use language, they always do so in a context, with an audience and for a purpose. Even in an experimental setting they are making assumptions about what their interlocutors know, understand and want, and what is relevant and what is not. Discourse psychologists propose that, in studying language, we can actually only study what language is used to do, and this forces us to revise the basic premises and methodologies of much other psychological research.

Recommended reading

Burr, V. (1995) *An Introduction to Social Constructionists*, London, Routledge.

Pinker, S. (1995) *The Language Instinct: The New Science of Language and Mind*, London, Penguin Books.

Aitchison J. (1997) The Language Web: The Power and Problem of Words, Cambridge, Cambridge University Press.

References

Aitchison, J. (1983) *The Articulate Mammal*, (2nd edn) Oxford, Blackwell.

Berry J.W., Poortinga Y.H., Segall M.H. and Dasen P.R. (1992) *Cross-Cultural Psychology: Research and Applications*, New York, Cambridge University Press.

Bransford, J.D. and Johnson, M.K. (1973) 'Consideration of some problems of comprehension', in Chase W.G. (ed.) *Visual Information Processing*, New York Academic Press.

Burleson, B.R. (1986) 'Attribution schemas and causal inference in natural conversation', in Ellis, D.G. and Donahue, W.A. (eds), *Contemporary Issues in Language and Discourse Processes*, Hillsdale, NJ, Lawrence Erlbaum.

Burman, E. and Parker, I. (1993) *Discourse Analytic Research: Repertoires and Readings of Texts in Action*, London, Routledge.

Burr, V. (1995) *An Introduction to Social Constructionism*, London, Routledge.

Edwards, D.E. and Potter, J. (1992) *Discursive Psychology*, London, Sage

Edwards, D.E., Potter, J. and Middleton, D. (1992) 'Towards a discursive psychology of remembering', in *The Psychologist*, vol.5, no.10, pp.439–46.

Fodor, J.A. (1983) *Modularity of Mind*, Cambridge, MA, MIT Press.

Forrester, M.A. (1996) *Psychology of Language: A Critical Introduction*, London, Sage.

Frazier, L. and Rayner, K. (1982) 'Making and correcting errors during sentence comprehension: eye movements in the analysis of structurally ambiguous sentences', *Cognitive Psychology*, vol.14, pp.178–210

Gardiner, R.A. and Gardiner, B.T. (1969) 'Teaching sign language to a Chimpanzee', *Science*, vol.165, pp.664–72.

Garfinkel, H. (1967) *Studies in Ethnomethodology*, Englewood Cliffs, NJ, Prentice-Hall.

Garrod, S. and Pickering, M.J. (1999) *Language Processing*, Hove, Psychology Press.

Gernsbacher, M.A. and Foertsh, J.A. (1999) 'Three models of discourse comprehension', in Garrod, S. and Pickering, M.J. (eds).

Gill, R. (1993) 'Justify injustice: broadcasters' accounts of inequality in radio', in Burman, E. and Parker, I (eds).

Goffman, E. (1976) 'Replies and Responses', *Language in Society*, vol.5, pp.257–313.

Greene, J. and Coulson, M. (1995) *Language Understanding, Current Issues* (2nd edn) Open University Press, Buckingham.

Grice, H.P. (1975) 'Logic and conversation', in Cole, P. and Morgan, J. (eds) *Syntax and Semantics: Vol 3 Speech Acts*, New York, Academic Press.

Kirschner, W.K. and Towne, W.F. (1994) 'The sensory basis of honeybee's dance language', *Scientific American*, vol.277, no.6, pp.52–9.

Harley, T.A. (1995) *The Psychology of Language: From Data to Theory*, Hove, Psychology Press.

Hockett, C.F. (1960) 'The origin of speech', *Scientific American*, vol. 203, pp.89–96.

Lorenz, K.Z. (1952) *King Solomon's Ring*, London, Methuin.

Kintsch, W. (1988) 'Role of knowledge in discourse representation: a construction integration model', *Psychological Review*, vol.95, pp.163–82.

Kintsch, W. (1994) 'The psychology of discourse processing', in Gernsbacher, M.A. (ed.) *Handbook of Psycholinguistics*, San Diego, Academic Press.

Marshall, H. (1991) 'The social construction of motherhood: an analysis of childcare and parenting manuals', in Lloyd, E., Phoenix, A. and Woolett, A. (eds) *Motherhood: Meanings, Practices and Ideologies*, London, Sage.

Marshall, H. and Raabe, B (1993) 'Political discourse: talking about nationalisation and privatisation', in Burman, E. and Parker, I. (eds).

Mayer, D.E. and Schvaneveldt, R.W (1971) 'Factors in recognizing pairs of words: evidence of a dependence between retrieval operations', *Journal of Experimental Psychology*, vol.90, pp.227–34.

McClelland, J.L. & Rumelhart, D.E (1981) 'An interactive activation model of context effects in letter processing. Part 1: an account of basic findings', *Psychological Review*, vol.88, pp.375–407.

McClelland, J.L. (1985) 'Putting knowledge in its place: a scheme for programming parallel processing structures on the fly', *Cognitive Science*, vol.9, no.115.

McKinlay, A. and Potter, J (1987) 'Model discourse: interpretative repertoires in scientists' conference talk', *Social Studies of Science*, vol.17.

Moss, H.E. and Gaskell, G.G. (1999) 'Lexical semantic processing during speech comprehension', in Garrod, S. and Pickering, M.J. (eds).

Parker, I. (1992) *Discourse Dynamics: Critical Analysis for Social and Individual Psychology*, London, Routledge.

Pearce, J.M. (1987) *An Introduction to Animal Cognition*, Hove, Lawrence Erlbaum Associates Ltd.

Pickering, M.J. (1999) 'Sentence comprehension', in Garrod, S. and Pickering, M.J. (eds).

Pickering, M.J. and Traxler, M.J. (1998) 'Plausibility and recovery from garden paths. An eye-tracking study', *Journal of Experimental Psychology, Learning, Memory and Cognition*, vol.24, pp.940–61.

Pinker S. (1994) *The Language Instinct*, London, Penguin.

Pinker, S. (1999) *Words and Rules*, Weidenfeld & Nicholson, London.

Pinker, S. (2000) 'Survival of the clearest', *Nature*, vol.404, pp.441–2.

Potter, J. and Wetherell, M. (1987) *Discourse and Social Psychology: Beyond Attitudes and Behaviour*, London, Sage.

Potter, J., Wetherell, M. and Chitty, A. (1991) 'Quantification rhetoric - cancer on television', *Discourse and Society*, vol.2, no.3, pp.333–65.

Premack D. (1971) 'Language in Chimpanzees?', *Science*, vol.172, pp.808–22.

Preuss T.M. (2000) 'The argument from animals to humans in cognitive neuroscience', in Gazzaniga, M.S. (ed.) *Cognitive Neuroscience*, Oxford, Blackwell.

Reicher, G.M. (1969) 'Perceptual representation as a function of meaningfulness of stimulus materials', *Journal of Experimental Psychology*, vol.81, pp.274–80.

Savage-Rumbaugh, E.S. and Lewin, R. (1994) *Kanzi: The Ape at the Brink of the Human Mind*, London, Doubleday.

Savage-Rumbaugh, E.S., Shanker, S.G and Taylor T.J. (1998) *Apes, Language and the Human Mind*, Oxford, Oxford University Press.

Scott, P. and Spencer, C. (1998) *Psychology: A Contemporary Introduction*, Oxford, Blackwell.

Schank, R.C. and Abelson, R.P. (1977) *Scripts, Plans, Goals and Understanding*, Hillsdale, NJ, Lawrence Erlbaum.

Seyfarth R.M., Cheyney D.L and Marler P. (1980) 'Vervet monkey alarm calls: Semantic communication in a free ranging primate', *Animal Behaviour*, vol.28, pp.1070–94.

Sperber, D. and Wilson, D. (1986) *Relevance: Communication and Cognition*, Oxford, Blackwell.

Sperber, D. (2000) 'Metarepresentations in an evolutionary perspective', in Sperber D. (ed.) *Metarepresentations: A Multidisciplinary Perspective*, Oxford, Oxford University Press.

Terrace H.S. (1979) *Nim*, New York, Knopf.

Von-Frisch, K. (1950) *Bees: Their Vision, Chemical Senses and Language*, Ithaca, NY, Cornell University Press.

Warren, R.M. (1970) 'Perceptual restoration of missing speech sounds', *Science*, vol.167, pp.392–3.

Wieder L. (1974) *Language and Social Reality*, The Hague, Mouton.

The psychology of sex and gender

Wendy Hollway, Troy Cooper, Amy Johnston and Richard Stevens

Contents

Aims:

This chapter aims to:

- present four different psychological perspectives on sex and gender, and evaluate their respective strengths and weaknesses
- enable you to understand the different meaning of the terms sex and gender and to use them appropriately
- introduce you to some influential pieces of psychological research on sex and gender
- examine the ways in which the four perspectives complement, conflict or coexist with each other
- provide a theoretical example to illustrate how biological and social perspectives can complement one another within a psychological account of the experience of sex and gender.

1   Introduction

The psychology of sex and gender is one of the most topical, important and engaging subjects that psychology must address. It has been a controversial topic since the inception of psychology as a discipline, and it powerfully illustrates some of the diverse approaches within the field. It demonstrates the numerous levels of analysis that psychology must accommodate – from genes and neurons, to language and socially-structured power relations. To add to the interest, the topic of sex and gender highlights the political and ideological implications that arise from explanations of differences between the sexes. Or should that be 'genders'? Every choice of word has different theoretical connotations and political implications!

In this chapter we are going to present four psychological perspectives with which you will be familiar from Book 1:

- biological sex differences: the sexing of bodies, sex differences in the brain, and biological correlates of behaviour;
- an evolutionary psychology account of differences in the behaviour of human males and females;
- social constructionist theories of gender differences;
- psychoanalytic accounts of the development and meanings of sexual difference.

To give you a feel for each perspective, we shall first briefly summarize the question that each one poses in this area. Despite the fact that they are all asking 'how do we understand the differences between men and women in sex and gender characteristics?', our four perspectives are posing the question in such different ways that the focus of their enquiry and conclusions are different in each instance. In this sense we can say that each has different *objects of knowledge:*

Biological psychology asks what effect biological processes have on behavioural differences between men and women, and in turn what influence behaviour has on the biological processes. Its object of knowledge is biological (physiological, cellular, biochemical and molecular) processes. It investigates the effects of these processes through scientific procedures.

Evolutionary psychology asks how evolution might have shaped human thinking and behaviour. We focus on why particular forms of sexual behaviour might have been selected for in different animal species, including humans. Its object of knowledge is how evolution has shaped human thinking and behaviour. It derives hypotheses based on evolutionary reasoning and, where possible, aims to test them empirically.

Social constructionist psychology examines how knowledge about sex and gender has been constructed within particular historical and social contexts. Its object of knowledge is these social constructions and their influences. It uses evidence largely taken from what people say and write.

Psychoanalytic psychology asks how girls and boys acquire a sexed and gendered sense of themselves, given that, at birth, infants appear to have no psychological awareness of either themselves or others as sexed beings. Its object of knowledge is psychic development and the consequent meanings of sex differences. The evidence for psychoanalytic theory is largely based on clinical observation, experience and testing through the interpretative work between analyst and patient.

These are not the only psychological perspectives that can be applied to studies of sex and gender. In Chapter 3 of Book 1, for example, the behaviourist, cognitive and sociocultural perspectives were applied to learning, while the discussion of life span development in Chapter 1 of this volume was informed by Piaget's genetic epistemology, and by developmental contextualism. All of these perspectives have also made contributions to our understanding of sex and gender.

By keeping an eye on the different objects of knowledge here, we want to encourage you to ask, following a theme in the first book of the course, in what ways can these perspectives complement each other, in what ways do they conflict, and in what ways do they just coexist? In the concluding section, we shall return to this theme by looking comparatively at the strengths and weaknesses of each account, arguing that none of them offers the whole story.

1.1 'Sex' and 'gender': what do they mean?

It is necessary to clarify the two central terms, sex and gender, and their relationship to one another. Why does the chapter title need to include both concepts? Take a look at Activity 3.1 and try answering the questions, then read the comment before reading on.

Activity 3.1

When you use the term 'sex', what are you referring to? Try to list several things you mean by the term.

When you use the term 'gender', what are you referring to? Try to list several things you mean by the term.

In constructing your lists think about the terms 'male' and 'female' and 'masculine' and 'feminine'. Do these pairs of terms have different resonances?

Comment

One response to the first two questions in this activity might be:

'Sex' means:

> the act of sexual intercourse

> the fact of being biologically male or biologically female

> 'being a man', 'being a woman'.

'Gender' means:

> the differences between the sexes (as they are manifested in behaviours, relationships, practices)

> coming across as, or feeling, 'masculine' or 'feminine'

> 'being a woman', 'being a man'.

These comments touch on two main themes: the range of different meanings between 'male/female' and 'masculine/feminine' and the either/or of being a man or being a woman. These are discussed further in the following sections.

First consider the definition of sex as the act of sexual intercourse. At first glance, the inclusion of this definition appears to mean something different from the sex or gender of a person. Why is the same term used? Presumably the connection is in the idea of sexual reproduction and the necessity of two different sexes (of fertile age and status) to take part in the act. This assumes heterosexual sex, however. The understanding of homosexual or heterosexual partner choice is one that deserves a whole chapter to itself and we cannot focus on it here. Our focus is on the meanings that cohere around the feeling of 'being a woman' or 'being a man'. Often 'sexuality' is used to refer to this more psychological object of knowledge, whereas 'sex' refers to a biological or anatomical differentiation. To complicate matters, 'sexuality' also commonly refers to sexual orientation, that is: homo or heterosexuality.

1.2 From 'male/female' to 'masculine/ feminine'

'Male' or 'female' is usually a simple assignment after the birth of a baby, based on visible genital differences. We use the terms to make a morphological distinction at the birth of a child and assume that other biological differences between the sexes (such as hormone levels, patterns of hair growth and loss, height, voice register and muscular strength) will fall into line in the course of sexual development.

However, these characteristics are not distributed in a strictly dichotomous way. It is only when averages are used that men and women come out looking so distinctly different. Many individual attributes that are characterised as 'typically' male or female, such as being tall or short and deep- or high-voiced, have *overlapping distributions*. Despite this, our perceptions, language and social practices place humans into one of two mutually exclusive categories – 'female' or 'male'.

The attribution of 'femininity' and 'masculinity' is also done on a dichotomous basis. The idea that these attributes are dichotomously opposed seems to be part of the straitjacket of gender difference, for are we not all a bit of a mixture? Carl Jung was probably the first psychological thinker to introduce the notion of *androgyny*: the coexistence of masculine and feminine characteristics in a single person. Later, Sandra Bem became well known for her measure of androgyny, published in 1974. She used a list of adjectives and asked people to decide if each word was referring to 'masculine' or 'feminine' characteristics (see Activity 3.2).

Activity 3.2

Which sex do you think each of the following adjectives from the Bem Sex Role Inventory (BSRI) refers to:

Affectionate, analytical, forceful, loyal, sympathetic, flatterable, individualistic, ambitious, compassionate, cheerful. (The answer is at the end of the chapter.)

Bem used *m* and *f* (masculinity and femininity) measures from scores on the BSRI and found high and low scorers on *m* and *f*, among both women and men (more specifically among Californian students of both sexes in a Hippie era). In other words, she found that masculinity and femininity did not necessarily tally with people being male and female. This is important because it makes clear that gendered characteristics do not follow biological sex differences. There is a world of difference between male/female and masculine/feminine: whereas the former are supposedly biologically prescribed, the latter are psychological characteristics, shaped by the experience of growing up within certain relationships, language possibilities, practices, role models, structures of expectation and opportunity. This has been the traditional distinction between 'sex' and 'gender': the distinction between the biological and the social (see Activity 3.1). There is a problem distinguishing between the two terms, however, because, as we shall see in this chapter, biological sex is expressed in behaviour that is influenced by social arrangements and psychological meanings. Therefore sex and gender can only be separated out for theoretical purposes.

As you read through this chapter notice the use of the phrase 'the other sex' rather than 'the opposite sex'? Avoiding the use of the term 'opposite sex' unsettles the idea that men and women can be defined by their opposite characteristics.

In using 'the other sex', you should note the active effect that words have. They do not simply reflect meaning, they also create it. For example, the common usage of 'opposite sex' serves to encourage us to forget the many characteristics that women and men have in common and the way that both sexes combine so-called masculine and feminine attributes.

Notice that, in Activity 3.1, 'being a man' or 'being a woman' was listed under the categories of both sex and gender. This is where the overlap is between the categories 'sex' and 'gender': in the 'being'. The idea of 'being' itself needs quite a bit of unpacking. This refers to the *experience* of being a woman or a man, living one's life from within a gendered identity, however taken for granted, however fraught with conflict. Sexual difference is a rule of human culture (a rule that is occasionally broken) and it is impossible to develop a sense of who one is without reference, not only to one's sex, but to one's gender, which includes the social meanings and practices that surround that sex. A *psychology* of sex and gender should have something illuminating to say about the *experience* of being either a woman or a man.

1.3 The either/or of being a man and being a woman

In 1970, in the US, Broverman and her colleagues conducted a study that explored the use of sex-role stereotypes in clinical judgements of mental health.

3.1 Sex-role stereotypes and judgements of women's mental health (Broverman et al., 1970)

Broverman *et al.* (1970) asked many clinically-trained mental health professionals (including both men and women and ranging from 23 to 55 years old) to fill in a 122-item questionnaire containing behavioural adjectives such as aggressive, independent, hides emotions, competitive, acts as leader, talkative, gentle, expresses tender feelings. Each adjective had two poles, for example 'very aggressive' and 'not at all aggressive'. The participants were asked to indicate, on each item, which pole would be closer to a 'mature, healthy, socially competent' adult. One third of the clinicians filled out the questionnaire for an adult, sex unspecified, one third for a man and one third for a woman.

Both the women and men described the 'mature, healthy, socially competent adult' and the 'mature, healthy, socially competent man' in virtually identical terms. The 'mature, healthy, socially competent woman' differed 'by being more submissive, less independent, less adventurous, more easily influenced, less aggressive, less competitive, more excitable in minor crises, having their feelings more easily hurt, being more emotional...'(Broverman *et al.*, 1970, p.4).

There are four important points to draw from this study:

1   Mental health professionals drew on common categories about differences between the sexes.
2   They equated what it was to be a man with what it was to be an adult. Men were taken as the human norm and women were contrasted to this.
3   The values contained in the judgements put women in a very contradictory position, namely that to live up to being a mature, healthy socially competent woman, she had to be suitably 'feminine', even though the traits associated with femininity were very different and often the opposite of those desirable in a mature, healthy, socially competent adult.
4   It is important to locate this study both in time and place and not to universalize its findings. It is unlikely that all of these stereotypes are still in use now at the start of the twenty-first century.

Sex role stereotype
Based on beliefs about typical masculine or feminine behaviour. Using sex-role stereotypes (also known as gender stereotype) tends to exaggerate the differences between women and men and underestimate people's individuality.

What is the difference between a descriptor, such as 'gentle', and a **sex-role stereotype***? In the 1970s, with the growth of feminism both outside and inside psychology, the study of sex-roles and stereotyping became influential in social psychology. Sex roles were seen as a product of socialization influences that* *imposed differences on girls and boys. Stereotypes were thought of as distorting lenses used to accentuate behavioural differences between the genders. The biological origins of these behavioural differences were strongly contested, because they made them appear unchangeable. However, socialization could presumably influence girls to be more 'caring' than boys, irrespective of whether 'caring' is a stereotype about women's behaviour. In this case, to use the adjective 'caring' might reflect reality – albeit a social constructed reality. The clinicians participating in Broverman et al.'s study might have been basing their judgements on clinical experience, rather than, or as well as, using stereotypes, which by implication means imposing distortions.*

The tendency to treat men and women as having separate and opposite characteristics was particularly pronounced in psychological research that employed the psychometric approach to measure sex differences. By the 1970s, this type of research was regularly reported in scientific psychology journals. Such studies would test both women and men, for example on spatial ability, then a statistical test of significance would be done to discover whether the two sexes had performed differently. Maccoby and Jacklin (1974) evaluated hundreds of published articles concentrating upon performance differentials between men and women. They called into question the interpretations of studies that often dwelt on girls' poorer performance – for example on intelligence tests and in maths. Their book became a reference point for feminists who were suspicious of the way in which psychological research was reporting so many sex differences that found boys and men doing better. The guidelines set out in Box 3.2 are the result of feminist psychologists' criticism of poor scientific practice in writing and publishing reports.

3.2 FEATURED METHOD

Guidelines for non-sexist research on gender differences

Janet Hyde (1994) pointed out that many studies of sex differences did not follow basic procedures of good science. She recommended that:

- Researchers and journal editors should take care that research that found no significant gender differences was published. (This is often not the case because journals tend to be interested only in findings of significant differences.) Failure to publish research that finds no significant sex differences has meant that publicly available knowledge in psychology has been biased towards highlighting gender differences not gender similarities.

- Published papers should take care to specify the magnitude of any gender differences.

- Interpretations of sex differences should be careful not to start off with the assumption of the male standard as norm and women's difference as problematic.

> - Researchers should not infer biological differences from performance tests based on behaviour. Biological differences should only be invoked if biological measures have been collected.
>
> Extracted and modified from J. Hyde (1994).

Feminists were wary of biological arguments because they were so readily used to suggest that women's and men's characteristics were unchangeable, although as we shall see, this is not an accurate extrapolation from biological psychology.

Hyde's guidelines are one example of the results of feminist politics taking a critical look at scientific psychology and questioning whether it had been as objective as claimed when measuring sex differences. She and many others concluded that science *could* be objective if practices were improved along the above lines (e.g. Eagly, 1994; Halpern, 1994). Other feminist psychologists became so sceptical about the possibility of an objective scientific psychology that they started developing alternative methods of inquiry and other criteria of evidence. While these challenges have affected all branches of psychology, the debate has raged most fiercely, not surprisingly, where psychologists are studying sex and gender. As you read the following sections, bear in mind, therefore, that the perspectives you come across vary not only in their theoretical forms but also in their political and ideological implications. These political implications can often be discerned in the object of knowledge and even in the use of a word (sex or gender?). We hope that this introduction enables you to read the following sections with an increased capacity to notice how these terms are being used, what effects they have for the understanding of what it is to be a woman, or to be a man, and how these relate to what we share as human beings.

Summary Section 1

- The psychology of sex and gender illustrates many of the difficult issues that psychological explanations must address, including the political implications of different perspectives and the challenge of integrating explanations including biological, evolutionary, social and psychoanalytic.
- The four perspectives presented in this chapter pose somewhat different questions, have different objects of knowledge and use different notions of evidence. These perspectives may be complementary, conflicting or may simply coexist.

- Sex is commonly used to refer to the biological basis of differences between the sexes, whereas gender usually refers to socially constructed categories pertaining to these differences.
- The psychological question of what it is to be a woman or a man provides a bridge between definitions of sex and gender.
- Masculine and feminine are categories that do not necessarily follow from being male and female. This idea is the basis of the concept of androgyny.
- In the 1970s, political differences were expressed about the measurement of sex differences, with challenges by feminist psychologists to scientific practices. These challenges have broadened and contributed new approaches to psychological investigation.

2 A biological psychology of sex and gender

This section describes some of the various methods used to 'sex' humans, and will identify some of the problems with each of these methods. It evaluates some of the evidence for structural (anatomical) differences in male and female human brains. Finally it illustrates the complex implications of approaching the question 'what enables us to become a woman or a man?' from a biological perspective.

2.1 Male or female? Sexing human bodies

It is surprisingly difficult to come up with universal and infallible biologically-based rules to define what is a male or a female human being. A part of this difficulty arises because a number of different methods are used to classify male and female humans and the results from one method do not always agree with the results from another.

Physical characteristics

The most obvious method, and the one that is most commonly used to 'sex' children after birth, is observation of the external (visible) genitals. In most cases (more than 98 per cent) this is a simple and reliable method of sexing babies. However, this method is not always straightforward. Neonates (newborn infants) are exposed to hormones circulating in their mothers' blood prior to and during birth, and these, together with the mechanical pressure associated with vaginal birth, can cause swelling of various portions of the genitals so as to make it difficult to identify male or female genitals clearly. Moreover, one person in every 500 is born with genitals that do not match their sex chromosomes, although they may never know it. Even when the assessment of the external genitals looks correct, the sex organs that are visible on the outside of the body may not necessarily match those inside the child. There are several recorded cases of boys who, early in development, have much reduced levels of an enzyme that would enable boys to produce a version of the typical 'male' hormone, testosterone. As a result, these boys have visible sex organs that look most like those of a female. They begin producing normal levels of this testosterone-like substance from (internal) testes at puberty, the penis grows and the testes descend from the groin, so in terms of external genitals, the children appear to switch from female to male at puberty. These cases are the exception rather than the norm. Nevertheless they do rule out observation of the external genitals at birth as a totally foolproof mechanism of determining sex.

Hormones

Sex organs, or at least their early external appearance, depend on hormones. Moreover, some psychologists suggest that the action of hormones during development also determines some behaviour patterns and the structure of some regions of the brain. Adult hormone profiles, or the relative levels of the various 'sex' hormones such as testosterone ('male'), oestrogens and progesterone ('female'), can also be used to help define male or female humans. However, a simple hormone screening test cannot be conclusively used to differentiate males from females for the following reasons.

- Sex hormones are produced in different amounts in different individuals and at different stages of development. For example, young children usually have lower levels of the sex hormones and more balanced sex hormone profiles than adults.
- Both males and females mostly have both 'male' and 'female' hormones and so it is the *balance* (the relative levels) of these hormones, rather than their mere presence, that generally produces the secondary sexual characteristics commonly associated with men and women.
- The 'male' hormones can be chemically converted to 'female' hormones within both the body and the brain, so it is not only the level of a specific hormone produced, but also what happens chemically to that hormone that is important for understanding its actions, particularly on brain structure and behaviour.
- Even if the hormone profile, assessed from a standard blood sample, falls into the normal range for one sex, the hormones may not be able to send the normal messages to the body tissues because they lack receptors for that hormone. (If you need to remind yourself what a receptor is, look back at Chapter 4 of Book 1). This means that the hormonal message is sent, but the

body does not have the receivers to be able to action the message. The most commonly cited example of this is **androgen insensitivity syndrome** (AIS).

- It is possible to ingest synthetic hormones and so alter the 'natural' hormone balance. For example oestrogens are sometimes used as a part of treatment for some cancers. Does this make men having this treatment female? The common answer is 'of course not' because most people recognize that it is more than just your hormone profile at a particular stage of life that makes you male or female.

Genes

Can biologists come up with a universal rule for sex determination using genetic screening tests? Humans usually have 23 pairs of chromosomes, one of which is used to direct the sex of the person. Males typically have different chromosomes in this pair; an 'X' and a 'Y' (so called because they are said to resemble an 'X' and a 'Y' under the microscope). Women typically have two 'X' chromosomes. In the vast majority of cases this sort of genetic test can show the pattern of sex chromosomes people have – defining them as men or women. But even genetic testing is not quite as conclusive as was originally thought. Estimates suggest that around 1 in 500 men have **Klinefelter's syndrome** – which means that they have an XXY genotype. AIS (referred to above) is even more rare (around 1 in 20,000), but it is interesting as some of those with AIS may look like women and have lived their lives as women but have an XY (or sometimes XXY) genotype.

Androgen insensitivity syndrome
Medical syndrome affecting 1 in 20,000 of those born with an XY genetic make-up and affecting the typical male/female bodily appearance. Symptoms include infertility and external genitalia that can range from completely male to completely female. Those with the syndrome may be raised as either male or female.

Klinefelter's syndrome
Medical syndrome affecting 1 in 500 males, in which the typical male chromosomal complement – XY – is replaced by XXY. Accompanying features are unusually tall stature, enlarged breasts, infertility and problems such as diabetes.

3.3 Genetic sex testing

At the Sydney Olympics in 2000, officials abandoned genetic sex testing. This was sparked, at least in part, by several cases of ostensibly female athletes who were found to have a Y chromosome. As such they had previously been excluded from competition. The rationale for this exclusion was that, because they had high levels of testosterone being produced from internal testes (a kind of inbuilt steroid treatment), they had an unfair advantage. But as these women had AIS, the testosterone did not significantly alter their physiology and so the claim that they had an unfair advantage was unfounded. This internally produced testosterone did not 'make' these women men, just as an extra X chromosome in men with Klinefelter's syndrome (XXY) does not 'make' these men women (though in both syndromes, the profile of genetic, hormonal and bodily characteristics is extremely atypical for the assigned sex).

While these genetic abnormalities are, by definition, unusual, they do make the point that it is not just our genes that make us male or female. Hormones are produced from the actions of genes and, while they usually fall into 'female' and 'male' patterns they are also not invariably a reliable measure of sex. Sex organs and secondary sexual characteristics depend on hormones and, as such, are also not completely reliable indicators of 'sex'. Yet, as we saw in the introduction, all human cultures divide people into either men or women. Is there a clear biological basis for sex differences?

2.2 Male or female brains?

As is generally recognized, adult women and men often behave differently. Just as with height or weight, the two populations overlap, but there are some behaviours more common to one sex than the other. Why is this? Could it be because they have different brains? As with height and weight, men tend to have larger brains than women. However, most evidence suggests that brain size in mammals, including humans, is proportional to body size and so it seems unlikely that sex differences are due to brain size alone.

It seems more likely that there are differences in the *parts* of brain that are involved in the processing of different tasks in which men or women seem to excel. This hypothesis is based, in part, on some experiments using rats. Male and female rats have very different sexual behaviours and scientists have shown that these behaviours depend on the balance of hormones that is present during a critical period of early development. Males usually mount females whereas receptive females adopt a lordosis position (with arched back and head up). However, by providing male rats with 'female-type' hormones, or female rats with 'male' hormones, during their critical period of early development, it was possible to show reversed sexual behaviours, so that treated females mostly attempted to mount other rats, while treated males mostly adopted the lordosis position (Young, 1964; Beach, 1938). These differences were shown to match differences in a brain structure called the *sexually dimorphic nucleus* of the *preoptic area* (SDN–POA). This area of the brain demonstrates **sexual dimorphism**.

Sexual dimorphism
Where a part of the body (including the brain) shows visible differences between males and females.

Testosterone was shown to be converted into a female-type hormone in the brain (estradiol) and to induce the SDN-POA to become larger. Thus, there was a difference in brain structure that correlated with a difference in sexual behaviour (Fitch and Denenberg, 1998). Of course, experimental studies of this kind cannot be conducted on humans. Is there any evidence of differences between human males and females in comparable brain regions?

Human brain region differences?

Biologists have examined a brain area in humans that is comparable to the SDN–POA, and the initial studies suggested that it may be larger in men than in women (the INAH-1 region; Swaab and Fliers, 1985). Later studies suggested that, while *this* brain region was not sexually dimorphic, two other adjacent regions, (INAH-2 and INAH-3), were indeed larger in males than in females

(Allen and Gorski, 1990). Still further studies have shown sexual dimorphism in only one of these regions – INAH-3 (LeVay, 1991). It therefore seems that sexually dimorphic brain regions are much harder to describe consistently in humans than in other animals (Cooke *et al.*, 1998). Researchers generally do not find sex differences in these brain regions in children less than 6–10 years old (Hofman and Swaab, 1991). We have to be careful how to interpret this finding. Although it suggests that the influences of genes and early hormones have not affected this brain region during childhood, this does not necessarily rule out the effects of genes and early hormones on later sex differences. Many later aspects of development – for example changes at puberty or patterns of ageing – are shaped by genes and early appearing hormones in interaction with environmental factors. In other words, the effects of both genes and hormones can be set up around birth but triggered later.

Before discussing the mostly commonly reported brain sex difference, it is worth considering the measurement methods such studies use. These methods are considered in Featured Method Box 3.4.

3.4 FEATURED METHOD

Techniques for measuring brain differences

Brain regions in people are usually measured either manually in post-mortem tissue or by brain imaging techniques, such as MRI in living tissue. Neither method is completely reliable:

- Using post mortem tissue dissection: this method needs to take into account any effects of the accident or disease that brought the person to the morgue on the brain tissue to be measured. Furthermore, chemicals such as formalin used to preserve brain tissue are known to induce uneven shrinkage.

- Using MRI measurements: these involve many individual observations which are averaged by a computer. This could potentially lead to errors, although these would be unlikely to have systematic effects on the identification of sex differences. The number of such studies completed thus far is relatively small, so we need to consider how well these results generalize. (For example, MRI studies are almost always conducted in developed countries and use participants from those countries. Any potential findings might conceivably reflect plastic changes due to Western social arrangements.)

As mentioned in the introduction, studies that do not show sex differences are less likely to be published than those that show differences. This applies also to these medical methods, perhaps skewing the available data towards findings of sex differences.

Corpus callosum
A thick tract of neurons connecting the two hemispheres of the human brain, which enables the two sides of the brain to 'talk' to each other.

Using these methods researchers have investigated the possibility of sex differences in the area of the brain called the **corpus callosum**, which enables the two sides of the brain to 'talk' to each other (see figure 3.1 below). Like any piece of brain tissue, the corpus callosum is divided into various sub-regions. Some researchers suggest that sex differences might lie in the thickness of various sections of the corpus callosum, such as the splenium. There have been a number of studies, some of which show some larger splenium regions in women, and others that fail to replicate these findings but show women as having other larger callosal regions (all regions aside from the splenium, see Rogers, 1999). The effect of a larger splenium region in females is hard to explain, because the splenium seems to carry visual information from one hemisphere to the other and thus aid in visuo-spatial ability, yet behaviourally, visuo-spatial abilities seem to be more developed in men (Fausto-Sterling, 2000). In general there appear to be difficulties in interpreting such sex differences in the size of the corpus callosum (Bishop and Wahlsten, 1997).

While the evidence for sex differences in the size or shape of brain sub-regions in adult humans is ambiguous, recent fMRI studies have shown that adult men and women do tend to use some brain regions differently (Schneider *et al.*, 2000). Again, this does not necessarily mean that these differences are present from birth. As you saw in Chapter 4 of Book 1, the brain is not fixed throughout life but rather is 'plastic' and able to change. The human brain continues to grow and change substantially after birth, the total amount of brain tissue not peaking until between 12 and 18 years old (Giedd *et al.*, 1999). Some smaller changes are possible even after this time. Animal studies have shown that brain regions, neuronal cell numbers and even synapse numbers can rapidly increase and decrease in direct response to both activity (use) and hormonal conditions throughout life. This is important because the plasticity of brain structures is consistent with the claim that sex differences in brain and behaviour are not due solely to what is specified either at conception (genes + maternal environment) or at birth (genes + early hormones + early environment). Sex differences could be the result of interactions between biological, psychological and social processes. All of these clearly play a role in the anatomy and functioning of the brain. In simple terms, genes, hormones *and* environment all interact in influencing women's and men's brains to become differentiated according to uses and experiences that are themselves gender differentiated.

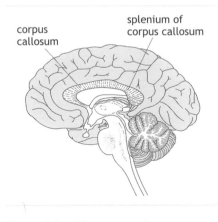

corpus callosum

splenium of corpus callosum

Figure 3.1   The corpus callosum

Imagine you decide to become a cyclist. To be successful, you will need well-developed thigh muscles, so you start training to build these up. You become successful and someone says that this is because you have well-developed thigh muscles. BUT is this because you have exercised or because you were genetically 'pre-destined' for physical excellence? Most likely it reflects an ongoing interaction between environment (e.g. training opportunities), genetic endowments (e.g. bone structure and muscle fibre types) and motivation.

It's clearly very difficult to separate these different factors as they work so closely together. As we learn more about genetics, physiology and psychology it is becoming increasingly clear that a simple dichotomy between nature and nurture is not tenable.

2.3 Biological factors in behavioural and cognitive gender differences

Are biological influences involved in generating differences in behaviour and cognitive skills between girls and boys? One famous study that examined this question was by Money and Erhardt (1972). In this study they looked at the 'masculinization' of the behaviour of girls who had been exposed to 'male-type' hormones *in utero* due to the administration of an anti-miscarriage drug progestin. They compared the behaviour of these girls with their sisters, who had not been exposed to progestin and also with girls who had adrenal hyperplasia (a condition in which girls have higher than average levels of the male hormone testosterone, produced by the adrenal glands). In all cases they asked the mothers to report whether the girls liked playing with 'girls toys' or 'boys toys', what sort of clothes they liked and the style of their play. (It's worth noting the 'implicit' understanding in this study of what is girlish and what is boyish.) They found that both the girls affected by hyperplasia and the progestin-affected girls seemed to play in a more boisterous 'tomboy' manner, that they preferred boys clothes, that they had higher IQ scores and showed a non-traditional pattern of preference for career over marriage. (This was at a time when most women felt that they had to choose one or the other.) However, the study employed directed questions (such as 'is your affected girl more tomboyish than your other girl?') which might have tended to bias responses. Moreover, some of the sisters of the affected girls also showed 'tomboy-like' behaviour patterns – suggesting that this was not just an effect of the altered hormonal profiles. In a follow-up study, which addressed these methodological difficulties, the only remaining difference found was that the hormonally affected girls seemed to play more energetically (Baker and Erhardt, pp.53–84, 1974).

Other research has reported differences between girls and boys in cognitive abilities, and particularly in mathematical ability. All of these findings, and especially those relating to mathematics, have generated controversy. In the US, Hyde conducted a large-scale meta-analysis of one hundred studies, representing the test results from over three million people. She found a very small difference in male and female distributions for cognitive ability and argued that the uncritical acceptance of these studies has promoted the idea that sex-based cognitive differences are more significant than they in fact are (Hyde, pp.207–23, 1990). However, those who accept sex-based differences in ability point to different **brain lateralization** between girls and boys as a causal basis for this result. There is evidence that the right and left hemispheres specialize in different cognitive functions: the left in language and the right in visuo-spatial and mathematical functioning. Relatively enhanced development of the left or right hemisphere respectively was thought to correspond with girls' and boys' respective strengths as measured on cognitive tests.

Brain lateralization
Structural or functional asymmetry in the brain.

In conclusion, the search for biological correlates of behavioural and cognitive differences between the sexes is a complex and confusing one. The main lesson seems to be that a single influence such as a sex hormone does not alone make the difference between becoming male or female. Indeed, only in non-human animals does it appear to have a clear-cut influence on particular behaviours, for example mounting or lordosis, and effects on specific brain regions. The effects of biological processes in human beings are likely to be more complex as a result of our unique capacity to reflect on our experiences, and modify our behaviour accordingly.

Summary Section 2

- Assigning a sex to humans is sometimes a complex process. Biological characteristics (genetic, hormonal or molecular), used to designate 'male' or 'female', are unreliable in a small proportion of cases.
- In humans, unlike in other animals such as rats, clear-cut differences in brain structures that correlate with differences in adult behaviour patterns have proved difficult to demonstrate.
- Nonetheless, imaging studies show some sex differences in brain functioning of Western adults. This is probably due, at least in part, to brain plasticity.
- While some sex differences are clearly established at birth for most individuals, bodies and brains may become *gendered* over a lifetime of use.

3 An evolutionary psychology perspective on differences between the sexes

What light can evolutionary psychology throw on the question – 'what is it to be a man or a woman'? Evolutionary psychologists would argue that there are few consistent differences between the sexes. However, one of the areas in which evolutionary psychologists do assert that there are some differences is in sexual behaviours and attitudes. This is because of the different reproductive strategies that have evolved in men and in women.

Activity 3.3

Before reading further, go back to Chapter 2 of Book 1 and remind yourself of the core concepts in evolutionary psychology. In particular, look at the Introduction, which discusses its functional approach and the idea of 'reverse engineering', and Section 2 on what evolution is and how it works.

3.1 Parental investment and its implications

To explain sex differences, evolutionary psychologists focus particularly on the processes involved in sexual selection. This, as you will remember, relates to the characteristics or patterns of behaviour that promote reproductive success (that is, **optimal reproductive style**). There are critical differences in the process of successful reproduction between males and females and hence in their optimal reproductive styles. Specifically, females have what evolutionary biologists (e.g. Trivers, 1972) call a greater **'parental investment'** in their offspring, in that considerable effort and energy is necessarily required for every infant they produce. For primate females, this involves a long period of gestation and most likely a long period of suckling and care. This means they can usually bear relatively few offspring during a limited period of their lives. For males on the other hand, only a few minutes of copulatory activity may be required. The only limit on the number of offspring they can have is the availability of potential mates. Evolutionary psychologists argue that this basic difference means that reproductive success for the two sexes in primate species would have been best achieved by different patterns of behaviour.

Evolutionary psychologists do not argue that animals or humans used conscious and deliberate strategies to achieve a particular type of behaviour in

Optimal reproductive style
Characteristics and behaviours that are most likely to result in producing children/ descendants.

Parental investment
The amount of energy and effort required to produce and rear offspring.

order to maximise reproductive success. Rather, they argue that the behaviour that just happened to result in reproductive success will have been selected for by evolutionary pressures precisely *because* of the reproductive advantage that it conferred. As modern primates are all the descendants of male and female ancestors who were successful reproducers, the sexual behaviours of males and females today are the result of reproductively successful behaviours that have been selected for over the history of the species.

Evolutionary psychologists infer that, given the relatively few offspring a female primate could produce (and thus her greater reproductive investment), being choosy would have been very important. For her, reproductive success depended on her selection of circumstances (including a mate) that were likely to ensure that her relatively few offspring would survive to sexual maturity and so in their turn pass on her genes.

By contrast, for a male, with his far more extensive potential capacity to reproduce, number of matings would have been the critical factor. For if these matings were sufficiently frequent, and particularly if they were with fertile and healthy mates, this would have been an effective reproductive strategy.

However, given that females would have been choosy about which males they mated with, male primates would have to compete with each other for females who, in terms of sexual availability, were in shorter supply. One result of this male competition would be much greater variability in reproductive success among males than among females. For while the majority of females would have had little difficulty in ensuring that they had offspring (as males would be competing to mate with them), some males would have succeeded in fathering many offspring but others may well not have produced any at all.

One consequence of this would be that characteristics promoting reproductive success in the face of competition, such as strength and size, would have been selected for in males. Thus ancestral human males evolved to have greater body weight and size in relation to females. In modern humans, men are on average 1.15 times bigger than women. The ratio in other species varies and (consistent with the reasoning above) appears to be related to the degree of sexual competitiveness. In the case of chimps, where there is considerable competition in selection of sexual partners, males are about 1.3 times as big as females. It is worth noting that there are a few species of birds and fish in which male investment in the caring and rearing of offspring is greater than that of females. In such species, there is female competition for males and females are often the larger and more aggressive sex. The kinds of difference we are discussing here are all average ones, of course. They derive from overlapping distributions and do not mean that all men are, for example, heavier and taller than all women.

Pursuing the same line of reasoning, if females evolved to maximize their own reproductive success, their choice of mate in particular would need to have been consistent with this. As well as selecting a fertile, healthy mate capable of producing healthy and reproductively successful children, a female would choose factors like status and resources, which would ensure a protective base for the long process of rearing her children. However, these would not be relevant unless the mate was prepared to commit such resources to the relationship and children. So male commitment would also have been a key criterion. In other words, those females who happened to choose males on the basis of such features would have been likely to produce most offspring and so the predilection to choose in this way would have been selected for in females. Note that, one of the difficult questions this raises is how female primates might have recognised characteristics such as commitment in potential mates.

3.2 Particular features of human evolution

So far, our discussion has concentrated upon primates generally, because, as with humans, their long gestation and suckling times suggest differences in parental investment between mother and father. But what about humans in particular? Are there any features specific to the evolution of our human ancestors that might have influenced their optimal reproductive styles and therefore, according to evolutionary psychologists, had some consequences for contemporary human sex differences?

One difference between humans and other primates is that, as a result of the evolution of an upright gait, the human pelvic girdle took on a size and shape that served to constrain the size of the neonate's brain at birth. So full development of the much larger brain, characteristic of the human primate, can only take place after birth. This, coupled with the need for sophisticated socialization that the development of language and culture made necessary, meant a longer period of dependency for human infants than for other primates. The upshot, evolutionary psychologists argue, is that behaviour that resulted in paternal investment (resources and support) would have taken on increased significance in ensuring survival of infants to sexual maturity.

The emergence of human sexual behaviour was also affected by the fact that human females have 'hidden oestrus': in contrast to other primates, there are no obvious signs of ovulation and human females may mate at any time during the menstrual cycle. A consequence of this is that pair bonding (which allows for consistent mating over time) and 'mate guarding' – ensuring that no other male has sexual access to his mate – also became important strategies for human males in ensuring their reproductive success. Whereas a female can be confident that a child is hers, for males paternity is never assured. Given this and human males' greater paternal investment, it is argued that human males have become particularly sensitive to female sexual infidelity.

The way that evolutionary psychologists seek to test their claims about the effects of genetic selection on contemporary human sexual behaviour is illustrated in a study on jealousy (Buss *et al.*, 1992). They found that, while both men and women reported experiencing jealousy at the thought of their partner being involved with another person, there were differences in the focus of their concerns. For men, it was the thought of sexual infidelity that triggered the most intense feelings of jealousy, whereas for women it was the possibility of their partner's emotional involvement with another. Similar studies have now confirmed this finding in a variety of cultures from China to Sweden (Geary *et al.*, 1995; Wiedermann and Kendall, 1999). Buss interprets this as in line with the evolutionary psychology prediction, namely that commitment would be valued by both sexes but for rather different reasons: for males it would be related to their particular concern for sexual fidelity, for females to the need to ensure continuation of support and resource.

3.3 Differences in sexual style

Evolutionary arguments have been further extended to explain observed differences between contemporary men and women in sexual attitudes and behaviours. Such differences are not only the regular diet of Western magazine discussions, media portrayal (e.g. Fielding, 1997; 2000) and popular psychology (e.g. Gray, 1993) but, as we shall see, have been documented in research studies involving both experiments and questionnaires with respondents from many cultures.

There is considerable evidence of difference between men and women, for example, in the *style of their sexual interest*, as exemplified in an experiment carried out on an American college campus by Clark and Hatfield (1989). An attractive stranger approached participants of the other sex, engaged them in conversation, and then made one of three invitations: to a) go out with them that night, or b) go back to their home, or c) have sex with them. Their results showed that while about 50 per cent of both men and women who were approached agreed to a date, only 6 per cent of the women who were approached compared with 69 per cent of the men were prepared to go to the stranger's college apartment. None of the women who were approached, compared with 75 per cent of the men, consented to sex. The investigators interpreted these results as being consistent with evolutionary psychology arguments about evolved optimal reproductive style. As it might be possible that women's greater physical vulnerability could better explain the difference found, the investigators analysed the reasons given by both women and men for refusing sex. They found these to be more or less identical (reasons such as they had a boy/girl friend or they did not know the person well enough) and the women's explanations placed no special emphasis on potential danger. Also, in a follow-up experiment (Clark, 1990), participants were given various assurances by friends about the integrity and trustworthiness of the stranger. These seemed to have the effect intended in that no woman participant expressed any concern about her safety, but the results remained essentially the same.

Could there be alternative explanations that make sense of this finding? One is that many men internalize social expectations that, in order to be successfully masculine, they should express constant interest in heterosexual sex. Most women, on the other hand, have internalized the idea that 'nice girls don't'. Some evolutionary psychologists (e.g. Dunbar et al., 1999) have proposed that evolved behavioural predispositions underlie many of the cultural patterns that we observe. So one possibility here is that evolution may have shaped cultural practices that in turn serve to reinforce patterns of evolved behaviour. Western morals that have regulated women's sexuality have been changing however. Consider recent British reports about 'ladettes' (young women who behave in laddish ways), who among other things have sex with many men who are strangers to them. Among a 'ladette' group of participants, the finding of Clark and Hatfield's study would perhaps not be replicated.

You may also like to consider the ethical issues raised by experiments designed along these lines. Guidelines drawn up by the British Psychological Society (BPS) can be found in the Introduction to Book 1.

Sex differences in number of sexual partners desired and readiness to have sex with strangers has been documented in confidential questionnaires and other research studies in different cultures and periods (e.g. Johnson, 1970; Buss, 1989). Evolutionary psychologists also point out that, consistent with their thesis, prostitution is predominantly for the benefit of males. The Kinsey report of sexual behaviour (Kinsey *et al.*, 1948; 1953), for example, indicated that about 70 per cent of American men had visited a prostitute at some time in their lives, while for women the incidence was negligible. The vast majority of prostitutes in all cultures are women and male prostitutes mainly service gay clients (Bullough and Bullough, 1987; McCormick, 1994). Most men who go to prostitutes are already in ongoing sexual relationships (Holzman and Pines, 1982). Evolutionary psychologists infer from such research that prostitution provides many male clients with an outlet for their need for sexual variety while enabling them to maintain an ongoing committed relationship; it thus offers them a way of coping with urges that evolutionary pressure has selected for in their behaviour.

The male preference for sexual variety is also manifested, evolutionary psychologists argue, in the extensive use of pin-ups in male magazines like Loaded and FM and in the high sales of soft-porn men's magazines. Where similar attempts have been made to produce magazines for women with photos of nude men, they have either foundered (e.g. Viva) or have largely tended to be purchased by gay men (e.g. Playgirl). If anything, women's magazines are dominated by photos of women rather than men.

It is worth remembering that evolutionary psychologists do not deny that evolutionary urges are overlaid by the effects of contemporary social arrangements or culture. They would therefore acknowledge that it is too simplistic to argue that evolutionary pressures are the sole explanation for some men's propensity to visit prostitutes or buy pornography.

Another area of contemporary behaviour which is claimed to be in keeping with evolutionary predictions is the *features in potential partners that men and women seem to find especially attractive*. Particularly salient dimensions for men are physical appearance and youth, which would both relate to reproductive capacity. All questionnaire studies on the topic suggest that, while for women physical attractiveness may be desirable, for men it is especially important. This finding runs across generations and cultures (Buss and Schmitt, 1993). While there is considerable historical and cultural variation in appreciation of different body types, Singh (1995) has found with participants from a range of cultures that what is consistently attractive to men is a ratio of waist to hip measurements of about 0.70. This ratio, he argues, differentiates the woman from pre-pubertal females and males (whose comparable ratio is more in the order of 0.90). It would also signal that a woman was not already pregnant.

For women across cultures, in contrast, height seems to be a particular attractor (Gregor, 1985; Jackson, 1992; Wiederman, 1993). A preference by female ancestors for taller and more powerful males would have been more likely to ensure protection and support and to result in taller male offspring who could in turn hold their own in the competition for both resources and sex. But most salient for women appear to be the situation and status of the prospective partner. A study of over 1000 personal ads, for example, found that women advertizing for partners mentioned good financial position as a desirable characteristic about eleven times more than did males (Wiederman, 1993). A major cross-cultural study (Buss, 1989) involving 37 cultures and 10,000 participants found that in all the countries studied, women more often rated financial prospects as a desirable attribute in a potential mate than did men. (There was some cultural variation however. In Japan, for example, women valued good financial prospects 150 per cent more than men: in the Netherlands the male/female difference was only 36 per cent). It has been argued that such differences are not explicable simply in terms of unequal economic power because financially successful women show an even more marked preference for wealthy men (Wiederman and Allgeier, 1992). Whereas poorer men show no greater preference for high income women (Buss, 1989).

In the Buss study, while the general trend is in the same direction across cultures there is some evidence of cultural variation. This would support the idea that the value placed on financial prospects reflects a complex interaction between biological predispositions and the particular social contexts of different cultures.

In most societies, social status is typically geared to the command of resources a person is likely to have (Betzig, 1986). So reasoning from evolutionary principles might lead you to think that women would also be more interested in the status of potential partners than males would be. This is indeed what Buss (1989) found in the cross-cultural study mentioned above. Numerous questionnaire studies in the USA (e.g. Langhorne and Secord, 1955) have also found that women value status and prestige in partners (as well as factors such as education and ambition that may signal future success) much more highly than do males. However, evolutionary psychologists accept that individuals and subcultures will vary in terms of which particular criteria (e.g. power, wealth, intelligence or popularity) they take as indices of status.

Evolutionary psychologists argue that all the criteria noted above (height, resource power and status of males) would have been related to the potential for protection and support; and thus, they reason, would have been selected for in the mate preferences of our female ancestors.

3.4 Concluding points

Evolutionary psychologists are not implying that the preferences and feelings discussed here are conscious strategies. Rather they are predispositions to respond and behave in particular ways which have been selected for in human ancestors, as in other species, because of the potential of these predispositions for facilitating reproductive success. However, note that it is not the goal of reproductive success in itself that has been selected for, but the kinds of behaviour that would have resulted in this in the past.

While the evolutionary approach outlined here may provide insights into certain differences in human sexual behaviour, sexual *relationships* generally involve a complex configuration of cultural and individual influences. Given this complexity, evolutionary psychology can provide only limited understanding of sexual relationships.

Finally, and importantly, evolutionary psychologists emphasize that there is no implication that because certain differences in sexual styles and preferences have an evolutionary underpinning they should therefore be regarded as desirable. Their argument is that human preferences evolved only because they were the optimal strategies for reproductive success in our distant past. Given the enormous success of human strategies for survival and reproduction, the further optimization of reproductive success is not a crucial or even desirable goal for humans as a species in the present time. In fact, Buss (2000) argues that the problem for contemporary humans is that this ancestral heritage of sexual styles and predispositions can impose considerable costs in feelings of rejection, jealousy and unhappiness. His view is that only by becoming aware of the origins of male and female sexual differences can we hope to alleviate their often painful consequences.

Summary Section 3

- Evolutionary psychologists argue that sexual selection and the different optimal reproductive styles of our male and female ancestors have resulted in some differences in the behavioural predispositions of the two sexes.
- These are seen to be particularly apparent in the area of sexual behaviours and attitudes.
- Their explanations would appear to be consistent with research findings from cross-cultural differences in male and female sexual behaviours.

4   The social construction of gender

In this section, you will be introduced to an explanation of gender differences that emphasizes their social origins. We ask how gender differences get reproduced and changed in specific social settings and use the example of contemporary British schooling to illustrate the kinds of research and argument that social constructionists offer of boys' and girls' preferences, behaviours and achievements.

In Chapter 1 of Book 1 and Chapter 2 of this book, you were introduced to a social constructionist perspective that proposed that the ways in which we understand the world and the things we consider 'true' are not just 'natural'. This perspective suggests that all knowledge – even knowledge that looks as if it is obvious and about reality – is constructed by people within their own particular historical and social contexts.

4.1 The social constructionist perspective

There is a postcard that shows a nurse holding up a newly born baby for the just-delivered mother to see, with the words 'Congratulations! It's a lesbian!' underneath. Jokes often work by taking our everyday, 'natural' assumptions and turning them upside down, contradicting or gainsaying them. Here the joke is about sex and sexuality. When a baby is born we usually congratulate someone not only on having a lovely baby, but on having a lovely little girl or boy. From the first moment of life the appearance of a baby's genitals is taken as a biological (natural) given that defines their reproductive role, and hence the sexual relations and behaviours that accompany that role. Gay sexuality presents a deep challenge to this notion of a causal chain between 'natural' biological (or reproductive) sex and sexuality, because it is not possible to tell from a baby's genitals whether s/he will identity themselves as gay in later life or have same-sex sex.

This joke could also prompt us to query other characteristics or attributes assumed to follow from the biological, reproductive status assigned from a baby's earliest moments. Social constructionists would argue that when we say 'Congratulations, it's a girl' we are using a shorthand that refers to the western stereotype of femininity (see Box 3.1). Of course there is a biological, reproductive sex encoded into a baby's genes and this, in interaction with the hormonal and physical environment *in utero*, will find physical expression in the baby's body. However, social constructionists also argue that an individual's behaviour cannot be directly explained by their biological, reproductive sex status alone.

Social constructionists argue that we construct the world to have two basic types of people, men and women, who are then produced as different in all kinds of other ways. This is partly achieved by the social identity processes described in Chapter 1 of Book 1. Social Identity Theory suggests that, when we see ourselves as belonging to a group or category, we try to maximize our perceived similarity to others in the group, and minimize it with others outside the group. In this way we derive a sense of social identity from our membership of groups, and from the differentiation of those groups and categories from each other. Gender is one of the most important and powerful of social categories by which individuals define themselves.

Activity 3.4

In the context of social identity theory, how might social constructionists explain the notion of the 'opposite sex' – that each gender is defined in terms of being opposite to the other?

In Chapter 2 of this book you were introduced to the ideas of discourse and subject positions through which individuals, as they engage with daily activities, create identities for themselves. Social constructionists suggest that there are many discourses of masculinity and femininity that are socially produced and reproduced through media, social relationships, the rules of institutions, and practices like applying for unemployment benefit, going to see a doctor, or (as we shall see below) going to school.

If you are finding these terms and ideas hard to remember, look back at Chapter 2 Section 4.2 to the worked example of the subject position, 'good mother'.

Individuals can use these discourses to create their own gendered subject positions as masculine or feminine in a variety of ways. Discourses will change as they are used in different circumstances and in relation to different contexts, but they are always produced and reproduced through language. The social constructionist position, as you saw in Chapter 2, is that language is used to construct the world and accomplish particular actions within it, and in this section we will explore gender as one very powerful discourse through which this is done. In the context of our attempt to understand the process of becoming a man or woman, we shall look at how gendered subject positions affect how children understand achievement at school, and in their school subjects. In particular we shall explore the notion that the 'oppositeness' of sex has become a key part of these gendered subject positions. Social constructionists would argue that, in the process of becoming a man or a woman, school occupies a very powerful place, providing a set of highly differentiated discourses about gender-appropriate positions for girls and boys that are incorporated into every aspect of life. It is argued that these will influence career paths in terms of choices about occupation, the aims and goals of personal relationships and responsibility for child-rearing (and hence access to income, social position and expectations of the future), which will have an enduring effect throughout adult life.

3.5 Social construction of gender

In the social constructionist account of what it is to become a man or a woman, reproductive sex is seen as an easily identifiable sign of difference between the sexes that provides the basis for building a whole edifice of constructed gender differences. It is these constructed gender differences, not sexual or reproductive status or potential, which constitute what it is to be a man or woman and explain our behaviours and experiences.

In certain cultural traditions, this social construction of a man or woman is made particularly clear when biological females live as men under certain conditions. For example, in remote parts of Albania, if the male line in a family cannot take on its traditional masculine duties, a woman, who becomes known as an 'avowed virgin', takes the place of the absent son. 'They obey an unwritten rule which requires them never to marry or have children. When a girl adopts the mantle of 'paterfamilias', she cuts her hair short, dresses as a boy and takes on a man's job. The men and village elders accord the 'virgins' all the rights and privileges of fellow males.' (The Guardian, May 7, 1996).

4.2 From gender as construct to constructing gender

Since the Second World War, Westerners have lived through a period of rapid social change in which women's and men's roles have been constantly transforming. Girls and women began to enter the workforce and higher education in increasing numbers and, in the 1960s, they gained access to a contraceptive pill that allowed control of their own fertility for the first time in history. Correspondingly some psychologists began to move away from seeing gender as simply the social expression of biologically grounded difference. Sandra Bem (1981) and others (for example, Spence, 1984) worked within an avowedly feminist framework to develop models of gender as related to identity construction. Bem's Gender Schema Theory proposed that individuals absorb culturally produced understandings of gender that they then use to interpret and make sense of themselves and their behaviour. These understandings are acquired as children learn to see the world through what Bem later described as the 'cultural lenses' of femininity and masculinity (1994). By this she means that masculinity and femininity are socially and culturally constructed dimensions that inform all the forms of our thinking, emotional experience and behaviour. In this analogy they literally condition and colour what we 'see' in our social and personal lives, constructing the world as a gendered place.

Social constructionists, however, do not see gender as a set of characteristics or properties that are acquired by the individual. They see it as something that exists only when it is being done or accomplished. Individuals establish and re-establish their gender continuously in actions, behaviours or experiences throughout their lives, both at the level of the individual and of the group or society. Gender therefore is an ongoing project, a construction of identity that is undertaken throughout one's life. It is dynamic because what is constituted as feminine or masculine will change with historical period or personal context and stage of life.

4.3 The (en)gendering of achievement and learning

From the age of two, children can identify clothes, toys and activities as designating gender, i.e. as 'girlish' or 'boyish'. As they get older, children play in increasingly gender segregated ways, with crossing of gender boundaries only allowed under particular circumstances (Thorne, 1993). This segregation is often explained as stemming naturally from the different reproductive roles of males and females, an argument which has been extended to explain the strong gender segregation of study and work. We discussed in Section 2 the claims that sex differences in visuo-spatial abilities were linked to differential brain lateralization. There have been similar claims about observed sex differences in olfaction (sense of smell), visual field attention and acuity, manual speed and skill performance. Some biological accounts of gender roles base these in differential development of the brain and processing of information between the sexes (Kimura, 1999) and claim this accounts for gender differences in academic subject achievement and occupational choice (Govier, 1998).

It is indeed the case that from early adolescence, children in the UK seem quite consistently to judge school subjects as either masculine or feminine. English and Humanities are preferred by girls, and PE and Science by boys (Colley *et al.*, 1994); French, English, Personal and Social Education and Religious Education are seen as most feminine and subjects like Information Technology, Design and Technology, Science and Maths as most masculine. There is an even stronger differentiation of vocational subjects where Typing and Cookery are seen as feminine and Metal and Wood Work as masculine (Weinreich–Haste, 1979; Archer and McCrae, 1991).

Social constructionists, however, propose that an important part of schooling is that children learn about the performance of masculinity and femininity, in terms of those things they can do to sustain their gender identity. In other words, the processes involved in schooling – the design of the curriculum, the apparent aims of learning and education, the way schools are organized and teaching is done, and how pupil interaction is regulated – act constantly to produce and sustain particular forms of masculinity and femininity.

Boys and academic achievement: 'real men' aren't girly

Social constructionists researching masculinity have used observation techniques and discourse analysis of interview material – a technique explained in more detail in Chapter 2 of this book – to explore how boys and young men understand their activities and achievements at school in relation to their gendered identity. In common with other social constructionist studies into adult masculinity (Mac An Ghaill, 1996), this research seems to indicate that, rather than there simply being one, there are several coherent masculine gender identities created within the school context (Connell, 1995;

Mac An Ghaill, 1994; Stainton-Rogers and Stainton-Rogers, 2001). Social constructionists interpret the evidence as suggesting two common themes across all masculinities. One is that they are relational: any particular gender identity used by boys or men is defined in relation both to feminine identity and also to the identities of other boys or men (see Chapter 1 of Book 1). The second is that masculine identities are constructed through power relations; that is, any masculinity is a privileged identity in that it is partly produced by having control over others, access to resources of some kind, or special social status or practices that others do not have (Wetherell, 1996).

UK primary school boys, as a group, achieve less academically than girls, and are less likely to conform to the rules of the school and demands for particular behaviours in the classroom. Because most teachers in the primary sector are female, it has been argued that boys fail to identify with the source of authority and that rebellion or rejection of authority – one of the defining features of masculinity – becomes in this way a form of masculine identification. While this relational production of identity is initially about being not-feminine, it generalizes to sub-cultures that develop within schools as boys start to identify consciously with particular groups or individuals representing those masculinities. In primary as well as secondary schools, female teachers are routinely exposed to sexual jokes and harassment from male pupils (Lloyd and Duveen, 1992). Social constructionist approaches have argued that experiencing power in relation to women is one way in which boys' masculinity is produced and sustained in schools.

It has also been suggested that girls' increasing academic success has led to a strengthening of an existing tendency to see academic achievement as linked to femininity (Willis, 1977). In a study of boys in a secondary school in the West Midlands, Haywood and Mac An Ghaill (1996) have identified four different masculine identities and how academic achievement and gender identity is constructed within them. The four groups were the 'Macho Lads', the 'Academic Achievers', the 'New Entrepreneurs' and the 'Real Englishmen'.

> *The Macho Lads rejected formal schooling. In contrast, the Academic Achievers legitimized and affirmed the schooling process, locating themselves within academic subjects. Meanwhile the working class New Entrepreneurs located themselves within the newly high status technical and vocational subjects as a resource to develop their masculinities. The Real Englishmen represented a group of middle-class students who, like the Macho Lads, rejected schooling but remained ambivalent as to its significance. Key elements of their masculinity included honesty, being different, individuality and autonomy, which they claimed were absent from the school's middle class culture.*

> *(Haywood and Mac an Ghaill, 1996, p.58).*

In this study, boys generally positioned academic achievement as feminine – as related to conformity and lack of self-assertion and individuality. Indeed the

Academic Achievers and the Real Englishmen groups involved in academic attainment were characterized by other groups as being literally feminized by it – turned into 'poofs' and 'ponces' i.e. feminized homosexuals. According to a social constructionist analysis of this situation, the way that boys can be involved in academic achievement is by being able to construct a gendered subject position that de-feminizes the activity, and reinterprets or reconstructs it in such a way as to fit with masculinity. In the case of the Real Englishmen group, this involved a sophisticated process of subverting and disrupting the teachers' authority and classroom activities while displaying an effortless academic achievement, which could not therefore be attributed to conformity and acceptance of the demands of formal schooling.

Girls and Information Technology: 'real women' relate to others

From a social constructionist perspective, the gendering of academic subjects does not lie in the subject itself, but in which types of knowledge, skills and activities are required by study (for example in the demands of the examinable curriculum). Properties like 'being about people' or 'technical' reflect choices that have been made about curriculum design. In other words, what a school subject is seen to be about, how it is to be used and the skills and abilities it involves, will be determined by the societal values and understandings of the wider culture at a particular point in history, using a particular lens of gender.

Despite the predominance of women in secretarial and clerical jobs involving Information Technology (IT) for word-processing or spreadsheet data, women and girls do not use computers as much for leisure as do men and boys. When they use computers in the domestic context it is more likely to accomplish specific tasks, like shopping, than the game-playing that men and boys do (Baines, 1991, cited in Kirkup, 1995; Cockburn and Furst, 1994). IT is one of the most segregated subjects in terms of voluntary enrolment and one of those subjects rated as most 'masculine'. (You will encounter a discussion of research on the use and understanding of computers in Chapter 6 of Book 3.)

In their review of current research in the area, Littleton and Hoyles (2001) note that, at school, boys seem to feel more confident in monopolizing space and resources. Where for example that means occupying the computer terminal physically, it seems that girls do not assert equal access. However, they argue that giving girls more access to machines, or experience with them, is not the solution. They conclude from the literature review and their own classroom study that most girls working on computers appear to want to work collaboratively, creatively (in terms of defining their own tasks), and carefully (rather than competitively to make the speediest response). However, both the curriculum and the way that IT is taught reflect a construction of it as an individualistic, competitive and set-task oriented practice, which fits well within a variety of masculine identities. Since part of the construction of masculinity is that it is also 'not-feminine' (and vice-versa), the subject is shunned by girls who see it as demanding attitudes that they do not have and activities that they do not want. Support for this interpretation comes from a study that found that when the IT curriculum encourages thinking of computers as animate, reflecting a relationship with the user, and with connotations of friendliness and interactivity, girls are significantly less likely to drop out of a computer studies course. The reverse is true for boys (Nelson *et al.*, 1991).

Activity 3.5

Think about someone – perhaps yourself or someone you know – who has taken up an occupation, interest or course of study that is currently unusual for someone of their gender. How well do you think the social constructionist account explains their involvement?

4.4 Conclusion

Since feminism became influential in academic research in the 1970s, feminine gender identities have been well researched. However, although femininity is relational to masculinity in its construction (i.e. as 'not-masculine'), it is not as strong a defining principle as 'not-feminine' is for masculinity. The struggle for greater equality between the sexes has involved women seeking access to social and economic privileges and this has been achieved partly by women becoming more like men in terms of performance and behaviour. For this, femininities had to develop flexibly to encompass elements that previously constituted masculine gender identity, including academic achievement.

Some gender theorists argue that, as many boys are rejecting educational achievement as a worthwhile goal because of its feminization, so men will find it increasingly difficult to find a socially productive 'not-feminine' masculine identity in a society where women have diversified and incorporated so many aspects beyond traditional femininity. This has been labelled a 'crisis of masculinity' (Connell, 1995; Faludi, 1992).

boys reject schooling due to female teachers =>

boys seeing edⁿ as feminine => underachievement => job problems

Summary Section 4

- According to the social constructionist perspective, biological sex is not central to explaining what it is to be a man or a woman, rather it is a signpost to which a whole set of socially constructed gender differences are attached.
- In this account, socially created discourses about masculinity and femininity are used by individuals to create their own gendered subject positions.

- Sandra Bem developed the idea of the 'cultural lens' of masculinity and femininity. This lens is a way of perceiving the world that makes behaviour and experience gendered.
- In social constructionism, gender is seen as continuously produced throughout their lives, as people construct and interpret their behaviour and experience through the cultural lens of gender.
- The gendering of subjects of study is shown in the gender segregation of subject choice and achievement. This is created through both the way curricula and learning and assessment activities are organized, and the nature of student activity required.
- Academic achievement has become 'feminized'. Current masculinities, traditionally defined as 'opposite' to femininities, have therefore involved schoolboys in attempts to reject academic attainment.

5   Sex and gender: a psychoanalytic perspective

5.1 Becoming and being gendered

What does psychoanalysis contribute to understanding how men and women come to be, and experience themselves as, gendered and different from each other? Psychoanalysis has a strong developmental focus; it concentrates much of its explanation on how young children make sense of their early experience, in particular their early experience of sexual difference as they absorb it from the world around them. Although the main focus is on 'becoming', psychoanalysis uses this developmental process to build explanations about how adults experience being men or women. According to psychoanalysis, sexuality and gender relations play a crucial role in the development of the self and identity.

The main source of evidence for psychoanalytic theories is the clinical experience that psychoanalysts have with their patients. This clinical experience produces different insights from perspectives that depend on experiments or social observations.

In this section, we shall see that psychoanalytic accounts of sexual difference have shifted from a reliance on physical (genital) difference as the key explanation, to an emphasis on meaning. Children attribute meanings to the differences that they perceive between women and men, in particular within the family. The meanings that they attribute are highly influential in the early years. We will also consider the processes whereby these meanings become internalized, so as to make up a person's sense of themselves, their gendered identity.

The psychoanalytic approach to sex and gender should be seen as the product of a movement of ideas that occurred over more than a century. Psychoanalysis moved from drive theory towards understanding 'the self-in-relation-with-others' and an emphasis on the internalization of meanings concerning sexual difference. You will find these different accounts threaded through this section. They add up to a contribution that is distinctively psychological in its understanding of sex and gender, in the sense that it does not reduce to either a biological or societal explanation.

So what do these various psychoanalytic theories of sex and gender have in common? According to psychoanalysts of all persuasions, we acquire the characteristic parts of who we are through identification with parental (and other close) objects.

Why does psychoanalysis use the term 'object'? Look back to Section 2.4, Chapter 9 of Book 1 to find a definition.

Identification involves a modification of identity that takes place through an unconscious process called *internalization*. We imaginatively take in, or **introject**, parts of people, whole people and their relationships and make them our own, over time. It is not a conscious or intentional process and does not depend on language. It is an unconscious, dynamic process that occurs more through inchoate feelings than through thoughts. It is through insight into these processes, using clinical evidence, that psychoanalysis has come to explain the role of sexuality and gender relations in the acquisition of self.

Introject
To incorporate the characteristics of another person into one's own self-image, during the development of one's own identity.

5.2 Oedipal conflict according to Freud

Freud's theory of Oedipal conflict is where psychoanalysis first tried to explain how anatomically differentiated babies develop a psychological sense of being a girl or boy, that is how they become gendered. According to Freud, all children will feel rivalry with the father (or other sexual partner of the mother) because, in their fantasy, the mother is the source of all care, love and pleasure and they want to keep this to themselves.

Psychoanalysts believe, based on infant observation and clinical evidence, that babies have omnipotent fantasies; that is, in their imaginations, fuelled by pleasure seeking, they believe they can do and be and have everything.

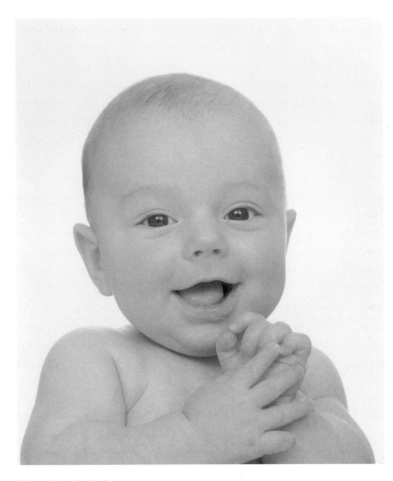

His majesty the baby

The baby therefore imagines it can have its mother completely. Babies are dependent on the mother figure, not just physically but for their psychological survival. There is a difference between physical and psychological survival. Both adults and children can survive physically yet experience themselves as being shattered, no longer with a workable identity. The idea of psychological survival highlights the importance of psychological well-being in providing a person with feelings that they can trust the world around them. This contributes to a secure sense of their capacity to survive without undue pain and anxiety.

In this sense, both boys and girls initially desire the mother and find themselves in competition with the father. Take as an example the occasionally reported little boys' claim 'when I grow up I'm going to marry my mother and have a baby'. This claim is the product of intense wishes: never to separate from his mother and, like her, be able to create a baby. He does not yet know that he is breaking two taboos with his wishes; the incest taboo and the rule of sexual difference. In time, the **reality principle** will make inroads into this fantasy of omnipotence, as successive experiences of frustration are organized meaningfully in a way that involves understanding the difference between self and other. The reality principle means that individuals can respond in an adaptive manner, as opposed to acting as if their desires will be automatically gratified. In the process, *differentiation*, the distinction between oneself and others (who do not necessarily want what we want), is more firmly established.

The reality principle means that, sooner or later, we cannot avoid the realization that our mother is not completely at our disposal, that others make claims on her, and we are jealous. We also come to the realization that we cannot be both boys and girls. These realities face us with loss. How do we cope with these losses – loss of the loved other (or at least the loss of a fantasy of omnipotent control over her) and loss of part of our imagined selves? According to psychoanalysis, the ensuing conflict provides early answers to the question 'who am I (as a girl/woman; as a boy/man)?' and 'who do I desire? (a man; a woman)' The first question is about the achievement of a gendered self; the second about **sexual object choice**. These acquisitions are part of the process of coming to terms with loss in facing the reality of sexual difference.

> *Consider the case of your own child or a child in a family you know. Think of an everyday example where that child has had to give up something it wants of the mother because of the father's (or father figure's) more authoritative demands. What lesson does the child learn about reality? Consider the common western arrangement whereby the parents sleep together in one bed and the baby sleeps on its own elsewhere. As a result, it is confronted with a disagreeable reality on a daily basis: namely, it is deprived of the comfort, reassurance and pleasure of sleeping next to the mother's body. In contrast, the father appears to have a right to just that position. When you come to ponder its significance, this arrangement is saying 'the father has rights and privileges over the mother that I do not have'. (It was all the more pronounced in the late nineteenth century heyday of patriarchal authority within which Freud worked and was a husband and father.)*

According to Freud, boys and girls embark upon different psychic paths because of the dawning awareness of their own sex, defined for them anatomically by the presence or absence of the penis, a *visible* source of considerable pleasure. Freud believed that girls' and boys' different psychic routes to achieving their sense of gendered identity hinged on their

Reality principle
The idea that, providing all goes well enough during the course of development, individuals are increasingly able to recognize the nature of the reality that they experience.

Sexual object choice
Whether we desire someone of the same or the other sex.

different responses to the realization that the boy (like the father) possesses a penis and the girl (like the mother) does not. Through this realization, boys typically can *identify with* their father. This entails the rights and privileges that boys experience fathers as having, especially in relation to the mother: 'when I grow up I can be just like him (we are the same in this vital defining respect)'.

Girls have to acknowledge that they do not possess penises and they also know that their mothers do not. According to Freud, girls identify with their mothers, which is less gratifying because of the status and assumed greater pleasure that attaches to the penis. As a result, girls envy those who possess one.

In this account, there is simultaneously a biological explanation and a cultural one. At first Freud thought that the mere difference – whether the child possessed a penis or not – was sufficient to explain the different psychological development of boys and girls. Later, he began to recognize the importance of the *meaning* of this difference if he was to provide a properly psychological account of the acquisition of gendered identity. If children perceive that adult men have more rights and privileges than women and if they also come to realize that the defining characteristic of a man – the thing that makes him different from all women – is the possession of a penis, then the anatomical difference comes to hold particular social meanings. It holds *symbolic significance*. This argument moves from an exclusive reliance on biology to an inclusion of the significance of social arrangements for how biological difference is experienced. However, it still does not provide a psychological explanation of what it is *to be* a man or a woman. For this, psychoanalysis also needed to explain how the symbolic significance of biological difference affects the sense of who we are as men and women, rather than just influencing how we make sense of the world around us. This is where psychoanalysis uses the ideas of *internalization* and *identification*. These are largely unconscious processes and they are important processes in the child's resolution of the oedipal complex.

If you cannot remember the details of why the oedipal complex occurs and what it entails, turn back to Chapter 9 of Book 1 and reread Section 2.

5.3 Critical developments

Feminists and other women theorists rejected the demeaning of women implied in the claim that women's sex is just lack; that women are constituted through envy of what men have that they do not.

In particular, two arguments have been influential in developing the psychoanalytic understanding of gender development. First, the symbolic significance of the penis emphasized that the organ itself was not the central issue, but rather what it symbolized about the father's power, rights and privileges within the family, in particular his authority over the mother. In this light, the theory looks less like a patriarchal slight on women and more like a recognition of how patriarchal relations affect boys' and girls' experience of what it is to grow up one sex or the other. Further, it is argued that girls do not have to give up their mothers in the traumatic way that boys do: they can continue to have and be her.

The second argument has criticized Freud's failure to consider the significance of women's genitals. Just because the boy's genital is more visible, does that mean that the girl's is unknown or gives no pleasure to her? Challenging Freud, many argue that girls do have knowledge of their vaginas as well as their clitorises and get pleasure from them. Both boys and girls associate a girl's internal reproductive organs with their mother's capacity to give birth. Karen Horney, an early colleague of Freud, was struck, in her clinical practice, by her male patients' envy of women's ability to give birth. In *Flight from Womanhood* (1926) she commented:

'When one begins, as I did, to analyse men only after a fairly long experience of analysing women, one receives a most surprising impression of the intensity of his envy of pregnancy, childhood and motherhood, as well as of the breasts and of the act of suckling' (Horney, 1926, pp.60–1)

Horney coined the idea of 'womb envy' and moreover pointed out that its neglect in psychoanalysis arose because, in a male-dominated cultural climate, the idea would more readily be repressed than the idea of penis envy.

A sculpture of the ecstasy of Teresa D'Avila, in the Santa Maria della Vittoria in Rome. Jacques Lacan, a French psychoanalyst, claims that it represents women's huge capacity for sexual pleasure, which radiates through their whole bodies, a capacity that rivals boys' pleasure in their penises and is accessible even to a celibate nun. The image also remains acceptable within the religious tradition of the time by ostensibly representing St. Teresa's ecstasy as she felt her heart pierced by 'the fiery arrow of Divine Love'

Karen Horney's claim has wide-ranging implications. From a psychanalytical perspective it suggests that if an idea – such as womb envy – is uncomfortable for a whole category of individuals – men in this instance – and if that group is influential in producing the knowledge that is available at a given historical period, then that idea it less likely to be produced; it will have been collectively repressed as too threatening. Other ideas will be appealing because they are satisfying to a person's beliefs about themselves and their group.

It seems likely that Freud's theory of gender development was limited by his 'phallocentrism' (the view that the penis was the only significant genital and hence girls' development was determined by their lack and by their envy). Following Horney's account of womb envy, we can see girls' identification with adult women in a more positive light than Freud did: 'I may not have the advantages of a man, but I can do something even more valuable: I can create a child'.

Melanie Klein analysed very young children using her version of play therapy. Her evidence helped to show that the Oedipus complex isn't simply about loving the parent of the other sex and hating the same sex (rival) parent. She found very mixed feelings where both boys and girls could love and identify with the same-sex parent. She also found that 'children often show, as early as the beginning of their second year, a marked preference for the parent of the other sex and other indications of Oedipus tendencies' (Klein, 1926, p.129). This meant disagreeing with Freud's positioning of the Oedipus complex at age 4 or 5, the genital phase. Increasingly, psychoanalysis has moved away from talking about drives or instincts to seeing the developmental history of the baby in terms of the quality of its *actually experienced* object relations and the effects of these on its identifications. According to psychoanalytic theory, people internalize objects and object relations, and then may or may not identify with them. This means that the process of identification with significant others is not automatic but allows for fluidity and changes over time. The process of identification does not stop after childhood. Rather it is a mechanism that continues throughout life and helps to explain how our identities (including our gendered identities) are continually subject to change and modification.

5.4 Changing gender relations and cross-sex identifications

Most psychoanalysts now agree that identifications with the same-sex parent are neither exclusive nor unambivalent. Jessica Benjamin's writings (1990, 1995, 1998) demonstrate how contemporary psychoanalytic theory has transformed Freud's ideas in a way that recognizes the importance of the meanings of sexual difference, as experienced through relationships, and how these are internalized to shape gender identity. She argues that it is no longer convincing to suppose that boys identify with fathers who are unambiguously masculine and girls identify with mothers who are unambiguously feminine. Perhaps because of the profound unsettling of traditional gender relations, when contemporary psychoanalysts look at what it means to be a man or a woman, they see a more complex picture.

If the significance of the penis is symbolic (that is, it becomes a source of pride or envy or fear of loss because it stands for the advantages of being a man) this has implications for how social changes in gender relations are incorporated into psychoanalytic theory. A common criticism of Freud's ideas is that he was constructing a theory that made claims about human nature in general whereas his evidence was limited to the gender relations of a particular place and time (nineteenth century mid-Europe). If so, as gender relations change towards equality of the sexes, will not the unconscious significance of anatomical difference change?

The answer to this question can be both 'yes and no'. Yes, because, if babies grow up experiencing maternal-type care from both a father and mother, then the time when they have to acknowledge sexual difference and give up the fantasy of being both will not involve as much loss. If this were the case, the boy, in giving up the mother, would not be faced with losing his source of love and care. Likewise, if both parents are active and powerful in the world, the girl's identification with her mother would not entail losses of those potentials. Consider too that if each parent already combines plentiful feminine and masculine attributes, then identification with one parent is not going to limit that child's potential in the way that it would in an era in which gendered divisions of labour and character were rigid and mutually exclusive.

The 'no' side to the answer refers to the significance of anatomy. Anatomy is not destiny in the sense of determining our psycho-sexual characteristics: one of Freud's greatest achievements was to distinguish between biological and psychological characteristics when it came to explaining gender development. However, anatomical difference in reproductive organs was, for Freud, part of reality that every child has to come to terms with. It is the bedrock of unconscious experience of sexual difference; difference that will not be erased by gender equality, but can be changed by it.

Summary Section 5

- Psychoanalysis, starting with Freud but not limited to his work, has contributed a psychological way of understanding sexuality and gender that takes into account both anatomical difference and social factors like family structure and meaning.
- Gender and sexuality came to be seen, through Freud's and later psychoanalytic work, as having far-reaching implications for the development of self.
- The concept of identification is common to all forms of psychoanalysis and illuminates the way people unconsciously acquire their characteristic identities from significant (gendered) others, especially from their parents and their experience of how their parents relate.
- Central to the process of acquiring a differentiated self is the task of coming to terms with the reality of two kinds of loss: loss of the mother as

an extension of the child's desires, and loss of the possibility of being both sexes.

- Important critical developments in the psychoanalytic theory of sex and gender include: the symbolic significance of the penis (and penis envy) as a symbol of men's privilege; the significance of women's creative capacity to give birth in understanding how envy affects gender identifications; and emphasis on the complexity of identifications with parental figures, resulting in the incorporation of multiple-gendered characteristics in both women and men.
- The symbolic significance of anatomical sexual difference cannot be erased in human beings' experience of gender, but it can change with changing gender arrangements.

6   Conclusion

The above four perspectives provide very disparate accounts of sex and gender and inevitably raise the question of whether together they are more useful than any single account is on its own. How can we deal with such diversity? Might it be acceptable to 'add together' the convincing or preferred parts of each perspective? In other words, using the '3Cs' theme from the first book of the course, do these perspectives *complement* each other, *conflict* with each other or *coexist* with each other? And on what grounds do we evaluate their claims when seen in relation to each other?

In this concluding section we shall address this fundamental question in the following ways. A logical first step will be to evaluate the strengths of each perspective in its own terms, because these will clarify what it is we want to hold on to in a general psychology of sex and gender. In identifying strengths, we will also touch upon weaknesses, because these suggest what to be wary of and what we shall need from the other perspectives to compensate. If, as a result of identifying strengths, we wish to put together parts of each perspective, we shall then have to work out whether they can be combined together, that is whether they are complementary or not. The second part of this conclusion therefore discusses ways in which it may be possible to combine different perspectives. It emphasizes compatibility at the level of thory. There are many different grounds, however, according to which perspectives can be complementary, conflicting or coexisting. Having discussed theoretical compatibility, we shall move on to the question of conflict between perspectives. Here the focus will be on political or ideological differences and the way they often lead to theoretical conflict. Finally, under the heading

'Coexisting methodologies', we discuss forms of knowledge that, due to the fundamentally different methodologies that produced them, can do no more than coexist with one another, perhaps.

First, however, it will help you to clarify your own understanding of the various positions by working through the following activity.

Activity 3.8

Look back to the summaries of each of Sections 2 to 5. Identify – if you find it appropriate – one or two aspects of the perspective that you are convinced by and one or two aspects that you are unconvinced by. Put them in your own words and note your reasons for each, if you can.

6.1 Strengths and weaknesses

The *biological perspective* has the strength of referring to material characteristics, using material data. Assuming that the methods are dependable (and biological research aspires to the rigour that is most attainable in natural science), evidence from biology can demonstrate sex differences (and similarities) in genetic make-up, hormones and brain regions. Section 2 made it clear just how complicated it can be to establish the relationship between biological processes, for example the effects of genes on hormones and of these on the sexed bodies of babies or adolescents. By carefully documenting these separate effects, biology shows us that biological difference between the sexes is not a simple fact, even before we take into consideration life history and experience. Biology's actions and effects are always in interaction, not just with other biological processes, but also with physical and cultural environments. Biological study can highlight developmental changes, for example, Hofman and Swaab found that sex differences that appear in certain regions of the adult brain are not found in the younger brains of children (see Section 2). The interpretation of this kind of finding is quite complex and the underlying causal sequence is not straight forward. In this case, changes in certain brain regions between childhood and adulthood could be a result, for example, of experience interacting with hormones that do not get triggered until puberty. An important message of biological psychology is that biological differences between the sexes can be a *product* of psychological experience as well as a *cause* of differences in behaviour.

However, although biological psychology can demonstrate the complexity of connections between biological mechanisms and behaviour, it cannot (and does not attempt) to say anything about the realm of human experience, or 'being' as this was defined in the introduction. By itself, then, it does not provide us with a psychology of sex and gender.

Evolutionary psychology has the strength of keeping in view the basic principle that the genetic make-up of human animals, like non-human animals, has evolved according to the principles of natural and sexual selection. The question that follows from this widely accepted principle is a valid and important one: can differences in sexual behaviour between men and women be explained – or partly explained – by genetic differences selected for in the course of evolutionary survival? It is a very ambitious question, because, to answer it, evolutionary psychology has to demonstrate ways in which contemporary behaviour is influenced by genetically programmed behaviours that were laid down many generations ago, notwithstanding all the other influences on the species during that time. Consequently, evolutionary psychologists do not address the detail of how particular forms of sexual behaviour have evolved among humans, but restrict their research to trying to show that contemporary differences in human sexual behaviour are consistent with their theoretical argument.

The difficulty with this is that the evidence gathered to support the argument cannot readily discount other explanations for the behaviours in question nor can it explain how other factors may influence and modify the behavioural outcome. Take as an example Clark and Hatfield's finding (see Section 3) that 75 per cent of American college men, as opposed to none of the women, consented to sex with an 'attractive stranger' of the other sex. This is consistent with the evolutionary psychology argument (always supposing that these men would have followed through on their claim, an outcome that was not tested). The finding would also be consistent with a social constructionist claim that men are motivated to position themselves in a discourse that constructs men as being 'properly masculine' provided that they are seen to be constantly in pursuit of heterosexual sex. Some evolutionary psychologists (e.g. Dunbar *et al.*, 1999) have proposed that evolved behavioural predispositions underlie many of the cultural patterns that we observe. So one possibility here is that evolution may have shaped cultural practices that in turn serve to reinforce patterns of evolved behaviour. In this way, evolutionary psychologists acknowledge social influences on sexual behaviour. However, their methods provide no systematic way of taking these into account in explaining the behaviour observed in their experiments with contemporary, culturally-situated, meaning-making human beings.

The strength of a *social constructionist* explanation of gender difference is its capacity to take into account the historical and cultural situation of human beings, and in particular their unique capacity, in the animal world, for meaning-making and communication of intentions. Its methods focus almost exclusively on the meaning-making activities of humans. Social constructionists would argue that the cultural lenses through which men and women filter their own sexual behaviours would be strong enough to account for Clark and Hatfield's findings. Many of them would probably argue that an evolutionary or biological account is superfluous because genetically-selected or hormonal influences would be comprehensively overlaid by the importance of cultural practices, meaning and intention in shaping human sexual behaviour.

Evolutionary psychology's rejoinder would probably be in terms of social constructionism's failure to explain the origins of these gender differences. How did the cultural lenses of gender come to construct the differences in men's and women's sexual behaviour in the first place? They point to the cultural universality of such human behaviours and argue that they cannot be explained entirely in terms of social influences. When evolutionary psychology considers genetic selection in human animals, how are the arguments modified to accommodate the unique features of human beings such as language and the existence of culture that survives through countless generations?

Psychoanalytic psychology's challenge would be different, namely that social constructionism over emphasises the role of external influences (identities being constructed by discourses and discursive practices) in determining people's behaviour. Consequently, it does not explain their agency and capacity for resistance and change.

The strength of *psychoanalytical psychology* is in addressing the question of 'becoming' and the processes involved in this: how the baby, sexed by its biology and gendered by society, takes on a *psychological* gender that becomes intrinsic to its later identity as a person. In this perspective, the social constructionist account (that social discourses concerning gender are consciously taken on board to comply with social pressures and group identity) is insufficient. For psychoanalysis, these meanings are transformed by unconscious and creative fantasies, born out of anxieties, desires and defences. These are unique to the human species. Meanings, then, are a crucial interface between the social environment that exists before any given individual, and the becoming of that individual. This can provide an explanation for how people resist and change the cultural meanings around them, so that people's gender is not seen as *determined* either by social discourses or by biology.

The criticism from most other perspectives would be to argue that psychoanalysis cannot demonstrate the validity of its claims. Critics point to its exaggerated or unlikely emphasis on unconscious experiences such as castration anxiety that cannot be empirically demonstrated, and its disregard for people's conscious explanations of their behaviour. This challenge raises questions about evidence and methods to which we shall return below.

In summary, as a result of considering the strengths and weaknesses of our four perspectives, it is possible to conclude that each has a valuable point of view, one that should not be lost sight of in a psychology of sex and gender. At the same time, no one perspective has the necessary breadth to provide a full explanation. Why, you may be asking, can we not combine these four to provide a full explanation? Would they not together take account of the full range of influences that make up being a man or a woman: biological, evolutionarily selected, social and psychic-developmental? Do not all these factors contribute?

6.2 Complementary perspectives

Most agree that there is necessarily some interaction among these influences. But how would such an interaction work? The idea of an interaction does not solve the problem if it is just a matter of combining theories that do not share any common theoretical ground. The challenge is to build a theory that *explains* how the different influences interact to produce some aspect of human behaviour.

So we need to establish whether the perspectives in this chapter are indeed complementary or not. Are there ways in which they can be combined to provide a better, fuller picture of human sex and gender differences or are they completely incompatible? Let me give an example in which biological and social explanations are rendered theoretically compatible within a psychological account: the *experience* of a girl's menarche (the onset of menstruation), which is a significant time in her experience of herself as becoming a woman. We have established that a properly psychological explanation must accept that hormonal and bodily changes take place in adolescence, because these impinge in some way on experience and are also affected by it. Likewise we must accept that the social context in which adolescents grow up is already awash with gendered meanings about adolescence that circulate in families and schools (and vary between cultures). It has also been argued that a psychological explanation needs to explain in detail how these social meanings become internalized and impinge on gendered 'being'.

The analysis would need therefore to examine the meanings that are made in the psyche of the experience of bodily and hormonal change, in the context of available social meanings. Some of these social meanings will have an effect, not just on the psyche, but on biological processes. If a girl starts her periods at an unusually early age, this will have been affected by genetic inheritance, triggering hormones into action that are expressed in the physical changes of puberty. But early periods have social significance that could well make them more anxiety-provoking. If – at whatever age – a girl absorbs from her mother or peer group the idea that menstruation is something to dread, or from her father that it is dirty or taboo, the anxiety can take a biological form that arguably can modify the biological processes giving rise to painful periods. Once biology is understood to be a two-way process, not just acting on individual behaviour, meaning and experience, but also being affected by it, then we can begin to see a way in which ovulation, for example, can be affected by social meanings.

However, we are not just combining hormonal change and social meaning (biological and social factors). The way that a particular girl experiences the social meanings concerning menstruation is *mediated* by her psyche. The psyche is not just a mirror of social meanings. We need to include the dimension of psychic development to make this 'bio-psycho-social' explanation properly psychological: that is, a girl's unique past experience and how she has, consciously and unconsciously, transformed its significance when it comes to an event that is central to becoming a woman. The meaning that menstruation has for her is not just dictated by the culture that surrounds her at the time, but by the inner meanings that her body, her gender and her sexuality have already acquired, meanings that are unique to her. Although related to those available in her culture, these have been creatively modified during her development through unconscious anxieties (for example about becoming like her mother) and desires (for example to have children of her own).

6.3 Political conflict among explanations

Throughout the twentieth century, biological and social explanations ('nature' and 'nurture') have been at loggerheads because of what has been seen as their opposite political implications. Those who were in favour of changing what they saw as women's disadvantaged position in society tended to favour social explanations because social influences can be changed. They saw biological explanations as dangerously deterministic: for example if women's caring capacity was naturally given, not socially given, would women ever win equal rights in the workplace? The kind of biology represented in this chapter, with its emphasis on plasticity and becoming, does not lend itself to this kind of political conclusion.

More recently, evolutionary psychology has been accused of the same politically conservative tendencies. Now, as then, it is difficult to separate out what responsibility lies in the explanation itself and what lies in the use to which it has been put by popularizers who oversimplify. One notorious example of such a conflict is the claim that evolutionary psychology 'excuses' rape by suggesting that sexually predatory behaviour is a genetically selected strategy because it maximizes male reproductive advantage by enabling them to inseminate as many women as often as possible.

In a book entitled *A Natural History of Rape: Biological Bases of Sexual Coercion* (2000), Thornhill and Palmer argue that rape is an adaptive strategy in animal species – and by extension in human males – which enables males who otherwise might be sexually unsuccessful to propagate their genes. The authors reported studies on forced sex in mallard ducks and scorpion flies. Supporters of evolutionary psychology do not accept the charge that this application of the evolutionary perspective 'excuses' the behaviour of men who rape. However, critics take issue with Thornhill and Palmer's failure to make the necessary conceptual distinctions between animals and humans in their use of the term 'rape'. Hilary and Stephen Rose (2000) point out that forced sex in animal species is always with fertile females, hence the reproductive potential. An account that omits the human capacity to make meaning (in this case out of violent intrusion of the body) is guilty of a serious conflation of humans with non-human animals. Some other criticisms are that Thornhill and Palmer's argument does not account for the behaviour of the vast majority of men who do not rape and who wish to be monogamous. Nor does it account for gang rape. However, evolutionary psychology *does* assume some individual (inherited) differences. Indeed, they are the very features on which natural selection operates. Moreover, as we have acknowledged, it accepts that environmental and social influences modify behaviour by operating on, or overlaying, existing genetic variation. Nevertheless, within this framework, evolutionary psychology as a perspective does not theorise about how individual differences arise. It considers universals as its object of knowledge.

There is one issue that it is important to disentangle when trying not to get sucked into a political argument that could be as unproductive as the history of the nature-nurture debate. Put simply, it is not acceptable to dismiss a theory on the grounds that it appears to legitimate behaviour that is morally repugnant to us. On the other hand, it would be surprising if morally repugnant arguments were not first in line for a very close examination of their assumptions, logic of argument and methods. As we saw in the introduction, feminists have long been suspicious of conclusions about 'natural' differences between women and men that male scientists discovered on the basis of so-called 'scientific evidence'. Many, especially social constructionists, have concluded from historical research that values inevitably underpin all knowledge. This should not mean, however, either that distasteful ideas are rejected out of hand, or that an equally partisan new set of ideas should be advanced that claims to explain the whole psychology of sex and gender.

6.4 Coexisting methodologies

Psychological methods have traditionally been based on scientific principles, derived from the natural sciences, that rely on systematic observation and measurement of phenomena. Such research derives testable hypotheses from current knowledge and theory, and draws on empirical data to test it.

Both biology and evolutionary psychology embrace this scientific approach. Evolutionary psychology inevitably relies in part on the principle of reverse engineering to construct theoretical models concerning the origins of human behaviour, and seeks empirical evidence from the behaviour of contemporary humans and other species to support them. There is controversy about whether this conforms to the rigorous procedures of science (see Herrnstein-Smith, 2000). Evolutionary psychology seeks to counter criticisms that it cannot provide 'direct' proof for its theories, arguing that the availability of different kinds of converging scientific evidence provides a suitable alternative.

Another criticism that has been levelled at evolutionary psychology is that it invokes the notion that particular patterns of behaviour are genetically selected without providing any evidence at the *genetic level*. Certainly we are a long way from identifying genes that might determine sexual behaviours. However, the existence of some genetically transmitted disorders, such as Huntingdon's disease, is well documented. In this case, as well as distressing degenerative effects, quite specific behavioural patterns are documented. For instance, patients seem unable to experience and recognise in others the emotion of disgust, while retaining the capacity to recognise emotions such as anger, happiness and fear. Animal models suggest that groups of genes can determine quite complex patterns of behaviour. It is highly unlikely that sexual behaviour in humans will be determined solely by genes; however, intricate interactions between inherited and acquired characteristics are to be expected. Thus, there will not be a gene for 'human females to have a predilection for wealthy men', but it could conceivably be that a gene complex, interacting with cultural determinants of 'high rank', predisposes some females to choose wealthy men.

The group of methods that are usually contrasted with scientific approaches are based on the hermeneutic (or interpretative) principle (see *Methods Booklet 1: Introduction to Research Methods*). Social constructionism and psychoanalysis are both based on the interpretation of meaning (symbolic data in the typology of data given in the Introduction to Book 1) and therefore, it is argued, cannot comply with natural science principles. Some psychologists regard this as 'special pleading' while others contend that the very criteria for what is scientific should be modified for psychological research to accommodate meaning-based interpretations of human behaviour.

Different psychologies use different methods, and this fundamentally affects what they can study and the knowledge that they produce. Such radical differences between different psychological approaches *can* lead to conflict but more usually result in coexistence. If two perspectives share some methodological principles, they have something specific to argue about, as when biologists, such as Herrnstein-Smith, argue that evolutionary psychology is not rigorous in its hypothesis testing, and evolutionary psychologists counter that hypothesis testing about evolution must necessarily take a different form. However, when the methodological principles are radically different, like those of natural science-based psychology and psychoanalytic psychology, useful debate is more difficult because they start from different principles and follow different procedures. For example, we saw that psychoanalytic psychology has been accused of being speculative and that psychologists have argued that concepts like repression and the unconscious cannot be tested according to scientific principles. Psychoanalysts counter that their methods derive from the clinical situation, where, they argue, the patient's free associations allow access to unconscious conflict and the way that, unintentionally, personal meanings influence behaviour.

Unlike natural science-based psychology, psychoanalysts, in common with social constructionist psychology, believe that the researcher's subjectivity is inevitably involved in research (see *Methods Booklet 4: Introduction to Qualitative Methods*); that its influence should be recognized rather than denied. It is not surprising then that this model of research has difficulty entering into meaningful debate with the natural scientific approach, either consensual or conflictual. Neither is it surprising that psychoanalytic methodology has generated such different knowledge from scientific psychology.

Where does this 'failure to engage' at the methodological level leave our nicely complementary theories of the menarche? Is such complementarity an illusion if theorists from different perspectives cannot agree on the status of each other's evidence? There is no easy answer to this question.

6.5 Last words

In the introduction to this chapter, we said that the topic of sex and gender illustrates many of the difficult and contentious questions that psychology faces. We have seen how these include the challenge of putting a range of very diverse perspectives alongside each other, of reckoning with the inevitable political dimension of psychological knowledge, of taking into account the importance of method to what knowledge can be generated. Above all, we must try to produce an account that convincingly does justice to the complexity of our experience as gendered human beings. All of these challenges are typical of those faced in the social sciences, although psychology faces the extra difficulty of incorporating the broad span of theories and methods entailed by biological and social accounts.

Is it reasonable to expect psychology to be able to solve all of these problems in its account of sex and gender? There is a lively debate in the social sciences as to whether an overarching explanation, a 'grand narrative', is either possible or desirable. At the moment the climate has shifted from those who believed in the possibility of dependable scientific knowledge to those who celebrate the multiple, unruly, often conflictual nature of different perspectives as they jostle for space in contemporary academic and cultural life. Certainly you should not expect, or try to produce, a single explanation of the psychology of sex and gender. It is also helpful to develop a critical capacity when confronted with the many accounts that are available. We hope that this chapter has helped you in this important area of academic study. It is a theme pursued throughout this book.

Summary Section 6

- The objects of knowledge of each of the four perspectives are all valid and useful in a general psychology of sex and gender.
- No perspective on its own can tell the whole story.
- Any explanation of human behaviour that draws from non-human animal behaviour must include a good understanding of specifically human characteristics.
- Perspectives and levels of analysis and explanation cannot just be combined without an account of how they interact.
- The experience of menarche provides an example of the potential complementarity of biological, psychoanalytic and social constructionist perspectives.
- Political differences are often exposed when conflicting accounts of sex and gender differences occur.
- The major differences between psychological methods based on natural science principles and those based on hermeneutic principles means that perspectives based on these methods may have difficulty achieving more than an uneasy coexistence.
- Don't worry if you cannot come up with a single psychological explanation of sex and gender. It might be more productive to enjoy the diversity. But cultivate your critical faculties.

Answer to Activity 3.2

female; male; male; female; female; female; male; male; female; female

Further reading

Buss, D.M. (2000) *The Dangerous Passion*, London, Bloomsbury.

This book focuses on sex differences in jealousy and is based on the findings of a large cross-cultural study. The book provides a readable up-to-date account of the evolutionary origins of sexual desires.

Minsky, R. (ed.) (1996) *Psychoanalysis and Gender: An Introductory Reader*, London, Routledge.

This is an accessible introduction that covers several important psychoanalytical theorists and includes significant extracts from their own work, with commentaries.

Rogers, L.J. (1999) *Sexing the Brain*, London, Weidenfield and Nicolson.

Stainton-Rogers, W. and Stainton-Rogers, R. (2001) *The Psychology of Gender and Sexuality*, Buckingham, Open University Press.

An accessible introduction to a range of perspectives on gender and sexuality, ranging from biology and evolutionary psychology to anthropology, psychoanalytical and feminist and critical perspectives.

Trew, K. and Kresemer, J. (1998) *Gender and Psychology*, London and New York, Arnold (Hodder).

An edited collection with chapters by specialists in every area, including cognition, biology and emotion.

References

Allen, L.S. and Gorski, R.A. (1990) 'Sex difference in the bed nucleus of the stria terminalis of the human brain', *Journal of Comparative Neurology*, vol.302, pp.607–706.

Baines S. (1991) 'Personal computing, gender and distance education', paper given to the International Federation of Information Processors (IFIP) conference, Helsinki, June. Cited in Kirkup, G. 'The importance of gender as a category of Open and Distance Learning', *Teaching and Consultancy Centre Report no.90*, Milton Keynes, The Open University.

Baker, S.W. and Erhardt, A.A. (1974) 'Pre-natal androgen, intelligence and cognitive sex differences', in Friedman, R.C., Richart, R.M. and van Deeds, R.L. (eds) *Sex Differences in Behavior*, New York, Wiley.

Beach (1938) 'Sex reversals in the mating pattern of the rat', *Journal of Genetic Psychology*, vol.53, pp.329–34.

Bem, S. (1981) 'Gender Schema Theory: a cognitive account of sex-typing', *Psychological Review*, vol.88, pp.354–64.

Bem, S. (1994) *The Lenses of Gender*, London and New York, Yale University Press.

Benjamin, J. (1990) *The Bonds of Love*, London, Virago.

Benjamin, J. (1995) *Like Subjects, Love Objects: Essays on Recognition and Sexual Difference*, New Haven and London, Yale University Press.

Benjamin, J. (1998) *The Shadow of the Other: Intersubjectivity and Gender in Psychoanalysis*, London, Routledge.

Betzig, L.L. (1986) *Despotism and Differential Reproduction: A Darwinian View of History*, Hawthorne, NY, Aldine de Gruyter.

Bishop, K.M. and Wahlsten, D. (1997) 'Sex differences in the human corpus callosum: Myth or reality?', *Neuroscience and Biobehavioral Reviews*, vol.21, pp.581–601.

Broverman, J.K., Broverman, D.M., Clarkson, F.E., Rosenkrantz, P.S. and Vogel, S.R. (1970) 'Sex-role stereotypes and clinical judgements of mental health', *Journal of Consulting and Clinical Psychology*, vol.34, pp.1–7.

Bullough, V.L. and Bullough , B. (1987) *Women and Prostitution: A Social History*, Buffalo, NY, Prometheus.

Buss, D.M. (1989) 'Sex differences in human mate preferences: Evolutionary hypotheses testing in 37 cultures', *Behavioural and Brain Sciences*, vol.12, pp.1–49.

Buss, D.M. (2000) 'The evolution of happiness', *American Psychologist*, vol.55, pp15–23.

Buss, D.M., Larsen, R.,Westen, D., and Semmelroth, J. (1992) 'Sex differences in jealousy: Evolution, physiology, and psychology', *Psychological Science*, vol.3, pp.251–55.

Buss, D.M. and Schmitt, D.P. (1993) 'Sexual strategies theory: An evolutionary perspective on human mating', *Psychological Review*, vol.100, pp.204–32.

Caplan, P.J., Macpherson, G.M. and Tobin, P. (1985) 'Do sex-related differences in spatial abilities exist – a multilevel critique with new data', *American Psychologist*, vol.40, pp.786–99.

Clark, R.D. (1990) 'The impact of AIDS on gender differences in willingness to engage in casual sex', *Journal of Applied Social Psychology*, vol.20, pp.771–82.

Clark, R.D. and Hatfield, E. (1989) 'Gender differences in receptivity to sexual offers', *Journal of Psychology and Human Sexuality*, vol.2, pp.39–55.

Cockburn, C. and Furst, D. (eds) (1994) *Bringing Technology Home*, Buckingham, Open University Press.

Colley, A., Comber C. and Hargreaves, D.J. (1994) 'Gender effects in school subject preferences', *Educational Studies*, vol.20, pp.379–85.

Cooke, B., Hegstrom, C.D., Villeneuve, L.S. and Breedlove, S.M. (1998) 'Sexual differentiation of the vertebrate brain: principles and mechanisms', *Frontiers in Neuroendocrinology*, vol.19, pp.323–62.

Connell, R.W. (1995) *Masculinities*, Cambridge, Polity Press.

Dunbar, R., Knight, C. and Power, C. (eds) (1999) *The Evolution of Culture*, Edinburgh, Edinburgh University Press.

Eagly, A.H. (1994) 'On comparing women and men', *Feminism and Psychology*, vol.4, no.4, pp.513–22.

Faludi, S. (1992) *Backlash:the Undeclared War against Women*, London, Chatto and Windus.

Fausto-Sterling, A. (2000) *Sexing the Body*, New York, Basic Books.

Fielding (1997) *Bridget Jones's Diary*, London, Picador.

Fielding (2000) *Bridget Jones: The Edge of Reason*, London, Picador.

Fitch, R.H. and Denenberg, V.H. (1998) 'A role for ovarian hormones in sexual differentiation of the brain', *Behavioral and Brain Sciences*, vol.21, pp.311–27.

Geary, D.C., Rumsey, M., Bow-Thomas, C.C. and Hoard, M.K. (1995) 'Sexual jealousy as a facultative trait: evidence from the pattern of sex differences in adults from China and the United States', *Ethology and Sociobiology*, vol.16, pp.355–83.

Giedd, J.N., Blumenthal, J., Jeffries, N.O., Castellanos, F.X., Liu, H., Zijdenbos, A., Paus, T., Evans, A.C. and Rapoport, J.L. (1999) 'Brain development during childhood and adolescence: a longitudinal MRI study', *Nature Neuroscience*, vol.2, pp.861–63.

Govier E. (1998) 'Brain, sex and occupation', in Radford, J. (ed.) *Gender and Choice in Education and Occupation*, London, Routledge.

Gray, J. (1993) *Men are from Mars, Women are from Venus*, London, Thorsons.

Gregor, T. (1985) *Anxious Pleasures: the Sexual Lives of an Amazonian People*, Chicago, University of Chicago Press.

Halpern, D.F. (1994) 'Stereotypes, science, censorship, and the study of sex differences', *Feminism and Psychology*, vol.4, no.4, pp.523–30.

Haywood, C. and Mac an Ghaill, M. (1996) 'Schooling masculinities', in Mac an Ghaill (1996).

Herrnstein-Smith, B. (2000) 'Sewing up the mind: the claims of evolutionary psychology', in Rose, H. and Rose, S. (eds).

Hofman, M.A. and Swaab, D.F. (1991) 'Sexual dimorphism of the human brain – myth and reality', *Experimental and Clinical Endocrinology*, vol.98, pp.161–70.

Holzman, H.R. and Pines, S. (1982) 'Buying sex: The phenomenology of being a john', *Deviant Behavior: An Interdisciplinary Journal*, vol.4, pp.89–116.

Horney, K. (1926) 'Flight from womanhood', *Feminine Psychology*, New York, Norton.

Hyde, J. (1990) 'How large are cognitive differences? A meta-analysis using ω^2 and d', in Nielsen, J.M. (ed.) *Feminist Research Methods: Exemplary Readings in the Social Sciences*, Boulder, CO, Westview.

Hyde, J. (1994) 'Should psychologists study sex differences? Yes, with some guidelines', *Feminism and Psychology*, vol.4, no.4.

Jackson, L.A. (1992) *Physical Appearance and Gender: Sociobiological and Sociocultural Perspectives*, Albany, State University of New York Press.

Johnson (1970) 'Some correlates of extramarital coitus', *Journal of Marriage and the Family*, vol.32, pp.449–56.

Kimura, D. (1999) *Sex and Cognition*, Cambridge, MA, MIT Press.

Kinsey, A.C., Pomeroy, W.B. and Martin, C.E. (1948) *Sexual Behavior in the Human Male*, Philadelphia, Saunders.

Kinsey, A.C., Pomeroy, W.B. and Martin, C.E. (1953) *Sexual Behavior in the Human Female*, Philadelphia, Saunders.

Klein, M. (1926) 'The Psychological Principles of Early Analysis', *The Writings of Melanie Klein*, vol.1, London, Hogarth Press.

Langhorne, M.C. and Secord, P.F. (1955) 'Variations in marital needs with age, sex, marital status, and regional composition', *Journal of Social Psychology*, vol.41, pp.19–37.

Levay, S. (1991) 'A difference in hypothalamic structure between heterosexual and homosexual men', *Science*, vol.253, pp.1034–7.

Lloyd, B.B. and Duveen, G. (1992) *Gender Identities and Education: the Impact of Starting School*, New York/London, Harvester Wheatsheaf.

McCormick, N.B. (1994) *Sexual Salvation*, Westport, CT, Greenwood.

Mac an Ghaill, M. (1994) *The Making of Men: Masculinities, Sexualities and Schooling*, Buckingham, Open University Press.

Mac an Ghaill, M. (1996) *Understanding Maculinities. Social Relations and Cultural Arenas*, Buckingham, Open University Press.

Maccoby, E.E. and Jacklin, C.N (1974) *The Psychology of Sex Differences*, Stanford, CA, Stanford University Press.

Money, J. and Erhardt, A. (1972) *Man and Woman: Boy and Girl*, Baltimore, Johns Hopkins University Press.

Rogers, L.J. (1999) *Sexing the Brain*, London, Weidenfield and Nicolson.

Rose, H. and Rose, S. (eds) (2000) *Alas Poor Darwin*, New York, Harmony.

Schneider, F., Habel, U., Kessler, C., Salloum, J.B. and Posse, S. (2000) 'Gender differences in regional cerebral activity during sadness', *Human Brain Mapping*, vol.9, pp.226–38.

Singh, D. (1995) 'Ethnic and gender consensus for the effect of waist-to-hip ratio on judgement of women's attractiveness', *Human Nature*, vol.6, pp.51–65.

Spence, J.T. (1984) 'Masculinity, femininity and gender-related traits: a conceptual analysis and critique of current research', in Maher, B.A and Maher, W.B. (eds) *Progress in Experimental Research in Personality*, vol.13, pp.1–97, Academic Press, New York.

Swaab, D.F. and Fliers, E.A. (1985) 'A sexually dimorphic nucleus in the human brain', *Science*, vol.228, pp.1112–5.

Thorne, B. (1993) 'Gender play: girls and boys in schools', Buckingham, Open University Press.

Thornhill, R and Palmer, C. (2000) *A Natural History of Rape: Biological Bases of Sexual Coercion*, Cambridge, MA, MIT Press.

Trivers, R.E. (1972) 'Parental investment and sexual selection', in Campbell, B. (ed.) *Sexual Selection and the Descent of Man*, Chicago, Aldine.

Weinreich–Haste, H. (1979) 'What sex is science?', in Hartnett, O., Boden, G. and Fuller, M. (eds) *Women: Sex-Role Stereotyping*, Tavistock, London.

Wiederman, M.W. (1993) 'Evolved gender differences in mate preferences: evidence from personal advertisements', *Ethology and Sociobiology*, vol.14, no.5, pp.331–51.

Wiederman, M.W. and Allgeier, E.R. (1992) 'Gender differences in mate selection criteria: sociobiological or socioeconomic explanation?' *Ethology and Sociobiology*, vol.13, pp.115–24.

Wiederman, M.W. and Kendall, E. (1999) 'Evolution, gender, and sexual jealousy: investigation with a sample from Sweden', *Evolution and Human Behavior*, vol.20, pp.121–8.

Willis, P. (1977) *Learning to Labour: How Working Class Kids get Working Class Jobs*, Aldershot, Saxon House.

Young, W.C. (1964) 'Hormones and sexual behaviour', *Science*, vol.143, pp.212–8.

CHAPTER **4**

Consciousness

Nick Braisby

Contents

▮ Aims

This chapter aims to:

- indicate how the study of consciousness relates to individual case studies as well as intuitions concerning everyday experience
- indicate the multi-faceted nature of consciousness
- explore how and why phenomenal consciousness has proved difficult to explain
- situate the contemporary study of consciousness in an historical context
- illustrate the multi-disciplinary nature of the study of consciousness, drawing in part on perspectives and material presented in Book 1
- outline key cognitive and biologically based perspectives on consciousness, and their relation to philosophical positions
- indicate the extent to which there is debate concerning the nature of consciousness
- illustrate some conceptual problems involved in the study of consciousness
- demonstrate the need for psychology to embrace conceptual and philosophical analysis
- show some of the limits of understanding in psychology.

1 Introduction

Consciousness presents us with something of a mystery. It is a pervasive feature of our mental lives: we all experience being conscious and we all know what it is to not be conscious, if only from periods of sleep. We do not need specialist training or knowledge to reflect on the differences between being conscious and non-conscious. Consciousness also appears to be a central aspect of 'what it means to be a person' and 'what it means to be me' – our conceptions of ourselves seem intimately tied to our conscious experiences and recollections. Consciousness helps differentiate us from other people – while we have to infer the experiences of others, we seem to be *immediately acquainted* with our own conscious experiences. So it seems as though we all know, at least implicitly, what consciousness is like. The portents could not be better, one might imagine, for psychology to provide an explanation of how we come to have consciousness, how consciousness relates to other topic areas within psychology, and what consciousness actually is. Yet despite this feeling that consciousness should present no mystery, it continues, as we shall see, to

[handwritten margin notes:]
Consciousness 'what it means to be me'
I know I am conscious when I infer other people's consciousness

frustrate all attempts at explanation; it is something of a theoretical bar of soap –
the firmer the grip we try to establish, the nearer it is to eluding our grasp
altogether.

This chapter introduces some of the puzzles and debates concerning the
nature of consciousness. Some of these are profound. They have implications
for how we understand the mind, and also for how we understand psychology
and the way in which it relates to the natural and social sciences. Many of these
implications have been elaborated within philosophy. Indeed, some stem from
a period when no real distinction was drawn between philosophy and
psychology. One could also regard this chapter therefore, as examining how
current psychology has sought to address some key philosophical concerns,
and how successfully it has done so. We shall see that contemporary research
reveals an intimate relationship between philosophy and psychology, one that
significantly enriches our understanding of consciousness.

Before we begin our examination of consciousness in earnest, you may
have noticed another source of insight. In *Mapping Psychology* (Book 1) and
in this book you have encountered a number of contrasting perspectives and
different topics, many of which relate to the topic of consciousness. At times
authors have been explicit in talking of consciousness and at others
consciousness has remained an implicit aspect of the topic under discussion.
But in nearly all of the topics you have examined, consciousness has played
some role. Consider, for example, Linton's diary studies (discussed in
Chapter 8 of Book 1) that helped inform our conception of autobiographical
memory. All of Linton's memories were ones of which she was conscious – at
least when she recorded them in her diary. Even later, when focusing on how
many memories had been retained, Linton was taking her conscious
awareness of what she could remember as evidence of her memory. Of
course, it is not unusual for 'memory' to be measured in terms of 'memories of
which one is conscious'. In the case of autobiographical memory, it is hard to
imagine how you could examine someone's memory for their own
autobiographical episodes without asking for conscious recollections of those
episodes. Yet, because of this, it can be easy to overlook the role of
consciousness. Indeed, as you saw in Chapter 9 of Book 1, Freud at least
believed repression could serve to render memories of certain
autobiographical episodes relatively inaccessible to consciousness. So,
consciousness could be said to play a pivotal role in this form of memory, yet
one that is not always made explicit. Consciousness is used, in this example, to
tap another hypothesized process – memory. This same observation applies to
many other topic areas too. When people are asked to state whether they find
sentences odd or ungrammatical (see Chapter 2 in this volume), they provide
conscious reports – they produce a verbal report of their consciousness. Such
reports *may* provide an accurate reflection of the processes of language

comprehension, but researchers will often employ other measures, such as the time taken to read sentences, to guard against possible inaccuracies in conscious reports. In Chapter 6 of Book 1, you examined top-down influences on perception. The Müller-Lyer illusion, for instance, showed how we do not always accurately perceive that two lines are of the same length. However, studies of the illusion also rely on consciousness, because the judgements participants make depend upon their conscious awareness of the lengths of the two lines. In cases like these, consciousness is used as a tool for investigating other aspects of the mind. Researchers in this tradition tend to adopt a working assumption of transparency – that is, that consciousness does not systematically distort the processes under investigation. So, for example, it tends to be assumed that the conscious verbal reports of autobiographical episodes reflect the state of autobiographical memory, and that a person's verbal reports of what they have perceived reflect their actual perceptions. Transparency is something that we all tend to assume too (though not all the time of course)– if someone tells you they are angry it is better not to question whether their consciousness accurately reflects their emotional state!

Of course it is not a criticism that the role of consciousness has not always been made explicit. It is a feature of psychology's explanatory strategy that different aspects of the mind and behaviour are first isolated, and treated separately from one another. It would presumably be far too difficult to try to explain memory and consciousness simultaneously! And, as we shall see, consciousness is not that easy to explain even when treated in isolation from other topics.

Besides using conscious reports to tap psychological processes, psychologists also use consciousness as a way of defining psychological processes. For instance, in Chapter 8 of Book 1, semantic and episodic memories are said to be declarative because both are 'consciously accessible and can be described in words'. Also, the author of Chapter 6 in the same course book indicates that the distinction between perception and sensation can be linked to consciousness. He distinguishes two kinds of perception: conscious perception, which involves conscious awareness of what one perceives; and non-conscious perception, where sensory information is processed below the level of conscious awareness. In these cases, consciousness is used to delineate or demarcate different kinds of mental faculty such as different kinds of memory, and different kinds of perception.

Despite these uses of consciousness the study of consciousness has a chequered history within psychology. Indeed during much of the twentieth century, consciousness was seen as a topic not fit for scientific enquiry, and some of this history will be considered later. However, the study of consciousness has since undergone a tremendous renaissance. There are new journals and major international meetings devoted entirely to consciousness. Of course, in this renaissance, some psychological approaches and some questions are receiving greater scrutiny than others. Although the work of Freud helped to emphasize the importance of the unconscious in the early part of the twentieth century, current work tends to emphasize cognitive and neuroscientific approaches to consciousness itself. The study of consciousness also tends to be multi-disciplinary, incorporating the analyses of philosophers as well as the studies and theories of psychologists. This is largely because consciousness presents such a difficult set of problems that it is not clear that we have yet settled on the most appropriate ways of thinking about consciousness. Philosophers have used a number of devices to help clarify what they see as the most important questions, as well as different ways of thinking about consciousness. These help to establish a framework that can be used to evaluate psychological explanations of consciousness relative to these foundational issues.

Having set the scene, we are in a position to begin our examination of consciousness. The next section begins by elaborating on our intuitive conceptions of consciousness, and then considers a number of real-life cases that serve to highlight different aspects of consciousness. The section also considers the ways in which the word 'consciousness' is used, and the fact that the word seems to take on slightly different meanings. A brief historical overview is also provided to help you situate some of the more contemporary debates. Section 3 then attempts to draw out theoretically important themes from the different issues in consciousness presented in Section 2. As we shall see, there is much convergence between researchers on what are the significant features of consciousness. There is much disagreement, however, concerning the best way of explaining these features and, more importantly, over whether they can be explained at all. Section 4 then outlines two psychological proposals that seek to explain consciousness, and remove some of the mystery with which it is associated. Consciousness can be studied from a number of different perspectives, and this section focuses on cognitive and biological viewpoints. Finally, Section 5 considers philosophical perspectives on consciousness and the extent to which the proposals developed in Section 4 fully explain the important features of consciousness outlined in Section 3.

Summary Section 1

- Though consciousness is something with which we have an intimate acquaintance, it appears to frustrate explanation.
- Consciousness is pervasive within psychology, though its role is usually implicit. It has been used both as a transparent measure of, and as a means for demarcating, distinct psychological processes.
- The contemporary study of consciousness brings together insights from disciplines such as cognitive psychology, neuroscience and philosophy.

2 Thinking about consciousness

Perhaps the best way to start thinking about consciousness is to do just that. Chapter 9 of Book 1 explicitly asked you to engage in the activity of reflecting on your own consciousness. Try the following activity – it is a little similar to the earlier one, though it focuses on generating descriptions of your consciousness.

Activity 4.1

Take a few minutes (no more than ten) to write down how you would describe your conscious experience at this very moment.

*[handwritten margin note:
- sitting in a room
- aware of people buzzing around
- studying
- glad of free period
- would like a cup of T]*

Just as with the exercise in Chapter 9 of Book 1, you may well have found this activity difficult. In spite of being so acquainted with our own consciousness, it is not easy to describe it in words. Nonetheless, you will probably have focused on the objects in your immediate environment. I did too. Right now, I am conscious of the green bushes outside my window, of the noise of my laptop computer, of the hard seat of my practical but not very comfortable chair, and the smell of fresh coffee and toast. I am also conscious of wanting to write more of this chapter, and of the telephone sitting on my desk, ominously quiet. Perhaps you have written of similar kinds of experience.

Strange though it may seem, through performing and reflecting on this activity, you will have already laid the foundations for a good understanding of consciousness. First, did you notice something strange to do with time? As I tried to formulate what I was conscious of, the conscious experience was already in the past. What I was describing was more like a *memory* of a conscious experience, rather than the conscious experience itself. This relationship with memory presents a curious contrast. Consciousness appears to be closely tied to our awareness of the 'here-and-now,' of our physical (the 'here') and temporal (the 'now') environment. Arguably, the sense that there is a here-and-now arises as a consequence of our being conscious. Yet the here-and-now also seems to elude our attempts to consciously reflect on, formulate or communicate our experience. Instead, we have to rely upon our memories of conscious experiences. That is, our descriptions depend upon our ability to store information that is consciously available, and then subject it to further processes. A similar conclusion is drawn in Chapter 9 of Book 1.

In performing the activity you possibly focused mostly on things of which you were conscious, though you may also have mentioned your feelings. I tended to describe some of the objects in my immediate environment as well as some of their properties (the shrubs were green, for example). In fact, I did not really describe *consciousness,* but rather the *things* of which I was conscious: I focused on the contents of consciousness but not the process. Consider an analogy. If we want to understand visual perception, listing all the things that visual perception allows one to perceive does not really help. Though of relevance, no great understanding of vision comes from listing all the things that can be seen. Instead, understanding seems to involve accounting for the processes and mechanisms that enable people to have the visual perceptions they do. It is similar with consciousness. It is as if we require an understanding of the *process* that gives rise to conscious awareness, not just a description of the *things* of which we are conscious. For our descriptions of consciousness to reveal anything of the processes involved, we would have to remove all reference to the objects and properties of which we have conscious awareness. From this perspective, verbal reports that focus on objects and properties seem rather unhelpful. Again, there appears to be a contradiction inherent within the notion of consciousness. Reflecting on consciousness invites us to think of the things of which we are aware. Yet an understanding of consciousness seems to be connected with the processes by which those things come into consciousness. Perhaps now you can begin to see why consciousness is a little like a bar of soap!

A further factor raised by Activity 4.1 concerns the language in which our descriptions of consciousness are expressed. Were there things of which you were consciously aware but have not written down? When pressed, I would say that I was aware of the distance between the telephone and myself, yet this does not figure in my verbal description. Perhaps you will also find that some things of which you were aware did not figure in your descriptions. One reason for this could be entirely practical. Language does not easily allow us to describe scenes completely – hence the proverb 'one picture is worth ten thousand words' – and so it is probably the case that some aspects of the environment of which you were aware were necessarily omitted from your description. However, another reason relates to the vexed question of the relationship between language and thought. A particularly controversial hypothesis, proposed by the linguists Edward Sapir and Benjamin Lee Whorf, is that the nature of our language determines the kinds of thoughts we can entertain. A strong version of the hypothesis holds that a language with no word or phrase for a certain kind of colour leads speakers of that language to think differently about that colour from speakers of a language which has such a word or phrase. Though controversial, could it be that *conscious* experiences depend upon the words and phrases that one's language makes available? For example, the Australian aboriginal language Pintupi has a single word 'katarta' that means 'the hole left by a goanna when it has broken the surface after hibernation' (a goanna being an Australian lizard). A Pintupi speaker, conscious of such a burrow in their immediate environment, could more easily convey some of the complexities of that experience than could an English speaker. Similarly, an English speaker whose car has broken down, conscious of their failing carburettor, might more easily describe their experience than could the speaker of a language that has no word for a carburettor. Could it be that a language might *determine* the kinds of conscious experience that speakers of the language have? Could it be that the linguistic resources available to you in constructing your descriptions have determined your conscious experiences? Perhaps if you possessed a very different language your consciousness would also have been different. Although we will not focus explicitly on this possibility, it is one to which we will briefly return towards the end of this chapter.

Lastly, my description of consciousness tended to revolve around other psychological processes, such as vision, hearing and thinking. For example, I noted the noise of my laptop computer. But of course that depends upon hearing, a perceptual process. I was also aware of trying to find words to describe my consciousness, but this process is usually thought of as specific to understanding and producing language. Is consciousness more than just the composite of these other psychological processes? If there is more to consciousness, what could it be? Try to imagine one of the things that you are conscious of, and consider what follows from your being conscious of it. For example, my consciousness of a green shrub outside my window seems to allow me to identify the object, to reason about it (perhaps to decide that it needs moving), and to communicate about it. To imagine something of the essence of consciousness we need to imagine what would be left of our descriptions if all references to other psychological processes and objects were stripped away. What would be left, if you can imagine it, is barely describable – it is perhaps something like a *'raw' feel* or *experience*, a feeling of being aware of, or experiencing the environment. The remainder of this chapter can be seen as an attempt to make sense of this characterization of consciousness as involving a raw feeling or experience. Before we consider these issues in more detail, however, let us consider some real-life examples that bear heavily on an understanding of consciousness. These, as we shall see, will add further dimensions to our emerging understanding and a complete theory of consciousness will need to account adequately for each of them.

language helps convey conscious experience

Would my conscious experience be different if my language were different?

2.1 Somnambulism

Sleepwalking or somnambulism raises a number of interesting questions concerning the nature of consciousness. If wakefulness and sleep are taken as exemplars of conscious and non-conscious states respectively, then where does sleepwalking lie? Sleepwalking seems to involve a degree of **automatism** on the part of the sleepwalker, wherein the sleepwalker seems to have no control over their behaviour. Yet there also appears to be some 'awareness' of the environment. The sleepwalker seems to be capable of interacting with objects in their environment. For example, in Shakespeare's Macbeth, Lady Macbeth was seen by her attendant to '… rise from her bed, throw her nightgown upon her, unlock her closet, take forth paper, fold it, write upon't, read it, afterwards seal it, and again return to bed; yet all this while in a most fast sleep' (Macbeth, Act V, Scene I). Watching Lady Macbeth sleepwalking, her doctor notes '… her eyes are open' while her attendant responds, 'Aye, but their sense is shut'. In this we see something of the puzzle of sleepwalking – to what extent do people have awareness during sleepwalking episodes?

Box 4.1 describes the case in Canada of Ken Parkes, a young man who committed an atrocious killing during an episode of sleepwalking. The case makes it clear that sleepwalkers are capable of sophisticated interaction with their environments, and of executing complex sequences of behaviour that would normally require consciousness (Broughton *et al.*, 1994). However, sleepwalking was critical to Ken's defence and this hinged entirely on the nature of consciousness. For someone to be convicted of murder, an *intent* to commit murder must be demonstrated. The Canadian legal system, however, assumes sleepwalking or somnambulism to be a state of automatism in which the individual has no awareness or control of his or her behaviour. Automatism is taken to imply a lack of volition on the part of the sleepwalker and so his or her behaviour, being involuntary, is assumed not to be guided by a conscious intention. As the appeal court judges noted: 'only those who act voluntarily with the requisite intent should be punished by criminal sanction'.

Automatism
A state in which the individual has no awareness or voluntary control of his or her behaviour.

Interaction with environment (whilst complicated behaviour) unconsc.

4.1 *Homicidal somnambulism*

The case of Ken Parkes came before the courts in Canada in the 1980s. He was 23 years old and married with a 5-month old daughter. He enjoyed good relations with his mother- and father-in-law. However, Ken had problems due to excessive gambling and, as a consequence, developed a pattern of delayed sleep (typically, he would go to sleep around 1:30 to 2:00 am and then enjoy four to six hours of good sleep). He embezzled funds in order to manage his debts, but lost his job and was charged with theft. Though Ken and his wife were concerned at the anguish that might be caused if his in-laws found out, they decided that Ken should tell them everything. At around 1:30 am on the night before Ken was due to visit his in-laws and explain his situation, he fell asleep in front of the TV. The next thing Ken said he could remember was looking down at his mother-in-law's face. In panic he got into his car but at that point realized that he had a knife in his hand and that he was bleeding. Seeking help, he drove straight to a police station and declared, 'I think I have killed some people'. Ken appeared to have no recall for the events between his falling asleep and his seeing his mother-in-law's face. Eventually police were able to reconstruct what must have occurred. They calculated that Ken must have got off the couch, put on his shoes and jacket, left the house, driven some 23 km to his parents-in-law's home, and there must have strangled (but not killed) his father-in-law, and then stabbed and killed his mother-in-law.

One year later, Ken was acquitted of the murder of his mother-in-law, and later acquitted of the attempted murder of his father-in-law. His defence team had successfully argued that Ken had been sleepwalking during the entire episode. This argument was vigorously contested, but was upheld on several grounds. One was that, in spite of being interviewed many times, Ken's testimony, even in the minor details, never altered. Moreover, to all involved, Ken seemed genuinely distraught at what he had done.

Thankfully for us, sleepwalking very rarely involves acts of violence. But somnambulism in general, and Ken's case in particular, show us the complexity of behaviour that can be achieved in the absence of conscious awareness. The state of automatism associated with sleepwalking suggests that consciousness itself is associated with awareness and the voluntary control of behaviour, these being guided by intentions. In fact, the Parkes case relates to an important philosophical argument concerning zombies, that is developed towards the end of this chapter.

The Parkes case also raises the moral dimension of consciousness. When we speculate on consciousness, and the criteria by which it differs from non-consciousness, we are also, like it or not, proposing when people may be held morally responsible in cases such as those of Ken Parkes. Similarly discussions of consciousness play a role in many other moral debates. For instance, the issues of abortion, animal rights, persistent vegetative state, and euthanasia, all raise questions concerning what it means for an organism to be conscious. Scruton (2000) argues that because animals have consciousness it would be immoral for people to deliberately inflict pain upon them. So, questions concerning consciousness are not solely of interest for the philosopher and psychologist. They have important implications for society at large.

2.2 Neglect

[handwritten: eg. flames from house (80%)]

Visual neglect
A condition brought
about by brain damage
involving a failure to
attend to or even perceive
certain aspects of the
environment. In unilateral
visual neglect only one
side of the visual field is
affected (see also
unilateral spatial neglect).

Visual neglect is most often associated with injuries to the right hemisphere of the brain causing damage to the parietal lobe, though it can also arise through damage to the frontal lobe (see Figure 4.1). It seems to involve a failure to attend or even perceive certain aspects of the environment (hence 'neglect'). A very similar idea was introduced in Chapter 6 of Book 1: as *unilateral spatial neglect*. The phenomenon of neglect is often described in slightly different ways, usually to emphasise particular features of the neglect. So for example, the Chapter 6 discussion emphasized the neglect of a region of space on one side only.

Marshall and Halligan (1988), for instance, report the case of a 49-year-old woman, referred to as PS, whose neglect was caused by damage to her parietal lobe. Since the neglect affected only one side of her visual field, due to damage to her right hemisphere, it is referred to as unilateral neglect. Marshall and Halligan presented PS with a series of picture cards. Each card contained two pictures of houses, one above the other. Sometimes the houses were identical and sometimes they differed only in that one of the houses had flames emanating from one side. Marshall and Halligan asked PS to judge whether the pairs of houses in each picture were the same or different, and indicate which she would prefer to live in. When the flames emanated from the right-hand side of the house, PS correctly identified pairs of pictures as being the same or different. She also correctly indicated that she would prefer to live in the houses that were not on fire. However, when the flames emanated from the left-hand side of the house, her performance was markedly different. When shown a pair of houses, one of which was on fire, one of which was not, she judged them to be the same. That might make you think that she would have no preference for living in one house or another. PS herself felt that the 'preference' question was silly, because the two pictures were the same. Surprisingly, on approximately 80 per cent of occasions, she *did* indicate a preference for the house not on fire. This pattern of behaviour is consistent with the visual information usually being processed, but somehow not being made available to consciousness – although PS is not conscious of the flames when they are on the left-hand side, the information is often able to influence her judgements of preference. Indeed, this view is apparently supported by the fact that, when presented once more with the houses with flames on the left-hand side, she again responded that they were the same. On the final trial, however, she reported 'Oh my God this is on fire'. Somehow, it seems, the visual information can influence her preferences but, apart from this final trial, is not generally available to consciousness.

Bisiach and Luzzatti (1978) demonstrated that this phenomenon is not due to a visual problem. They reported data concerning two patients with damage to their right parietal lobes. They asked their patients to imagine standing in the

[handwritten left margin: Visual info. processed but not accessible to conscious but when making decisions this info. influential

which means we must use our unconscious in making decisions in the same way as using our consc. to tap memory to help make decisions]

[handwritten: 80%]

Piazza del Duomo in Milan (the patients were from Milan), facing the cathedral, and to describe the buildings in the square. The patients tended to name only those buildings on the right-hand side of the square. Since the patients were *imagining* the square their performance could not be directly related to visual problems. Nor could the difficulty be a lack of knowledge of the buildings on the left-hand side. Bisiach and Luzzatti asked their patients to imagine walking to the cathedral, turning to face the square, and again describe the buildings. This time the patients described the buildings that would have been on their left-hand side the first time (but which of course were now on the right-hand side of the square). You might like to compare this behaviour with that of patients described in Chapter 6 of Book 1 who, when asked to draw a clock face, would cram all the numbers on one side.

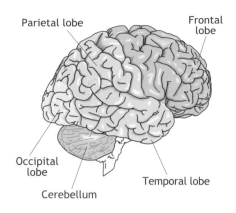

Figure 4.1　A side view of the brain (right hemisphere) showing the position of the parietal lobe and frontal lobe (Source: adapted from Martini et al., 2000, Figure 15–9 (a), p.395)

The case studies of PS and Bisiach and Luzzatti's patients show that it is possible for information to be perceptually processed normally, but not enter into consciousness. Although the information may be available to certain kinds of process (as in judging preference for example), it does not enter into conscious awareness. Although this does not tell us what consciousness is exactly, it gives us some detail of the relationship between consciousness and brain structures and processes, and indicates a complex relationship between consciousness and information processing.

It should be noted that Bisiach and Rusconi (1990) failed to replicate the findings of Marshall and Halligan when testing four similar patients. Farah (1997) suggests that PS may have based her judgements on minor differences on the right side of the picture, or on very dimly perceived details of the left side. Whichever interpretation is correct, the case of PS gives us insight into the phenomenon of neglect, even if the appropriate theoretical explanation is not yet evident.

2.3　Blindsight

Blindsight is not unlike visual neglect in that those affected seem to experience a kind of blindness without actually being blind. It was first brought to prominence by Weiskrantz and colleagues (1974). A blindsight patient will generally report being unable to see anything in a significant portion of their visual field, yet more detailed examination will reveal some access to visual

Bindsight
A condition in which those affected seem to experience a kind of blindness without actually being blind. Patients appear to perceive stimuli but generally believe they have not perceived anything in a region of their visual field.

information presented in that region. In particular, blindsight patients can make eye movements towards stimuli that they claim they cannot see. Unlike the case of neglect, blindsight patients apparently perceive the stimuli that they cannot report seeing.

Young and De Haan (1993) discuss the studies conducted with Weiskrantz's patient, DB. During surgery to remove an abnormality from his right occipital lobe, DB had a section of his right visual cortex removed. This left DB with an area of blindness (called a scotoma), which reduced in size over time, but never entirely went away. DB's own reports of his experience signalled that he could not see in the region of this scotoma. It was as if he was partially blind. Nonetheless, a series of ingenious experiments conducted by Weiskrantz and colleagues showed that DB was capable of detecting visual information presented in the scotoma. First, they discovered that DB could detect flashes of light. When DB was asked to move his eyes towards where he guessed the lights had flashed, his performance was somewhat better than you might expect if DB had been guessing. When DB was asked to point to where he would guess the light flashes occurred, his performance was much better still. Weiskrantz *et al.* went on to show how DB could in fact detect other aspects of visually presented stimuli (e.g. DB could detect whether stimuli were vertically or horizontally oriented). Note that DB made all of these 'guesses' still insisting that he was unable to see anything in the region of the scotoma. In fact, when asked whether he knew how well he had performed, DB responded, 'No, I didn't because I couldn't see anything. I couldn't see a darn thing' (Weiskrantz, 1986, p.24). These original findings have since been confirmed and much extended. Stoerig and Cowey (1989), for example, show that the capacity to make colour discriminations can be preserved in blindsight.

There are a number of interesting observations to be made in connection with blindsight. First, though blindsight patients can access visual information without conscious awareness, their ability to access this information still lags behind the performance of people who do not have blindsight. Further, a blindsight patient will generally perform less well in the region of their scotoma than in their unaffected field of vision. Therefore, although such patients seem able to access visual information without an accompanying awareness or feeling, their access is still somewhat limited. Second, although blindsight patients *can* access visual information, typically they do not. As Tye (1995) reports, blindsight patients do not appear to use their abilities to detect visual information in the scotoma spontaneously. It is only when they are encouraged to give verbal reports, or required to perform certain tasks, that they show evidence of accessing this visual information. Moreover, blindsight patients appear to believe that the 'guesses' they produce are simply that – guesses.

Blindsight

access to subconsc. awareness limited + slow compared with consc. awareness

access to subsc. only made when required to do so – it doesn't happen autom.

Tye (1995) discusses the possibility of a phenomenon he calls super-blindsight. No such phenomenon exists – the possibility is intended to stimulate our thinking. Super-blindsight is a hypothetical possibility in which blindsight patients would be trained to produce verbal reports of events occurring in the region of their scotoma. Even though the patient would feel that they could see nothing in this region, the training would encourage them to guess where objects were, what orientation they were in, and so on. Now imagine the training was so successful that blindsight patients spontaneously produced such reports and came to believe them. Suppose that the training was so stunningly successful that the blindsight patients became behaviourally indistinguishable from normally sighted people. Now, under these conditions, would there be a difference between the consciousness of blindsight patients and the consciousness of normally sighted people? If we were unable to distinguish a blindsight patient from a normally sighted person in terms of their behaviour, would we not have to agree that both *were equally and fully conscious?*   Yes

Activity 4.2

Consider the possibility of super-blindsight outlined above. Suppose you encountered someone with super-blindsight. Would you think they had a full and complete consciousness? What would influence your judgement? Keep a note of your answers to these questions. We will return to them later in this chapter.

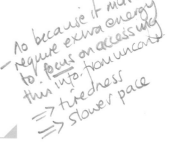

(handwritten margin note) No because it must require extra energy to focus on accessing this info. from unconc. ⇒ tiredness ⇒ slower pace

Visual neglect and blindsight clearly tell us something about how people experience the visual world, and how this information is made available to other psychological processes. It may also shed light on the nature of consciousness in at least two ways. First, for these patients, certain aspects of their visual world are not available to consciousness, although the information may be available to other processes. We thus have the opportunity to compare cases where information is available to consciousness with cases where it is not. This might enable us to understand better the benefits to be gained from information being consciously available. Second, visual neglect and blindsight show us that our consciousness is tied in some way to the nature of activity in the brain. Although later, we will consider arguments that the brain cannot be responsible for consciousness we will still want to explain these links between consciousness and brain activity. Visual neglect and blindsight may help us to identify specific regions of the brain that play a role in consciousness.

(handwritten margin note) Benefits of info being consciously avail.

(handwritten margin note) link between consciousness + brain ?

2.4 Post-traumatic amnesia

The final example we will consider is a memory disorder in which the conscious experience of the patient is dramatically transformed, often in the space of a very few hours. This can often happen after a head injury and, if you have been unfortunate enough to experience this, some of what follows may resonate with your own experience. Antonio Damasio is an eminent neurologist who has investigated consciousness drawing extensively on his experience of working with patients who show impairments in their conscious experience. Damasio reports a patient referred to as DT who was injured in a riding accident. DT was knocked unconscious and remained so for approximately ten minutes. He woke feeling agitated and confused, though he later recalled seeing faces peering down at him. He had no clear sense of who he was, why he was on the ground or to whom these faces belonged. As his sense of identity began to return, he announced he wanted to go jogging (his original intention before the riding accident). Finally, when he was in the ambulance, his normal sense of self returned more fully. Damasio suggests that DT went through a range of different kinds of consciousness during this period: non-consciousness; a level of consciousness not unlike automatism; a form of consciousness in which awareness of the environment returned, but no proper sense of self; and finally full consciousness.

These examples show that consciousness may usefully be thought of in terms of different degrees. There does not appear to be a simple dichotomy between states of consciousness: between being conscious or non-conscious. Rather, it seems as if there may be different *kinds* of consciousness, perhaps being qualitatively distinct, and perhaps being distinguished in terms of their similarity to full consciousness and full non-consciousness.

Notice that here we have been deliberately talking of 'non-conscious' states as opposed to the unconscious states that Sigmund Freud argued were so important. This is because Freud's views of the unconscious differ somewhat from the 'non-conscious' as viewed by contemporary consciousness researchers. For Freud, unconscious processes provide motivations for our behaviour. The notion of non-conscious states and processes adopted here, like the humanistic conception discussed in Chapter 9 of Book 1, does not assume that they play a motivational or psychodynamic role. In contrast, they are assumed to be informational in nature and inaccessible to consciousness. It is because of such differences that Freud's work does not figure centrally in this chapter. Accordingly, throughout, I will largely talk of non-conscious as opposed to unconscious processes.

2.5 Talking about consciousness

Activity 4.3

Take a few minutes to go through the discussion so far and list as many different key words as you can that I have used to describe consciousness, such as 'awareness'. What implications might there be for the study of consciousness of having so many different words for describing it?

Comment

I have used a number of different ways of describing consciousness, and the different degrees of consciousness and non-consciousness associated with some of the conditions highlighted above. Predominantly, I have made a distinction between consciousness and non-consciousness. I have also talked of 'conscious awareness', 'intentions', 'voluntary control of behaviour', 'feeling', 'experience', and 'sense of self', raising issues concerning self-consciousness and self-awareness (these latter issues were discussed at length in Chapter 1 of Book 1). Perhaps you found other ways of talking about consciousness too.

It is perhaps unsurprising that we can find different ways of talking about consciousness. After all, our focus so far has been to uncover an understanding that is established prior to the development of theories of consciousness. At this 'pre-theoretic' level we have not really considered sharpening our terminology. Nonetheless, there are two difficulties associated with looseness in vocabulary of which we need to be aware. First, using different words tends to imply that different things are being talked about. So we might have the feeling that consciousness and awareness are somewhat different, if only because the *words* 'consciousness' and 'awareness' are different. Consequently, when multiple words are used in this way, we should always consider whether they have the same or different meanings. Second, the same word can be used to describe a constellation of phenomena. This is exactly how I have used the word 'consciousness' so far. That is, I have taken the word to refer to something that is involved in a raw feeling or experience as well as in conditions such as somnambulism. Yet it might be that what is involved in each case is actually somewhat different. This possibility has become something of a talking point in contemporary research into consciousness. Some researchers suggest that we need to interpret theories of consciousness very carefully in light of the difficulties of terminology and vocabulary. Their argument is that such theories are nearly always partial – while they may address some of the phenomena associated with 'consciousness' successfully, they do not address others. It might be that a 'theory of consciousness' turns out, on closer inspection, to be a theory of only some limited aspect of consciousness, or that 'consciousness' turns out to be many phenomena.

We will return to this issue again towards the end of this chapter. However, throughout our discussions of consciousness, we will need to bear in mind the difficulties that can arise when terminology and vocabulary have not been agreed.

2.6 An historical perspective

This section outlines some of the historical antecedents to our contemporary thinking on consciousness and shows why, arguably, it is a core problem for psychology.

Chapter 4 of *Mapping Psychology* briefly introduced the views of the French philosopher, René Descartes, in particular his belief that the mind and body (including the brain) are fundamentally distinct kinds of entity. Although most psychologists and philosophers now reject this dualism, the question as to how minds relate to bodies has not been satisfactorily resolved. Indeed, the mind–body problem is particularly acute for consciousness since it is unclear how anything so apparently non-physical as a raw feeling or experience could be reduced to something so physical as a brain state.

Descartes adopted what has become known as his 'method of doubt' in trying to uncover the very *essence* of his being. The method involves rejecting as part of one's essence any and all aspects of experience where the reality of the experience could be doubted. For example, right now I am typing on a keyboard, and looking at my computer screen. Though I do not doubt the reality of my perceptions, it is *conceivable* to me, though sadly not likely, that I am instead relaxing on a tropical island. That is, because I can coherently imagine an alternative state of affairs, my experience can be doubted: perhaps I am experiencing a very complex perceptual illusion. Using this method, Descartes concluded that his senses and even the existence of his body could be doubted. However, Descartes was unable to doubt the fact of his own thinking. He thought that it was not possible that he could think that he was not thinking. Descartes therefore concluded that his essence was a thinking thing, a conclusion that gives rise to the well-known argument 'I think, therefore I am'. In this conclusion lie the seeds of the contemporary problem of consciousness. If the essence of a person is a thinking thing, and the body is not part of the essence, then it seems that it is conceivable that minds might exist independently of brains. Whatever the mind is, it seems that its physical basis could be immaterial. For Descartes, minds do not appear to be made of anything, nor do they ultimately depend upon there being a brain.

Descartes' method does not appeal to empirical data to settle the question of how minds and bodies relate. Instead, he pursues an approach often taken by philosophers of trying to scrutinize our conceptualizations, examining their implications and consistency with other beliefs. This method provides a useful complement to the empirical methods most often favoured by psychologists –

by examining in detail how we conceptualize an entity or process we may find our ways of thinking to be impoverished or even incoherent, results that may not ever be established by focusing purely on collecting new empirical data. By his method of doubt, Descartes is asking whether our conceptualization of the mind *requires* minds to be embodied. Philosophical analyses such as this may require researchers to engage in more theoretical work in order that their explanations are complete. If a psychological theory implied that minds require bodies, for instance, Descartes' conclusion would suggest that the theory and the explanations it provides are at best incomplete.

Descartes' conclusion is deeply problematic for conventional assumptions of science. One assumption is that the universe and everything in it is physical – ultimately, it is made up of space, energy and matter. We too are composed of matter – its organization is breathtakingly complex but, at base, we are comprised of molecules and atoms. A related assumption is that the physical universe, and all the physical objects within it, can ultimately be *understood* in purely physical terms (e.g. as in physics). On this assumption, complex phenomena such as consciousness could ultimately be 'reduced' to, or explained by, purely physical phenomena, such as being in a certain kind of brain state (this is similar to the reductionism of Crick (1994), discussed in Chapter 4 of Book 1).

These assumptions are in opposition to Descartes' conclusion. One way of thinking about the mystery of consciousness is that it arises from attempting to respect both Descartes' view that the mind transcends the brain, and the conventional assumptions that all things in the universe are physical and can be explained in physical terms. Suppose you are attracted by Descartes' position – perhaps you are suspicious of the scientific view. What would it mean to say that minds are *not* composed of matter? Certainly, sciences such as chemistry and physics would then have no bearing on the problem of explaining the mind. But what would a non-physical mind be like? It seems impossible to say. Perhaps this is because so much of our understanding of the world is rooted in an understanding of physical matter. Once we have said that minds are not made of matter, what more can we add?

On the other hand, if we embrace the claims that the universe is ultimately physical in nature and can be understood in purely physical terms, then we appear to be faced with another problem. If people could be understood in purely physical terms, then our use of psychological terms to understand people would be dispensable. Instead of saying that someone is *thinking* of home, for example, we perhaps ought to concede that what we mean is that his or her brain is undergoing a certain kind of activity. When we say that someone is *in love*, perhaps we ought merely to say that they are in a certain kind of brain state. Yet it seems that trying to express concepts such as 'love' solely in terms of brain states would fail. Wouldn't such brain state descriptions necessarily miss some quality of the concept, perhaps the *feeling* of what it is to love?

Trying to combine the idea that the mind may not be explicable solely in terms of brain activity, with the assumption that everything in the universe is ultimately physical in nature, leads to a tension. It is a tension that characterizes much of contemporary psychology and helps explain why consciousness has presented such a deep and abiding mystery. The challenge is to explain how it is possible for matter, which is presumably non-conscious, to give rise, when suitably organized (as in human beings), to something as seemingly non-physical as raw feeling or experience.

The mind–body problem is not the only historical antecedent of the contemporary discussion of consciousness. William James (1890/1984) considered consciousness to be an essential feature of our mental lives, and linked consciousness to perception and attention. Most significantly, he distinguished two aspects of consciousness that seem to be in tension. There is a sense in which our consciousness is continually in flux, changing moment-by-moment. An intuition that emerged from Activity 4.1 was that consciousness has changed the moment you come to reflect on it. It is as if its connection to the here-and-now means that it cannot stay still. James called this the 'stream of consciousness'. Yet, he pointed out, this continuous flow of consciousness seems strangely at odds with our sense of self: we have the sense that, in spite of changes in our consciousness, a stable entity – the self – persists throughout (though note that Chapter 1 in Book 1 presents the argument for a fluid and constructed identity – perhaps what James describes as the stable self is stable only relative to the ever-changing stream of consciousness).

With the ascendancy of the behaviourist tradition (see Chapter 3 of Book 1), the study of consciousness was almost entirely neglected. Indeed, because consciousness cannot be directly observed, some doubted its very existence (though not all – Skinner, for example). Belief in a consciousness that could not be objectively observed or measured was seen as speculative at best, and a rejection of the scientific approach to psychology at worst. In spite of the fact that cognitive psychology assumes one can scientifically study mental processes that cannot be observed, it too tended to disregard consciousness as a topic of study, favouring instead other components of mind such as memory, language and attention. The reasons for this are complicated, but in part stem from the complexity of consciousness. However, researchers from perspectives such as cognitive psychology and neuroscience and disciplines such as philosophy became increasingly concerned that consciousness might resist attempts at scientific explanation and, since the 1980s and 1990s, the study of consciousness has assumed a much greater urgency. Research has tended to be multi-disciplinary, bringing together philosophers, cognitive psychologists, neuropsychologists, neuroscientists, physicists and others in an attempt to learn from the research conducted from these different perspectives.

Thought experiments

This chapter draws upon an unusual methodology for considering the validity of certain claims about consciousness. We have used *thought experiments* (also known as Gedankenexperiment, from German), such as Tye's discussion of super-blindsight in Section 2.3.

A thought experiment is a device that is designed to make us question our own thinking. Often, a thought experiment asks one to imagine an hypothetical situation or event. The purpose of the experiment is to question whether the situation or event is truly possible. Whatever we decide, the experiment should shed light on the concepts with which it was framed. For example, Descartes believed that his thought experiment, involving doubting his senses and body, showed that minds do not require a corresponding body. Note that the thought experiment is not concerned with the plausibility, likelihood or even truth of the described situation. It is only concerned with whether the situation is possible, and what this reveals about the concepts in which the situation was described. So, even though Descartes' situation is almost certain never to occur, if we accept his reasoning then we could not deny the *possibility* of a mind existing without a body. This does not mean that the thought experiment *proves* that minds can be disembodied. Instead it shows that conceptualizations of the mind do not require them to be embodied; it shows that there would be no incoherence in a theory proposing that there are minds that exist outside of bodies – of course there may never be empirical evidence in favour of such a view, but that would be another matter.

In essence, the thought experiment helps us to work out the implications of our current modes of thinking. Accepting the conclusions of a thought experiment can mean having to change the concepts used to frame the issues. Denying the conclusions of the thought experiment involves having to show what is wrong with it. Why is the described situation impossible? Have the issues been wrongly described? Again, this might mean changing the concepts originally used to describe the situation, or it might lead us to recognize as important something that had previously been overlooked. A good thought experiment should teach us something whichever conclusion we come to.

To see how this might work in practice, consider how Tye's thought experiment concerning super-blindsight could lead to one of the two following conclusions.

You might be impressed by the fact that blindsight patients typically believe that their reports about the location of objects in their scotoma are guesses. You might further believe that the training of such patients as in super-blindsight would never change this subjective experience. Even if the training were successful in other respects, so that patients spontaneously produced reports about the location of lights in their scotoma, you might believe that the patients would always regard these as guesses. If this were the case then such a patient would not be behaviourally indistinguishable from a normally-sighted person. Asking both people, 'Are you guessing where the light is in your visual field?' would lead them to produce different behaviour, one would say 'yes' and the other would say 'no'.

Alternatively, you might believe that training as in super-blindsight would alter the blindsight patient's subjective experience of their reports – as they found, over time, that their guesses were accurate, perhaps they would come to regard these not as guesses at all but as reliable reports. If training could produce this outcome, then asking both a super-blindsight patient and a normally-sighted person, 'Are you guessing where the light is in your visual field?' would yield the same behavioural outcomes – both would say 'no'. In which case super-blindsight would be possible.

Notice the first option requires us to explain why training could not alter the subjective experience of the blindsight patient, whereas the second option requires us to explain why it could. Although in this case neither option seems to require us to revise our conceptualization of consciousness, they do highlight something that was not so obvious before. Namely, that an important feature of blindsight is the fact that blindsight patients subjectively regard their reports as guesses.

Summary Section 2

- Consciousness is difficult to describe. When descriptions of it are stripped of reference to objects and other psychological processes, they suggest consciousness is associated with an almost intangible raw feeling or experience.
- Insight into the nature of consciousness comes from real-life cases. Somnambulism suggests that consciousness is associated with awareness and the intentional, voluntary control of behaviour. Neglect and blindsight show that information may be processed by the senses and yet not made available to consciousness, and that consciousness seems linked to activity in the brain. Post-traumatic amnesia shows that there may be degrees of consciousness and non-consciousness.
- Consciousness is difficult to analyse, in part because it is not clear what terminology should be adopted in describing it. Our existing terminology might lead us to mis-characterize or mis-analyse consciousness.
- The mystery of consciousness may stem also from the difficulty in explaining how the mind relates to the brain. How should we explain the relationship between a feeling or experience and the physical medium of the brain?

3 Different kinds of consciousness

Thus far, we have considered a number of aspects of consciousness. We have also moved from discussing our own intuitions about consciousness to arguments mounted by others in part on the basis of their own intuitions. This section outlines some of the key qualities of different kinds of consciousness as expressed by contemporary researchers.

3.1 Access consciousness

access consc.

Block (1991) distinguishes two kinds of consciousness, or at least two distinct phenomena that are referred to by the word 'consciousness'. The first is what he calls **access consciousness**, which refers to the kind of conscious experience involving access to information from different kinds of mental process, including verbal reports. If, for example, in reasoning about a problem, I report on my reasoning to another person, my report is taken to reveal something of the nature of my access consciousness – a kind of conscious awareness involving access to information about my own reasoning. For example, in solving a crossword puzzle, I might indicate that I am thinking about an anagram for a particular clue. I might speak out loud the letters I am using, and how I am arranging them. These reports are evidence that I have some conscious access to the processes I am using to solve the puzzle. Of course, there might be times when the solution comes as a flash of insight – another way of saying that I don't have access consciousness to the process of arriving at the solution.

Access consciousness
The kind of consciousness we have that involves accessing information from different kinds of mental process. Our verbal reporting on mental processes involves access consciousness.

Verbal reporting such as this is the foundation of techniques involving **protocol analysis** (Ericsson and Simon, 1980). In these, people are encouraged to report out loud while performing a task, and their conscious reports are taken as evidence of the processes involved. Access consciousness is involved in many types of mental process. Young and Block for example, suggest that we are conscious in the sense of being access conscious whenever we think about a mental state, 'report its content, and use it to guide action' (Young and Block, 1996, p.156). The notion can be extended to include feelings and memories. Acts of recognition and recall involve access consciousness; perception also, as when we are conscious of accessing perceptual information about the world around us. In Chapter 6 of Book 1 a distinction was drawn between non-conscious and conscious perception. Conscious perception was defined in terms of awareness of aspects of the environment because of the integration of stored knowledge and sensory information. Now we can see that conscious perception is also a kind of access consciousness. In conscious perception we have access to information derived from our perception of the

Protocol analysis
This involves a cluster of techniques in which participants report on their concurrent activity. The analysed reports are taken as evidence of the nature of mental processing.

world. So, for example, when looking at Figure 6.1 in Book 1, the author of Chapter 6 was able to give you a verbal report of what he saw. Similarly, you could offer verbal reports of what you saw and compare these to that of the author. The reports may differ. All this is evidence of access to our perceptions.

Recalling Activity 4.1 in this chapter, we can now say that much of what we sought to describe concerned the objects and properties of which we had access consciousness. In fact, we noted there that consciousness seems to allow other mental processes access to the same information. Being conscious of a shrub outside my window allows me to identify the object, to reason about it, and to communicate about it.

3.2 Phenomenal consciousness

Phenomenal consciousness
The kind of consciousness we have that involves the 'raw feel' or experience associated with consciousness. This is distinguished from information or knowledge that might be gained whilst conscious. We experience a loud noise, for example, in a certain way, and this is independent of the information the noise conveys.

Block's second kind of consciousness – **phenomenal consciousness** – is the aspect of consciousness that we have so far referred to as 'raw feel' or experience. To appreciate something of what is meant by phenomenal consciousness, imagine that you are tasting fresh coffee (or, better still, make some and savour the experience while reading!). At one level, your conscious experience could be described in terms of the information you have access to – your perceptions deliver sufficient information that you can recognize the liquid as being coffee. Depending on how you take your coffee, you may be able to discern the flavour of milk or the taste of sugar. You may be able to judge its temperature, albeit coarsely. If you are more skilled and experienced than I, you might conceivably be able to judge what type of bean it is made from! However, phenomenal consciousness goes beyond this kind of information – it encapsulates the *experience* or *feel* of tasting coffee. Nagel (1974), in an article entitled 'What is it like to be a bat?' expanded on this sense of phenomenal consciousness. He suggested that if an organism is conscious then there must be something 'that it is like' to be that organism. If a bat is conscious, then there must be something that it is like to be a bat. Nagel's view helps us to frame some of the issues involved in the example of tasting coffee. To understand our conscious experience of tasting coffee we would need to be able to state what it is like to taste coffee. This is different from merely stating the information that can be gained from tasting coffee, information that could be gained in other ways. For example, the temperature could be judged using a thermometer, the sugar content by a hydrometer. We might see that milk was present (or absent), and we might be told what bean the coffee was made from. Since the information could be gained without tasting coffee, it does not help us understand the experience of tasting coffee. In Nagel's terms, it does not tell us what it is like to have the experience or feel of tasting coffee.

Our consc. exp. is what it is like to ...."

(handwritten margin notes: Access Phenomenal; Monitoring (reflecting) actions; self consc (past, present, future) 'self' awareness)

3.3 Monitoring consciousness

Young and Block distinguish these two types of consciousness (access and phenomenal consciousness) from a further two: **monitoring consciousness** and self-consciousness (Section 3.4). Monitoring consciousness refers to the conscious experience that arises from reflecting upon one's own actions and mental states. This form of consciousness allows us to monitor our own mental states, and perhaps take action where the monitoring reveals some discrepancy with previous goals. Even the simple action of unwrapping a sweet and popping it into your mouth involves a form of monitoring. Usually, we take this monitoring for granted, and it is only when things go wrong that we notice that we should have monitored our actions more closely.

James Reason conducted a diary study of errors in everyday actions. He asked his participants to make an entry each time they made an error in their intended actions. He gives a number of examples of errors that are attributable to a lack of monitoring (Reason, 1979, pp.72–3). One respondent reported: 'I unwrapped a sweet, put the paper in my mouth and threw the sweet into the waste bucket'. Another wrote: 'When I leave for work in the morning I am in the habit of throwing two dog biscuits to my pet corgi and then putting on my earrings at the hall mirror. One morning I threw the earrings to the dog and found myself trying to attach a dog biscuit to my ear'. Yet another reported: 'I was just about to step into the bath when I discovered that I still had my underclothes on'. Reason's explanation of these errors invokes a distinction between two kinds of mental process – we can think of these as automatic and controlled processes. Chapter 6 of Book 1 discussed this distinction in some detail in conjunction with attention, and pointed out that even automatic processes require some cognitive resources. Reason's explanation of these errors is similar. He notes that complex sequences of actions are likely to contain some highly automatized processes. However, in order that action sequences are executed successfully, he suggests that at certain key points in the sequence controlled processing is required – perhaps to choose between two competing automatic processes for example. That is, attention or the conscious monitoring of the action sequence is required.

The failure of monitoring consciousness can also be seen in people with **anosognosia**, an inability to recognize one's own disease, illness or impairment. Damasio describes one of his patients, DJ, who has complete left-side paralysis. Despite being unable to move her left hand and arm, she would report that it was healthy and no longer impaired. Doubt would only appear to creep into her account when she was asked to move her arm, and found herself unable to do so. She might say that the arm 'doesn't move much by itself' (Damasio, 1999, p.211). In cases like these, patients seem to retain some aspects of consciousness, but seem impaired in their conscious ability to monitor the behaviour of their bodies.

Monitoring consciousness
The kind of consciousness we have that involves monitoring one's own actions and mental states, and allows one to take action as a consequence.

Anosognosia
This is a condition in which the patient is unable to recognize and deal with his or her own disease, illness or impairment.

3.4 Self-consciousness

Young and Block's (1996) fourth major type of consciousness is **self-consciousness**, a form of consciousness that involves a concept of self and its use in thinking and reflecting on oneself. Self-consciousness involves awareness not just of the self in the present (the 'here-and-now'), but also in the past and in the anticipated future. Self-consciousness therefore suggests a wider sense of awareness, one that encompasses an autobiographical sense of self. Unsurprisingly, cases of amnesia where autobiographical memory is disrupted, suggest some of the aspects of self-consciousness. In Section 2.4 we discussed Damasio's patient DT who experienced temporary amnesia after sustaining a head injury. After the accident, DT awoke agitated and confused and with no clear sense of who he was. Slowly, over a period of minutes, his sense of self started to return. In Chapter 8 of Book 1, the authors describe the case of HM who was apparently unable to form new long-term memories after undergoing surgery for epilepsy. This has had major consequences for HM's sense of self. Even in old age, he believes that he is a young man and that his friends and family, who are dead, are still alive. Apparently his identity is frozen at the time of the surgery – in his twenty-fifth year (Carter, 1998). The effects of head injury on the sense of self are also discussed in Chapter 1 of Book 1.

Asomatognosia also gives a feel for what can be involved in self-consciousness. This is a condition in which the patient is seemingly unable to recognize his or her own body and, more strikingly, unable to recognize even that he or she has a body. Damasio describes the patient LB who experienced episodes of asomatognosia after having sustained a stroke. In one episode, LB was apparently unable to feel her body, in spite of her mind being alert and active. Although she could pinch her skin, she apparently felt nothing as a consequence, though feeling did return after some minutes. She reported a further episode thus: 'I didn't lose any sense of being, just my body' (Damasio, 1999, p.214). LB apparently lost her conscious awareness of having a body, lost her sense of being an embodied self. DT may not have lost this sense exactly, but seemed to lose a sense of his own personal autobiography. Again, perhaps there are different kinds of self-consciousness, or different kinds of self.

3.5 A framework for consciousness

The four types of consciousness discussed in this section seem to fare well in accommodating some of the intuitive themes raised in Section 2. For instance, there we explored the importance of language and memory. We also talked of the fact that our descriptions of consciousness are dominated by descriptions of the objects of which we are conscious. In Block's analysis then, we were describing our access consciousness – the awareness that arises from

Access cons — arising from PtM ⟹ verbal reports
Phenomenal cons — what it was like — hard to describe

perception and memory, and that is involved in giving verbal reports. We also looked at something much harder to describe – a process of experiencing or feeling. Now we can see that we were trying to describe phenomenal consciousness. We were trying to describe *what it was like* to have the awareness we did (compare this to the endeavours of humanistic psychologists to describe the phenomenology associated with conscious awareness – see Chapter 9 in Book 1). This framework of types of consciousness also gives us a better understanding of some of the real-life cases we have examined. During episodes of somnambulism (such as Ken Parkes' as discussed in Box 4.1) for instance, we can now say that there is probably no access consciousness and presumably no self-consciousness either. Perhaps there is a form of monitoring consciousness; otherwise it might not be possible to explain complex action sequences. Whether Ken Parkes experienced phenomenal consciousness we can only speculate, though we return to this question towards the end of the chapter. The cases of neglect and blindsight are perhaps most obviously cases where phenomenal consciousness is impaired, while there is some preserved access consciousness – patients are unaware of seeing certain visual stimuli, but can, under appropriate circumstances, report their presence. Lastly, post-traumatic amnesia seems to involve different kinds of impairment, although there seems to be a stage in which the patient has all forms of consciousness except self-consciousness.

One possibility raised by this framework of four different kinds of consciousness is that a complete theory of consciousness will have to explain quite different kinds of phenomena. Indeed, when we consider some specific theoretical accounts, we may feel that they explain some aspects of consciousness well, but explain others poorly, or fail to explain them at all. This is a possibility that we raised in Section 2.4, where we considered the pitfalls of loose ways of talking about consciousness. Here we can see how real the possibility is. Given that there may be different kinds of consciousness, different ways of talking about the phenomena multiply the possibilities for confusion. Yet, if there are different kinds of consciousness, an obvious question that arises is whether one single theory could ever offer a comprehensive explanation. We will also consider this question at the end of the chapter.

Summary Section 3

- Consciousness appears to involve a number of distinct aspects:
    access to information provided by other mental processes (access consciousness);
    what it is like to have the experience or the raw feel associated with consciousness (phenomenal consciousness);

Somnambulism
— no access. consc
— no self consc.
— monitoring ✓
— ? phenomenal

Neglect + Blind S
— no/impaired phenomenal
— some access cons

Post Traumatic Amne
— all lost except self consc.

monitoring consciousness, in which mental states and actions are monitored;

and self-consciousness, involving awareness of the self.

- It needs to be clear, in talk of consciousness, which kinds of consciousness are under discussion.
- Distinct kinds of consciousness may eventually require different kinds of theoretical explanation.

4   Explaining consciousness

In the introduction to this chapter, it was noted that the contemporary study of consciousness is multi-disciplinary, drawing on research from disciplines such as cognitive psychology, neuroscience and philosophy. The different disciplines tend to ask slightly different questions and expect answers to take on correspondingly different forms. For example, cognitive psychologists tend to consider mental processes in terms of the ways in which information is manipulated – how it is input, stored, transformed and output. A cognitive analysis of memory, for example, might break it down into the information processing that operates at encoding, in storage, and in retrieval of memories (see Book 1, Chapter 8). As Chapter 3 (sub-section 3.1) of Book 1 pointed out, the cognitive psychologist is concerned more with a functional analysis, and less so with how mental processes are physically realized in the brain. Conversely, biological psychologists tend to focus on how functions are physically realized in the biological hardware of the brain and body. They may also focus on such questions as the evolutionary basis for a mental process and how changes to the underlying biology influence these processes – in brain damage and in development, for example. Again, in contrast to these perspectives, philosophers tend to focus on whether the conceptualization of a mental function is appropriate. They may develop arguments, and exploit thought experiments, in order to examine the coherence of a conceptualization. They may draw out implications of a view, perhaps showing that a position leads to counter-intuitive or incorrect predictions. Philosophers may also consider the appropriateness of existing explanations.

The different approaches also involve different criteria of evaluation. Whereas the cognitive and biological psychologists typically make empirical claims about the mind, brain and behaviour, philosophers typically claim that certain modes of theorizing and conceptualizing are more appropriate than others. The claims of cognitive and biological psychologists may therefore be examined empirically – key predictions can be examined by collecting new empirical

data. Where the data contradict or fail to support the predictions, we can
conclude that the claims need modification. Philosophical accounts proceed via
logical argument and conjecture, and through considering possible scenarios,
such as the thought experiments we have discussed. Of course, this is a
simplified picture. Psychologists often make claims that are not empirical – that
is, where it would be impossible to collect data that would decide whether the
claim is true or false – and philosophers often do make empirical claims. So
perhaps the boundaries between these two disciplines are rather more blurred
than appears at first glance.

You may then wonder why there are different disciplines – involving
different personnel, different institutions, different conferences, journals and
book series, and even different funding arrangements – attempting to address
these rather different questions about consciousness. Any response to this
question will necessarily make reference to the historical and political contexts
of these intellectual enterprises, but, of course, there are also practical reasons.
It takes a considerable length of time to grasp a particular literature, and so
much longer for any individual to approach a problem through a full
understanding of the different perspectives that are taken. However, the study
of consciousness has become multi-disciplinary because researchers have also
come to believe that the problems consciousness poses are broad-ranging. It is
not yet clear that we have conceptualized consciousness appropriately. It may
be that our concepts for analysing consciousness are in need of revision.
Cognitive psychology has made progress in understanding mental processes,
yet even our basic talk and thought about consciousness suggests that its
information processing role is unclear. Perhaps most pressing of all, questions
as to the physical realization of consciousness have remained outstanding since
the time of Descartes. If Descartes were right in suggesting that minds have a
fundamentally different constitution to the rest of the physical universe, then
consciousness would appear to lie beyond the limits of scientific explanation.
At a time of otherwise dazzling scientific progress, observations such as these
have encouraged researchers from different disciplines to work together, and
seek a unified understanding of consciousness.

This chapter attempts to show something of what the ingredients of a unified
understanding might be. Though presumably many perspectives will ultimately
help to form a complete picture of consciousness, most progress has been
made in relating the views of cognitive psychologists, neurologists, and
philosophers. It is on the first two of these perspectives that this section focuses.
We will first consider an account developed within cognitive psychology, and
then one from a biological perspective. Both of these accounts claim to be able
to explain a broad range of empirical data. However, it should already be clear
that it is our theoretical understanding of consciousness, rather than a paucity of
empirical data, that is in most urgent need of attention, and so this section
concentrates more on the theoretical picture of consciousness that emerges

from these accounts than on how in detail they explain empirical data. In Section 5 we will consider some philosophical perspectives on the problem of consciousness and we will see how these raise challenging questions concerning the very possibility of studying and understanding consciousness. While we will want to think about how all of these different views might relate to one another, it should be noted that these are not the only views developed within cognitive psychology, biology or philosophy. Just as differing approaches within psychology stand in different relations to one another (e.g., coexisting, complementing), it is likely that the disciplines we will consider in this and the following section do not stand in a single relation to one another. One particular philosophical view, for example, might complement a cognitive account, while another may conflict with it. So, the relations between the specific theories we will look at will not necessarily reflect the general relations between the disciplines they represent. Working out these general relations between explanations from different disciplines is no easy matter, and not something we can hope to achieve in this chapter. Instead, we will draw some characteristics from the theories that exemplify features of their host disciplines. In this way we can hope to gain some insight into the multi-disciplinary nature of consciousness studies, and an idea as to how psychology relates to other disciplines.

4.1 A cognitive perspective: global workspace theory

Bernard Baars (1988) offers a cognitive theory of consciousness, in which consciousness is seen as arising from the interplay between a number of different cognitive processes, such as perception, attention, language and memory. The essence of Baars' account is that consciousness involves a common 'workspace' that can receive input from a large number of specialized processors, all of which are operating non-consciously. There are limits to what can be put onto the workspace, but whatever is there appears in our conscious awareness. The contents of consciousness, then, correspond to the contents of this workspace. Baars' model (see Figure 4.3) has a number of basic components.

1 *Specialized input processors.* These process information non-consciously and in parallel. Each is dedicated to a particular kind of information that needs processing. Some may be dedicated to perception, others to language, and so on. Each processes information efficiently, but only within a specialized domain.
2 *The global workspace.* Whatever appears in the global workspace is in consciousness. The workspace is like a message board on an Internet site or a blackboard in a classroom. It is a place where different non-conscious processors can 'write' the results of their processing, and so communicate

and share information with one another. This communication enables a degree of coordination and cooperation between the different processors. However, only a few messages can appear in the workspace at any one time – it is limited in its capacity. Multiple messages can only be displayed serially – one at a time. Some will need to be erased before more are displayed.

3   *Specialized receiving processors.* Information in the global workspace can be sent to specialized receiving processors. By these means, the contents of the global workspace can change the way in which the processors process information. Note, however, that the workspace is not active. It does not direct processing. The workspace is more like a memory where the different receiving processors can read information. These receiving processors are also dedicated, computationally efficient and operate in parallel.

The components of Baars' model are described in terms of further characteristics (such as computational inefficiency). Let us consider what these characteristics are.

1   *Computational inefficiency* refers to the fact that conscious processes are unable to perform large or sophisticated computations. Mostly we find it difficult to perform long division 'in our heads'. Yet our visual processes are capable of performing much more complex computations on the images that fall on our retinas.

2   Consciousness has a *wide range of possible contents.* I can be conscious of this week's cricket test match, the buzzing of a bee outside my window, or the problem of trying to perform long division consciously. There appears to be no limit to the kinds of thing that can figure in our consciousness. In contrast, our non-conscious processes seem highly specific in the types of content on which they operate. Whatever processes we have for performing the analysis of visual stimuli, they presumably are dedicated to the task. It is unlikely that they get involved in the processing of other senses nor do we seem able to put them to use in other ways – in solving physics problems, for example. The non-conscious processors are not unlike modules (Fodor, 1983) as discussed in Chapter 2 in Book 1, that operate only with regard to dedicated types of information (e.g. a module in visual perception will operate only on incoming visual information).

3   It seems that consciousness is required to be *consistent* unlike non-conscious processors, which could conceivably come to mutually exclusive results. For example, since two interpretations of the Necker cube (shown in Figure 4.2) are available, presumably the non-conscious processes of visual perception are generating conflicting views as to which points in the visual field map to the front vertices of the

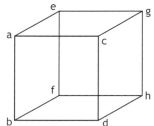

Figure 4.2   Necker cube (Note: The cube can be seen in two distinct orientations – either the vertices a, b, c and d form the front face of the cube, or the vertices e, f, g and h form the front face.)

cube, and which map to the back. Yet consciousness seems to require these inconsistencies to be resolved: in consciousness we seem forced to 'see' the cube in only one way at any one time.

4   Consciousness seems to operate in a *serial* fashion, while non-conscious processors can operate simultaneously, that is, in parallel. It is as if consciousness can only be directed to one or a very few things *simultaneously* – though consciousness can be directed to many different things this must be done sequentially over a short period of time.

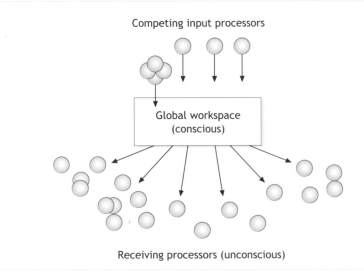

Competing input processors

Global workspace
(conscious)

Receiving processors (unconscious)

Figure 4.3   Baars' model (Source: Baars, 1988, p.88)

Figure 4.3 shows how the different processors are meant to interact via the global workspace. The specialized processors operate in parallel, relatively independently of one another and in particular domains. They each may try to present information to the global workspace. However, whatever information goes into the workspace must be consistent. If different processors present competing pieces of information, these will not get into the workspace. Likewise, there is a constraint on the amount of information that can be put into the workspace. If the workspace becomes full, further information can only be added by removing other pieces of information. These constraints provide an alternative way of formulating a capacity limitation.

You may wish to reread Section 2.3 of Chapter 6 in Book 1 and compare this notion of capacity limitation with that developed there concerning attention.

Once information has entered the workspace, the information is then globally broadcast to all of the specialized processors and so can influence their behaviour. Baars likens this broadcasting of information to the operation of a committee, where individuals combine to solve problems they cannot solve on their own. Thus the broadcasting of information enhances cooperation between the otherwise independent processors.

Baars' theory is presented as a way of unifying a variety of related concepts and metaphors. One of these is activation: consciousness has been thought to involve certain aspects of mind (such as memories or perceptions) becoming more active than others, and eventually crossing a threshold – things more active than the threshold become conscious, things less active do not. This notion is lent some support by studies and accounts of perception and memory that appeal to the concept of activation. A second concept is novelty: it has also been suggested that consciousness is required for appropriately dealing with novel objects, and reacting in novel situations. Non-conscious processes tend to operate in a fixed or rigid manner and, while this is adequate for highly predictable situations, an organism's success in dealing with novel objects and situations will depend upon its identifying new and appropriate behaviours. Consciousness has often been seen as the prime means by which this could be done. A third concept motivating Baars' account is that of non-conscious processes: psychologists have accumulated considerable evidence concerning the operation of non-conscious processes, for example, in perception, language and memory.

We are now in a position to consider the extent to which Baars' account helps explain different aspects of consciousness. Relatively easily, we can see how the theory might explain phenomena of access consciousness. Specialized processors will deal with information coming from different senses and, where the sensory information is consistent with information from other processors, the information will be broadcast on the global workspace. That is, it will become conscious. In this way we can see how perception might involve conscious awareness, as suggested in Chapter 6 of Book 1. Specialized perceptual processors would process sensory information and, ultimately, this information would be placed onto the global workspace. Broadcasting of the same information to other processors allows this perceptual information to be processed further – perhaps by a language processor so that the perception can be communicated to others.

Monitoring consciousness might be similarly explained. Specialized processors that guide action, for example, might send their results to the workspace. So long as there are no competing messages from other processors, then these results will be broadcast. The broadcasting might be sufficient to ensure that any additional processing required for a complex action sequence actually occurs. In the case of the errors noted by Reason, perhaps at the critical point in the action, there are too many competing messages trying to get onto the global workspace, or perhaps the critical message is too weak to exceed threshold.

consc. flexible
non-consc. – rigid

↗ what it is like to experience

In further refinements of the model, Baars discusses how distinct senses of self might be incorporated so perhaps aspects of self-consciousness can also be explained by his account. However, there seems to be no obvious way of accommodating phenomenal consciousness. It is reasonable to ask how, for example, taste information passing from specialized processors to the workspace and then being globally broadcast could possibly explain what it is to taste coffee. How could a feeling or experience arise from this process? Baars does not really provide an answer and, in its absence, we may conclude that it is unlikely that Baars' account can explain phenomenal consciousness.

4.2 A biological perspective: core and extended consciousness

Antonio Damasio presents an account of consciousness rooted in an understanding of humans as biological organisms. Damasio proposes three distinct kinds of self that help explain different kinds of consciousness. First, there is what Damasio calls a proto-self. For Damasio, the proto-self is what gives us a sense of stability, a sense that, in spite of changes over time, we remain the same entity. William James discussed this facet of consciousness. He viewed consciousness in terms of a tension between what appears as a stream of continuous flux and an invariant sense of self which experiences this ever-changing stream. Though our conscious experience may change radically moment by moment, our sense of self by and large does not. Damasio proposes that this sense of stability arises because of invariance in the organization and structure of the body. Though bodies change markedly over the life span, 'the 'design' of the body remains largely unchanged' (Damasio, 1999, p.141). Bones, joints, muscles and organs all seem to carry out the same function moment-by-moment, year-by-year. Moreover, the body possesses mechanisms by which sameness and stability are enhanced. Chapter 4 of Book 1 introduced the notion of homeostasis, referring to the tendency of certain parameters of the body to remain stable, there being mechanisms to restore parameters to their normal values when they deviate. For example, body temperature is regulated. When we become too cold we take control actions – for example, we turn on the heating or put on extra clothing. Indeed, as the author of Chapter 4 noted, sometimes the need to restore body parameters to their normal, stable level, can come to dominate the contents of our consciousness – we can think of nothing other than getting warm!

Somatosensory mechanisms
These mechanisms provide the brain with information from different areas of the body, so allowing it to maintain a representation of the body's condition.

The brain embodies what are called **somatosensory mechanisms** – these mechanisms enable the brain to receive information from different areas of the body, and so maintain a coarse picture of the body's condition. Damasio's view is as follows. The proto-self is a collection of these brain representations of the body and so maps '... the state of the physical structure of the organism'

(Damasio, 1999, p.154). The proto-self is not available to consciousness, but, as we shall see, forms the precursor to consciousness. We can think of the proto-self, then, as a neural representation of the state of the body. Because it is not conscious, however, we should not confuse it with any of the types of consciousness outlined earlier, or any richer sense of self.

For Damasio, consciousness arises from the relationship between two kinds of neural pattern. Damasio believes there are neural patterns in the brain that represent the organism (organism-representations which, as we have seen, are described as the proto-self). He also believes that there are neural patterns that represent the outside world (external-representations, which are produced by perceptual mechanisms). Because these are both representations of types of object, Damasio calls them first-order representations. The core self then arises from a further set of neural patterns. This set of patterns represents the relationships between these two first-order representations. Since these represent representations, Damasio calls them second-order – though he could equally call them meta-representations as discussed in Chapter 2 of this volume. The second-order patterns can then represent changes in the proto-self that arise from the formation of external-representations. The external-representations are thought to include sensorimotor information (representing, for example, different actions for the object), and their formation brings about changes in the organism-representations (i.e. the proto-self).

Though technical, Damasio's view can be simplified thus. Suppose we see a ball hurtling towards us at some speed. As perceptual processing of the ball takes place, so representations of the outside world are formed. In particular, the world is represented as containing a ball hurtling towards the body. As a result of this representation, bodily changes occur. These might relate to the preparation for an appropriate action. Muscles might begin to contract, for instance. Because the body undergoes changes, so the proto-self changes – because the proto-self represents the state of the body. For Damasio, core consciousness is involved in representing the relationship between these changes within the body and the representations of the outside world. The second-order patterns that represent these relationships capture something of the relationship between the body and its environment.

Finally, Damasio believes there is an autobiographical self (and an extended consciousness) that arises from the long-term storage of the contents of core consciousness. The organism is thought to possess an extended sense of self, stretching back over its lifetime and, via plans and expectations, forward into the anticipated future. When these stored contents are brought into core consciousness together with a representation of a particular object, then extended consciousness occurs. This enables us to think about an object not just in terms of the 'here-and-now', but also in a broader context. (You might wish to compare this notion of an autobiographical self both with the discussion of autobiographical memory in Chapter 8, and with the discussion of identity in Chapter 1, both in Book 1.)

There are a number of appealing features of Damasio's account. His view of core consciousness helps us to make sense of why objects in the environment appear to dominate our conscious awareness. If core consciousness is constituted by representations of how the organism changes in response to objects in the environment, then this dominance seems less surprising. Damasio's account also appears to offer help in framing phenomenal consciousness. Perhaps the raw feel associated with consciousness is related to changes in the proto-self, to the feel of how our bodily representations change with perceptual experience. The notion of extended consciousness allows self-consciousness to fit into the general picture. The account also offers an explanation for William James's contrasting views of consciousness. The neural patterns that constitute core consciousness are, of course, transient: they change as the organism's perception of the external world changes. A sequence of such patterns seems to form a continuous stream, ever changing, as suggested by James. However, the autobiographical self, being based on long-term storage of information about the organism's history, provides for a stable sense of self. Damasio's account is also supported by much neuropsychological observation. Patients with very different kinds of disorder seem to fit Damasio's scheme for describing consciousness. He explains amnesia, anosognosia and asomatognosia as disorders of autobiographical self. Automatism is explained in terms of disorders of core consciousness. Lastly, Damasio has also made detailed proposals about how these different components of consciousness are physically realized in different regions of the brain.

In spite of these positive features, there is one clear difficulty. In Section 2.6 we considered the problem of relating consciousness to physical matter. It might seem as though Damasio has gone some way to solving this problem. Nevertheless, a closer examination reveals a different story. Damasio tells us that core consciousness arises from the relationship between representations of the organism and representations of the external world. However, he tells us nothing about how this occurs. How does feeling or experience arise from representations? It is as if, at the crucial stage in the argument, just when we are on the edge of our seats, desperately anxious to hear how consciousness really arises, we are told only 'somehow it emerges from these representations'. This is, of course, not really an explanation at all. Perhaps this is our first candidate theory to fall into the trap of loose vocabulary we identified in Section 2.5 – it is presented as a theory of consciousness yet it does not really address the heart of the problem. Perhaps Damasio's account should be interpreted as an account of self-consciousness, monitoring consciousness and access consciousness, and not of phenomenal consciousness. In fact this is an option of which Damasio seems aware: '... I am open to the criticism that I am just addressing the problem of so-called self-consciousness and neglecting the remainder of the problem'

(Damasio, 1999, p.19). Unfortunately, without an explanation of how consciousness can arise from representations, the criticism seems valid.

Summary Section 4

- Consciousness has been studied from different perspectives. Cognitive psychologists have been concerned with the information processing involved in consciousness. Biologists have been concerned with how the functions of consciousness may be realized by the physical brain and body. Philosophers studying consciousness are concerned with whether theorists have adopted the most coherent and appropriate conceptualization of consciousness.

- Baars' account of consciousness assumes that autonomous processors, working in parallel, send information to a global workspace that can broadcast information to other processors. Consciousness corresponds to the contents of the workspace.

- Damasio considers core consciousness to be rooted in representing relationships between representations of the body and representations of the external world. An extended consciousness arises from the long-term storage of core consciousness.

- Both Baars and Damasio have difficulties explaining phenomenal consciousness, though access, monitoring and self-consciousness are explained more successfully by their views.

5   Consciousness explained?

In contrast with the previous section which outlined a cognitive psychological and a neurological account of consciousness, this section focuses on the attempts made by philosophers to make sense of the very notion of consciousness. One reason for doing this is that neither of the accounts of the previous section seems to deal adequately with one core intuition: that consciousness involves something like a raw feeling or experience or, in Nagel's terms, something that it is like to be conscious. In fact, we could have considered many other proposed explanations of consciousness, and this intuition would always stand out as a stumbling block. Why?

Chalmers (1995, 1996) suggests that explaining consciousness presents a number of difficult problems, but that one problem stands out as being especially hard – explaining how experience (feeling or phenomenal consciousness) arises from a physical basis. Sometimes this is also known as the problem of **qualia**, a term coined by philosophers to describe the individual feelings or experiences that come under the general heading of phenomenal consciousness. For example, we have already discussed the nature of qualia associated with drinking a cup of coffee. The problem is thus almost exactly that which Descartes raised in the seventeenth century – how do we explain the relationship between a conscious mind and a material body? Why is the problem so difficult?

Searle (1999) emphasizes three aspects of our conscious experience: conscious states are inner, qualitative and subjective. They are inner in the sense that conscious processes go on inside persons, and in the sense that they exist in the context of a 'stream' of conscious processes, such as described by James. Conscious states are qualitative in the sense that each has a qualitative character – a way that it feels to be in that state. In Nagel's terminology, there is something that it is like to be in a conscious state. Finally, conscious states are subjective, in that it is necessarily a subject (e.g. a person) who experiences them.

The reason why the problem is so hard is encapsulated in these three features. To provide an objective, scientific account of phenomenal consciousness or qualia, we need to understand 'what it is like' to be in a conscious state. The fact that conscious states are 'inner' poses severe difficulties. We cannot objectively observe what it is like for others to be in a conscious state, so we have to infer what it is like. This leads to the second difficulty: that phenomenal consciousness is qualitative – it is a feeling or experience, and there are few if any outward signs in people's behaviour to indicate the nature of this experience. The subjective character of conscious states raises the final difficulty. Many researchers have expressed the worry that attempts to study consciousness objectively involve disregarding its subjective character. Nagel (1974) claimed that consciousness possesses an essential point of view. This is sometimes described as a 'first-person' character (referring to the first person singular pronoun 'I'). Nagel's claim is that consciousness always seems to involve an 'I' who does the experiencing from a particular point of view. What is a point of view, and why might it pose difficulties for an objective scientific account of consciousness? Davies and Humphreys describe a point of view as constituting 'a kind of limitation upon what is conceivable for an individual' (Davies and Humphreys, 1993, p.15). For example, our perceptual systems set limits on how we view the world. If we were not capable of seeing the visible spectrum, but x-rays instead, we would have very different points of view on the world. Bats navigate the world using a form of sonar echo location and presumably have a very different 'view' of the world. To begin to construct an objective account of phenomenal conscious, it seems we would have to understand something of the point of view of other organisms. This may be relatively unproblematic in humans – though think back to some of the neuropsychological case studies – how easy did you find it to understand the points of view of the patients we described? But in the case of very different kinds of organism, such as bats, the task may be hopeless.

Where does this leave our exploration of consciousness? We have seen that explaining phenomenal consciousness is difficult, very difficult. Chalmers thinks that it is the 'hard problem' of consciousness. We have also seen how many accounts of consciousness do not seem to begin to explain it. Perhaps, as Nagel suggests, the intrinsic 'first-person' or perspectival character of consciousness places insurmountable obstacles in the way of an objective account. How could we objectively describe another's conscious experience without describing their point of view? Yet, how can we describe their point of view when we are not the subjects of their conscious experience? This does not mean that there are no ways of perceiving and understanding other people's minds – from Book 1 recall the discussions of theory of mind in Chapter 2, and of attribution theories in Chapter 7. It is just that giving an objective account of another's point of view may involve much more.

Nagel helps us to understand why consciousness is proving to be such a fiendishly difficult problem. Faced with real difficulties in explaining consciousness, researchers have increasingly been drawn to quite extreme positions in an attempt at some resolution. The remainder of this section focuses on some of these positions. The material is some of the most difficult in the whole field of consciousness – you should not be put off if some points are difficult to grasp at first.

5.1 Does phenomenal consciousness exist?

Daniel Dennett, a philosopher, offers an approach to the problem of consciousness which is very different from that of psychologists like Baars and Damasio (Dennett, 1991). They have taken their primary goal to be to account for psychological evidence, and the development of a theory expressed in terms familiar to psychologists (e.g. information processing and biological structure). In contrast, Dennett's concern is with the very notion of consciousness and whether our conceptualization of it is coherent. His goal is to consider whether a theory of consciousness is at all possible and, if so, what form it should take.

Dennett proposes that the mind consists of a series of specialized processors or circuits all working in parallel. These processors may be in conflict, and may compete. His account of consciousness is therefore broadly consistent with Baars'. However, the two accounts differ on one central claim. With regard to phenomenal consciousness, Dennett believes that there is no such thing. From Dennett's viewpoint, some of those intuitions we expressed in Activity 4.1 were mistaken. Although we may have been convinced that there was some aspect of feeling or experience involved in our consciousness, according to Dennett, we were wrong. In our discussion of those activities, we considered the difficulties in stating what was involved in consciousness as opposed to other processes such as hearing and vision. According to Dennett, there we simply assumed that something else – phenomenal consciousness – existed over and above these other processes, even though it was difficult to describe.

In this regard Dennett's position has some similarities with our earlier discussion of the importance of language in describing our consciousness. There we noted the possibility that the nature of language might determine the kinds of conscious experience that we have. So it could be that a Pintupi and an English speaker would have different conscious experiences of the very same hole in the ground. If we accept the possibility that language could determine the nature of our conscious experience, then it seems we can hardly deny a stronger possibility: it may also be that out language misleads us into thinking that phenomenal consciousness exists when, perhaps, it does not. So Dennett takes an extreme position on the role of language in shaping our consciousness. He believes that our talk of experience and the like lead us into the mistaken belief that phenomenal consciousness, feeling and experience actually exist! Dennett's view, then, is that talk of phenomenal consciousness is nothing more than a conceptual confusion, and that careful unpacking of the notion reveals it to be bogus.

One decidedly positive consequence of Dennett's position is that it suggests that accounts of consciousness such as Baars' and Damasio's may well be rather more complete than we previously thought. That they are unable to explain phenomenal consciousness can hardly be a criticism of these accounts if there is no such thing! So if Dennett is right, some or all aspects of these accounts may well turn out to provide a good explanation of consciousness.

On the other hand Dennett's argument does not adequately address our strong intuition that phenomenal consciousness exists. The following thought experiment from Frank Jackson (1982) is intended to show that phenomenal consciousness must exist (though Dennett disapproves of this example).

> Mary is a brilliant scientist who is, for whatever reason, forced to investigate the world from a black and white room via a black and white television monitor. She specializes in the neurophysiology of vision and acquires, let us suppose, all the physical information there is to obtain about what goes on when we see ripe tomatoes, or the sky, and use terms like 'red', 'blue', and so on. She discovers, for example, just which wavelength combinations from the sky stimulate the retina, and exactly how this produces via the central nervous system the contraction of the vocal chords and expulsion of air from the lungs that results in the uttering of the sentence 'The sky is blue' ... What will happen when Mary is released from her black and white room or is given a colour television monitor? Will she learn anything new or not?

(Jackson, 1982, p.130)

What do you think? Do you think that Mary would learn something about colour she has not learned already in her monochrome environment? If so, what would she learn? If you think Mary would learn nothing, why do you think this?

Many people think that Mary *would* learn something when she sees for the first time, for example, a red rose, or a blue sky. She would already know that the rose is red, but she will learn for the first time what it *feels like* to experience 'red'. For the first time, she will be able to say 'so that's what red looks like' – or, in other words, 'so that is what it is like to experience red'. Jackson thinks that it is *obvious* that Mary will learn something from experiencing colour as opposed to just knowing about colour, and that this shows there is more to conscious experience than acquiring information via the cognitive and biological mechanisms of the brain and body. After all, since, by hypothesis, Mary already possessed all physical information concerning colour, her learning something demonstrates there is more to the experience of colour than merely the acquisition of information. What more could there be? Phenomenal consciousness.

Jackson's argument is controversial. Dennett for one believes that the thought experiment is fundamentally misconceived. He thinks that it is just too difficult for us to imagine and work out the implications of someone knowing all the physical information there is about colour. Nevertheless, the thought experiment is extremely useful in trying to clarify the intuition that phenomenal consciousness exists.

5.2 Does everything have phenomenal consciousness?

An equally bold alternative treatment of consciousness is suggested by Chalmers. He suggests that experience or phenomenal consciousness may be a 'fundamental feature' of the physical universe. What might this mean? Just as mass, electromagnetic charge, space and time are fundamental features of objects – all objects have a mass and charge, and occupy space and time – Chalmers proposes that all objects have a further feature, 'experience'. Chalmers' argument is based in part on considering a thought experiment, one that examines whether it is conceivable for there to be zombies – molecule-by-molecule replicas of human beings which do not have consciousness. This is developed in Box 4.3.

4.3 Zombie thought experiment

Imagine that there are creatures that not only look identical to human beings, but are in fact molecule-by-molecule replicas of conscious human beings. Suppose further that these creatures are behaviourally identical to their human counterparts. Consequently, there is no way of telling one of these creatures from a real human being. Now the question is this: is it conceivable that these creatures are not conscious? Could they be zombies, entirely without any mental life? What do you think?

If you believe that non-conscious zombies are not conceivable, then you are committed to saying that a molecule-by-molecule replica of a conscious human being would have to be conscious also. This amounts to saying that consciousness is a product solely of a person's physical composition. However, if you think that non-conscious zombies are conceivable (you can imagine them existing, no matter how unlikely), then the thought-experiment seems to show that consciousness does not arise from the physical nature of an organism's composition. After all, a human and a zombie might be identical in every detail including their molecular composition and yet the former would be conscious and the latter not.

The zombie thought-experiment relates to our earlier discussions: of automatism, sleep walking, super-blindsight, and the unfortunate case of Ken Parkes. At this stage, you may also want to revisit Activity 4.2 and recall your answers to that activity.

You will recall that Ken Parkes produced complex behaviour consistent with his possessing the various aspects of consciousness described earlier in this chapter. Yet Parkes' successfully argued that the death of his mother-in-law and wounding of his father-in-law took place without his voluntary intentions or his conscious awareness. Both his physical make-up and his behaviour appeared to match that of a fully conscious-if violent- human being, yet the court accepted that he had neither the experience of being conscious, nor the capacity to choose his actions. If we accept the court's interpretation of events, we must also accept that during his 'sleep walking' incident Ken Parkes was in the same state as a hypothetical zombie-lacking the key experience of being conscious. In terms of our earlier discussion of phenomenal consciousness, there is nothing that it was like to be Ken Parkes 'sleep walking' (or a 'zombie'). He was without phenomenal consciousness. Similarly if we return to the hypothetical possibility of super blindsight (Section 2.3) , whilst the super blindsight patient can successfully describe a scene perceived in the visual area affected by the scotoma, there is nothing that it is like to see that scene.

The implications of accepting that Ken Parkes was a 'zombie' while sleepwalking, or that, in our theoretical thought experiment, super blindsight patients could exist, are considerable. The logical consequence appears to be that consciousness does not arise directly as a result of the brain and its physical state. This is a startling and unsettling conclusion to those committed to the view that all elements of consciousness are amenable to scientific investigation. So much so that some psychologists and philosophers would argue that non-conscious zombies are inconceivable, and that super blindsight could not even be a theoretical possibility. Chalmers however responds to this problem by suggesting that objects possess, in addition to physical fundamental features (such as mass), the non-physical fundamental feature of experience. There are very substantial challenges for Chalmers' view however. One is to explain how the 'experience' features of things like neurons, which we do not ordinarily consider to be conscious, combine in the brain to give the experience that we ordinarily do call consciousness. Another, already implied, is to explain how neurons and other physical objects such as chairs and thermostats do not achieve what we call consciousness. Perhaps the most difficult problem, however, concerns the extent to which we can make sense of Chalmer's account. Researchers have questioned what it really means to say that experience is a fundamental feature, one that we share with all other physical objects. If Chalmers' account leaves you with unanswered questions and feeling somewhat confused, then you are not alone. Perhaps the fairest way of regarding his position is as an extreme option, a logical possibility that is, as yet, not fully intelligible, chosen because it might help circumvent the really hard problem of consciousness – how consciousness arises from non-conscious matter.

5.3 Might we never understand phenomenal consciousness?

One further option for treating consciousness is known as **mysterianism**. This is the view that consciousness may not be a natural phenomenon, that is, it may not be amenable to the methods of science. Colin McGinn has put forward a form of this kind of argument. He has argued that consciousness may be so complex that it transcends our understanding. Just as cats might never have the intellectual resources to 'understand' the causes of their behaviour, so we may not have the resources to understand our own consciousness.

The three options we have considered serve to illustrate the range of positions that have been taken in response to the difficulties in explaining consciousness. In essence, the difficulty arises because though there are reasons to believe in phenomenal consciousness, it has not been possible to give an adequate account. Indeed, there are reasons to believe that if phenomenal consciousness exists it may not be possible to explain it objectively and scientifically. This possibility has presented researchers with a genuine dilemma. While access, monitoring and self-consciousness seem amenable to

Mysterianism
This is the view that consciousness may not be a natural phenomenon amenable to the methods of science.

psychological and philosophical accounts, phenomenal consciousness seems to transcend the explanatory abilities of science (as mysterianism suggests). It is this conclusion – profoundly gloomy to those who would hope to explain consciousness – that has led researchers to suggest new ways of conceptualizing consciousness in order to escape the problem of phenomenal consciousness. It is perhaps in this context that we should interpret what otherwise seem to be the extreme views of Dennett and Chalmers.

The options proposed by Dennet and Chalmers fall into two broad categories. On the one hand, we might agree that there is no such thing as phenomenal consciousness over and above what is explicable in terms of the kinds of cognitive and biological theories we have examined. Talk of phenomenal consciousness might be a device that helps us to think about people and their behaviour, an invention of a particular social, cultural and linguistic milieu. This is what Dennett argues and it links to our discussion of the relation between consciousness and language in Section 2 (and to discussions in Chapter 3). If language appears to shape the nature of our conscious experience then perhaps there is no such thing as phenomenal consciousness, and our ways of thinking and talking about it are in error.

On the other hand, we might decide that phenomenal consciousness seems to involve going beyond the information we obtain from our biological constitution and our cognitive organization. Although there are good arguments for this possibility, it is difficult indeed to spell out what else there might be that could explain experience. Appeals to 'experience' being a fundamental feature do not really help, since it is so difficult to make sense of this notion.

Perhaps McGinn's argument is less problematic, but its negative conclusion – that we may never be able to explain consciousness – should be resisted. Whatever the prospects for explaining consciousness, it is clear that there is much lively debate ahead. Almost certainly, findings from different approaches to psychology, as well as philosophical re-examinations of our existing conceptualizations, will be key to making progress.

Summary Section 5

- Phenomenal consciousness is difficult to explain scientifically because of its inner, qualitative and subjective character.
- Dennett argues that phenomenal consciousness does not exist – it is a consequence of our faulty conceptualization of consciousness, a conceptualization which he believes needs revision.
- There are alternative options for treating phenomenal consciousness, including: assume it is a fundamental feature of the universe (Chalmers); assume it transcends our explanatory abilities (mysterianism).

[handwritten annotations:]

Processes not content   Ken Parker   Kinds of

3 levels of Consc.
— Reflective
— Pre-reflective *Sonnambulism*
— Non Consc. *blindsight*
visual neglect
DM

4 kinds of cons

Access Cons.
Phenomenal Cons
Motor Cons.
Self Cons.

6 Conclusion

This chapter has explored territory that is widely acknowledged to be challenging for psychology. There appear to be no easy answers to the questions posed by consciousness. Yet, in spite of the debates, considerable progress is being made in investigating consciousness. Accounts such as Baars' and Damasio's make positive proposals concerning the notion of self, and for the accessing and monitoring of information in conscious awareness. These are important aspects of our conscious experience too, and, in spite of disagreement on precisely how to explain these phenomena, researchers are developing theories and beginning systematically to explain considerable bodies of evidence. Neuropsychological evidence concerning the experiences of patients has helped us to understand some of the different elements involved in consciousness, as well as their possible physical basis in the brain.

The chapter has also explored your own intuitions as much as the scientific literature. I hope you can now see why. How we regard positions such as mysterianism and others depends in part on how we are prepared to treat our intuitions concerning conscious experience. Dennett believes our intuitions are leading us to make mistakes, and they must be retuned – we need to clear up some of our own conceptual confusions. Other researchers are adamant that our intuitions are well founded, and that they raise genuine difficulties for a scientific approach to consciousness. At this stage, we can only hope to appreciate the arguments on both sides, and understand their implications.

We are left with two important questions. First, given the different kinds of consciousness, is it reasonable to think that a single theory can explain all of them? The evidence we have discussed suggests that phenomenal consciousness may require a very different kind of explanation from access consciousness, monitoring consciousness and self-consciousness. Second, how should we treat phenomenal consciousness? Answering this question will have *[handwritten: qualitative aspect of experience]* quite profound implications for our understanding of the mind and of psychology. If we decide that phenomenal consciousness can be explained scientifically (either by denying qualia, or attempting to explain them through cognitive or biological function), then psychology may be viewed as a science of the mind, in much the same way as physics and chemistry are considered sciences. If, however, we decide that phenomenal consciousness will always elude the scientific approach, then we are faced with two choices. The first is to maintain a scientific approach within psychology, but concede that psychology will only ever offer a partial explanation of mental life – it would not explain phenomenal consciousness, nor would it ever completely explain the mind.

The other is to concede that, while consciousness lies within psychology's remit, psychology must stand apart from the natural sciences, and offer somewhat different kinds of explanation.

In our deliberations we have come full circle. We began by trying to tease out an intuition that in being consciously aware of our environment, we not only pick up information about the environment, but we also experience the environment in a certain way. We have ended on the horns of a dilemma concerning how we should treat this intuition. While our current state of knowledge does not really allow this issue to be resolved, when it does there will be profound implications for our understanding of the mind and how it should be studied.

Further reading

Baars, B.J. (1988) *A Cognitive Theory of Consciousness*, Cambridge, Cambridge University Press.

Damasio, A.R. (1999) *The Feeling of What Happens: Body and Emotion in the Making of Consciousness*, London, Heinemann.

Dennett, D.C. (1991) *Consciousness Explained*, Boston, MA, Little, Brown & Company.

These authors provide readable but comprehensive treatments of their own accounts of consciousness.

Davies, M. and Humphreys, G.W. (1993) 'Introduction', in Davies, M. and Humphreys, G.W. (eds) *Consciousness: Psychological and Philosophical Essays*, Oxford, Blackwell.

This is a good introduction to various psychological and philosophical perspectives on consciousness.

Farah, M. J. (1997) 'Visual perception and visual awareness after brain damage: a tutorial overview', in Block, N.J., Flanagan, O.J. and Güzeldere, G. (eds) *The Nature of Consciousness: Philosophical Debates*, Cambridge, MA, MIT Press.

This book provides a thorough review of the literature on changes in visual perception and awareness following brain damage, and the implications for consciousness.

Young, A.W. and Block, N. (1996) 'Consciousness', in Bruce, V. (ed.) *Unsolved Mysteries of the Mind: Tutorial Essays in Cognition*, Hove, Erlbaum.

This chapter provides a brief review of the topic of consciousness from both a philosophical and psychological perspective.

References

Baars, B.J. (1988) *A Cognitive Theory of Consciousness*, Cambridge, Cambridge University Press.

Bisiach, E. and Luzzatti, C. (1978) 'Unilateral neglect of representational space', *Cortex*, vol.14, pp.129–33.

Bisiach, E. and Rusconi, L.L. (1990) 'Break-down of perceptual awareness in unilateral neglect', *Cortex*, vol.26, pp.643–9.

Block, N. (1991) 'Evidence against epiphenomenalism', *Behavioural and Brain Sciences*, vol.14, pp.760–2.

Broughton, R., Billings, R., Cartwright, R., Doucette, D., Edmeads, J., Edward, M., Ervin, F., Orchard, B., Hill, R. and Turrell, G. (1994) 'Homicidal somnambulism: a case report', *Sleep*, vol.17, no.3, pp.253–64.

Carter, R. (1998) *Mapping the Mind*, London, Weidenfeld & Nicholson.

Chalmers, D. (1995) 'Facing up to the problem of consciousness', *Journal of Consciousness Studies*, vol.2, no.3, pp.200–19.

Chalmers, D.J. (1996) *The Conscious Mind: In Search of a Fundamental Theory*, Oxford, Oxford University Press.

Crick, F. (1994) *The Astonishing Hypothesis: The Scientific Search for the Soul*, London, Simon and Schuster.

Damasio, A.R. (1999) *The Feeling of What Happens: Body and Emotion in the Making of Consciousness*, London, Heinemann.

Davies, M. and Humphreys, G.W. (1993) 'Introduction', in Davies, M. and Humphreys, G.W. (eds) *Consciousness: Psychological and Philosophical Essays*, Oxford, Blackwell.

Dennett, D.C. (1991) *Consciousness Explained*, Boston, MA, Little, Brown & Company.

Ericsson, K.A. and Simon, H.A. (1980) 'Verbal reports as data', *Psychological Review*, vol.87, pp.215–51.

Farah, M.J. (1997) 'Visual perception and visual awareness after brain damage: a tutorial overview', in Block, N.J., Flanagan, O.J. and Güzeldere, G. (eds) *The Nature of Consciousness: Philosophical Debates*, Cambridge, MA, MIT Press.

Fodor, J.A. (1983) *The Modularity of Mind: An Essay on Faculty Psychology*, Cambridge, MA, MIT Press.

Jackson, F. (1982) 'Epiphenomenal qualia', *The Philosophical Quarterly*, vol.32, no.127, pp.127–36.

James, W. (1890/1984) *The Principles of Psychology*, New York, Harvard University Press.

Marshall, J. and Halligan, P. (1988) 'Blindsight and insight in visuospatial neglect', *Nature*, vol.336, pp.766–7.

Martini, F.H., Timmons, M.J. and McKinley, M.P. (2000) *Human Anatomy*, Upper Saddle River, NJ, Prentice Hall.

Nagel, T. (1974) 'What is it like to be a bat?', *Philosophical Review*, vol.83, pp.435–50.

Reason, J. (1979) 'Actions not as planned: the price of automatization', in Underwood, G. and Stevens, R. (eds) *Aspects of Consciousness, Volume 1: Psychological Issues*, London, Academic Press.

Scruton, R. (2000) *Animal Rights and Wrongs* (3rd edn), London, Metro Books.

Searle, J.R. (1999) *Mind, Language and Society: Doing Philosophy in the Real World*, London, Weidenfeld & Nicolson.

Shakespeare, W. (1978) *The Complete Works of William Shakespeare*, London, Abbey Library.

Stoerig, P. and Cowey, A. (1989) 'Wavelength sensitivity in blindsight', *Nature*, vol.342, pp.916–8.

Tye, M. (1995) *Ten Problems of Consciousness: A Representational Theory of the Phenomenal Mind*, Cambridge, MA, MIT Press.

Weiskrantz, L. (1986) *Blindsight: A Case Study and Implications*, Oxford, Clarendon.

Weiskrantz, L., Warrington, E.K., Saunders, M.D. and Marshall, J. (1974), 'Visual capacity in the hemianopic field following a restricted occipital ablation', *Brain*, vol.97, pp.709–28.

Young, A.W. and Block, N. (1996) 'Consciousness', in Bruce, V. (ed.) *Unsolved Mysteries of the Mind: Tutorial Essays in Cognition*, Hove, Erlbaum.

Young, A.W. and De Haan, E.H.F. (1993) 'Impairments of visual awareness', in Davies, M. and Humphreys, G.W. (eds) *Consciousness: Psychological and Philosophical Essays*. Oxford, Blackwell.

'Normal' development?
The case of dyslexia

Clare Wood and Alex Richardson

Contents

Aims

This chapter aims to:

- give a critical account of the issues that relate to the definition, explanation and remediation of 'abnormal' psychological functioning
- give a critical account of the identification of dyslexia, its suggested explanations and management strategies.

1 Approaches to the definition of 'abnormality'

You may have noticed that we often discuss people with the assumption that there is a 'normal' pattern of behaviour, which some people do not conform to, while the rest do. This idea of 'normality' is implicitly subscribed to in many of the areas of psychology that you have already covered. We theorize about 'normal development', 'normal memory functioning', 'typical perceptual experiences', 'gender appropriate behaviour', and refer more explicitly to examples of unusual psychological functioning as being of interest, because of what they can tell us about 'normal' functioning.

The concept of psychological 'normality' is not simple. This chapter addresses the issues surrounding the idea of 'normal' psychological development, and shows that how we define 'normality' will influence the way we think about and deal with 'abnormal' psychological functioning. To illustrate how 'abnormality' is defined in practice, and what issues are important when considering its causes and treatment, we will refer to the specific example of developmental dyslexia. However, these issues will also apply to many other types of 'abnormal' functioning, some of which you will encounter in Book 3, *Applying Psychology*.

Book 2 has introduced you to areas of psychology that are particularly associated with 'being human' and each one has required you to think about more than one psychological perspective. In the introduction to this book it was proposed that we need to consider multiple perspectives in psychology, as our understanding of a topic is enhanced by the comparison of research findings from different perspectives. This final chapter consolidates this theme by showing how research from cognitive, biological and neuropsychological perspectives can be combined to offer a more complete account of conditions like dyslexia. The chapter therefore presents dyslexia as a 'case study' in how different perspectives might be complementary to each other.

1.1 Definitions of 'normality'

What do we mean when we say something is 'normal'?

Activity 5.1

Write down what you would consider to be 'normal' for each of the following examples:

- women's height;
- eyesight;
- behaviour when waiting for a bus;
- consumption of alcohol.

Each of your answers to Activity 5.1 will reflect a different approach to defining 'normality'. We will examine each of these approaches in turn. Note that there are quotation marks around the word 'normality'. This is to show that we are exploring the meaning of the word, and accept that there is no one unproblematic definition. Throughout the chapter, quotation marks around any word indicates that there are issues or debates about the definition of the word.

Statistical approaches to 'normality'

What did you base your idea of 'normal' height on? It might have been based on your own experience, reflecting the *average* height of women in your community. Similarly, 'abnormality' can be defined in terms of low statistical frequency. If what is most common in the general population is considered 'normal', then any behaviour or psychological characteristic that occurs only rarely may be regarded as 'abnormal'. From this viewpoint, above average individuals are just as 'abnormal' as those who are below average. This approach is particularly suited to variables that are **dimensional**, such as height or scores on a test. These variables lend themselves to measurement on a continuous scale. You can relate this to what you have already learned about the normal distribution. If you look at Figure 5.1, you can see the normal distribution curve with the mean value in the middle.

Dimensional
Used to refer to variables that lend themselves to measurement on a continuous scale (e.g. height is dimensional, but eye colour is not).

If you cannot remember what the normal distribution is, or what the term 'standard deviation' refers to, pause now and reread Sections 2.5 and 2.6 in Statistics Without Maths for Psychology *(Dancey and Reidy, 2002).*

You will recall that about 68 per cent of all values are within one standard deviation of the mean (see Section 3.2 in Dancey and Reidy, 2002). This is termed the 'normal' zone of the curve. Note that this choice of the percentage of values which comes under the 'normal' zone of the curve is arbitrary in the sense that it was defined by statisticians, and does not reflect any natural circumstance or law.

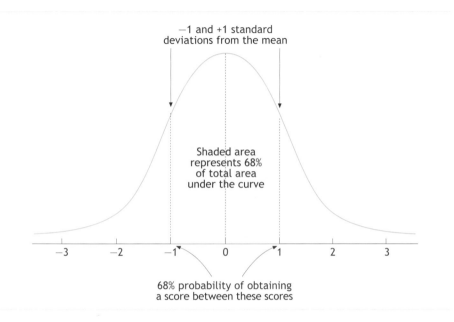

Figure 5.1   The normal distribution curve (Source: Dancey and Reidy, 2002, p.89)

The standard deviation for a set of scores can therefore be used to define the boundaries of what 'normal' might be. Another example is that of IQ scores, which are constructed to be normally distributed with a mean of 100 and a standard deviation of 15. This means that IQ scores between 85 and 115 are considered to be 'normal'. Scores lower than 85 are regarded as abnormally low (the bottom 16 per cent), and scores higher than 115 are seen as abnormally high (the top 16 per cent).

This seemingly simple and objective approach to defining 'normality' is in fact quite problematic. If deviation from statistical norms is used to define 'abnormal' functioning, then the following questions about measurement must be answered.

1   How are psychological characteristics (such as intelligence) quantified? Can they be measured on a continuous scale or are they better captured by discrete categories?

2   Do the relevant measures have a normal distribution? If not, mean scores and standard deviations are likely to be inappropriate reference points (see Section 2.2 in Dancey and Reidy, 2002).

3   Are the assessments reliable? Tests that are going to be used for diagnostic purposes need to have extremely good internal and external reliability.

4   Are the assessments valid? To address this, we need to be clear about the purpose of measurement and consider different types of validity (see Chapter 5 of Book 1).

5   How is a behaviour classified as 'abnormal'? The 'one standard deviation away from the mean' criterion can be a rather over-inclusive indicator of abnormality for some tasks, especially if the consequences of such an assessment would be to give that person a negative label. More extreme boundaries of 1.5 or 2 standard deviations from the mean are sometimes chosen instead. Any cut-off point for classifying people into discrete categories of 'normal' and 'abnormal' is arbitrary if the characteristic in question really is dimensional.

6   Does it matter if someone is scoring higher than the average population? On some measures very high scores may be just as worrying as very low scores (e.g. persistent over-arousal, reflecting stress or anxiety). On other measures, only one extreme of the distribution may be considered 'abnormal' in the sense of problematic. The statistical approach to defining normality does not make these kinds of judgements, so clearly other criteria are being applied in these situations.

Medical approaches to normality

What did you write for 'normal' eyesight? The ability to see clearly without glasses? It is unlikely that you wrote down short- or long-sightedness as an example of 'normal' eyesight, even though they are very common. However, they are not seen as 'normal' because having to wear glasses is perceived as a limitation or even a form of disability. This relates to one of several so-called 'medical models' of normality, which centre on the idea of uniformity of physical and psychological functioning across individuals. These models are often reductionist, proposing that disease or physical disorder of some kind can explain 'abnormality', although such explanations frequently acknowledge social and external factors that may trigger the physical 'cause' of a problem. Psychological conditions like depression can be viewed using medical approaches as the result of 'abnormal' functioning of the brain systems that govern mood and arousal. As a result, medical models often provide the rationale for many drug treatments (e.g. anti-depressants) aimed at correcting the presumed biochemical imbalances to restore 'normal' functioning. However, these simple reductionist approaches have proved unsuccessful because:

1   The identification of many psychological 'disorders' can be very difficult in practice, because they appear to fall on a continuum with 'normal'

functioning, so any clear distinction between 'normal' and 'abnormal' is frequently difficult to draw.

2   Biochemical (drug) treatments often go hand-in-hand with a medical approach. However, there is still considerable uncertainty about the precise nature and origins of any biochemical abnormalities associated even with well-studied conditions like depression or schizophrenia, for which various drug treatments are in routine use. For others such as eating disorders, even less is known about possible biochemical contributions, if any exist at all.

3   It is evident that many of our most common diseases are actually **systemic** – they arise from a breakdown of many complex interacting systems, and medical approaches acknowledge this. They should not be thought of as simple or reductionist explanations for physical or psychological disorders. For example, both heart disease and cancer arise from the interaction of genetic predisposition with environmental and lifestyle factors that include both biological and sociocultural influences. There is no reason to suppose that psychological disorders are any simpler.

Systemic
Belonging to or affecting the system or body as a whole. For example cardiovascular disease, with origins involving many interacting sub-systems, is usually seen as systemic, whereas tuberculosis, caused by a single infectious agent, is not.

The sheer complexity of the many interacting systems involved in human development and functioning means that even in physical disorders, realistic medical approaches are rarely simple or reductionist. In the same way that good medical models reflect complex interactions between different factors, so too should our models of psychology.

Cultural approaches to normality

What is normal in terms of the simple act of waiting for a bus? In the UK it is expected that people will organize themselves into a queue, so those who have waited the longest can board the bus first. However, this is not true of all cultures. Yet, if someone from a culture that does not queue were waiting for a bus in Manchester and did not wait her turn, she would be chastised for it. So, another approach might be to define as 'abnormal' any behaviour that contravenes social norms, values or expectations.

Using a cultural approach, what is defined as 'abnormal' will depend on expectations and standards of the society, and thus on political and economic as well as social factors. The criteria used may differ between societies, over time within the same society, and between groups within the same society.

One thing to consider is whether a 'deficit' or 'abnormality' is defined as such by context. For example 'deficits' in one area may be linked to 'abnormal' strengths in another. We shall consider this in more detail in relation to dyslexia later in the chapter. Another issue is whether what is considered 'normal' should then also be considered as 'natural'. Human behaviour is complex and is determined by interactions between a variety of influences, internal and external. Consequently, the idea that some behaviours are 'natural' because they are determined in some part by our physiology, is not a satisfactory justification on its own for considering them 'normal'.

Personal distress

Another way of defining psychological 'abnormality' is to ask whether certain behaviours or styles of functioning cause distress to the individual concerned. Think about your response to what you consider to be 'normal' alcohol consumption. Perhaps you specified a maximum number of units per day or week? If so, why did you do this? Is it because of the health problems associated with excessive drinking, or because of its association with antisocial behaviour? Some of you may believe that any alcohol consumption is inappropriate, for medical, cultural or religious reasons. Alternatively, some of you might have specified an age criterion that reflects the legal age for alcohol consumption in your country. These are not trivial points. Many people see 'excessive' alcohol consumption, even if within cultural norms, as 'abnormal' because of the personal distress it will cause. They believe that heavy drinking can lead to alcohol dependency or health problems that have the potential to ruin a person's life.

An obvious difficulty with the criterion of personal distress is that in some cases, such as alcoholism or drug use, personal distress is not necessarily manifest. Whose distress are we considering? Are we really intervening in the interests of the person showing the behaviour, or in the interests of their family or society? Moreover, who makes the decision to intervene will vary depending on what the behaviour is. The degree to which individuals are pressurized to comply will also vary depending on whether it is a doctor or a friend who is trying to intervene. Clearly this criterion raises some complex issues to do with the imposition of other people's values and the acceptability of setting limits to individual freedom.

Tobacco use is associated with substantial health risks and social issues, but would intervention, in the form of bans on its use, infringe personal freedom? If the answer is 'yes', then why does this not equally apply to behaviours such as eating disorders? Is it because of sociocultural notions of what constitutes 'normal' behaviour? Furthermore, does the large number of people engaging in a behaviour, such as smoking, make it somehow more 'normal'?

1.2 Overview of 'normality'

Before we can specify what might be 'abnormal', we must first have a clear idea of what we mean by 'normality'. However, within psychology this is much more difficult than it first appears. As our discussion has shown, psychological 'normality' can be defined in terms of:

- what is 'average' or 'typical' with respect to statistical frequency;
- 'lack of disability' – where 'normality' is defined by reference to an 'ideal' or 'perfect' state of functioning;
- conformity to social, cultural or historical expectations or norms;
- individual well-being or lack of personal distress.

It is important to recognize that these approaches are not mutually exclusive. Thus, 'normality' can be defined by calculating statistics on what is most common, as well as by trying to find valid, biologically based criteria of 'healthy' functioning. It can also be culturally defined, encompassing social values and expectations, as well as involving appreciation of individual differences and personal well-being. Each of these factors may carry more or less weight, depending on the circumstances and the behaviour(s) being considered. There is so much natural variation in human behaviour and psychological functioning that it is almost impossible to arrive at any universal definition of 'normality'. This means that attempts to define 'abnormal' psychological functioning can be problematic and misleading unless careful consideration is given to the reasons for seeking such a definition.

Why do we need to make a distinction between 'normal' and 'not normal' when we are acutely aware that human psychological life is so diverse? Do you think that society or the individual within it benefits from identifying some types of behaviour as 'abnormal'?

1.3 Experiencing dyslexia

To illustrate just how problematic the idea of 'abnormality' is in practice, we will consider the condition of **developmental dyslexia**, *dyslexia* for short. Dyslexia is relatively common and you may have knowledge of it from friends or personal experience. The following section illustrates many of the difficulties experienced by people with dyslexia, and it also highlights more generally some of the problems that can occur if you are not, in some sense, 'normal'.

Developmental dyslexia
Refers to a congenital condition that results in a primary difficulty in learning to read and write.

Alexander Faludy is severely dyslexic. Dyslexia is a condition that is primarily manifested by a difficulty in learning to read and write, although its behavioural symptoms are far more wide ranging than this. At the age of 15 Alexander was still only able to write two legible words per minute, and coped with reading by using book tapes intended for blind people, which he would listen to while following the text of the book. He was also extremely clumsy and uncoordinated. Unable to read at all for a long time, he suffered bullying at school. In these respects his story is not untypical of many people with dyslexia. However, Alexander is also 'not normal' in another respect – he has an extremely high IQ. By the time he was 11 he had passed GCSE and A-Level English Literature and had begun a foundation course with the Open University. To achieve all this, Alexander and his parents had to persuade schools and examination boards to change their thinking about the ways they assessed and examined dyslexic students' work. Alexander dictated his work to his parents who would copy down what he said verbatim. At 15 he won a place at Peterhouse College, Cambridge as the youngest student since Pitt the Younger, studying Theology and History of Art.

Alexander's story in his own words, aged 15

> At playschool, other children were taught to read. They tried to teach me, but I was never any good at it, and even when I did learn to read I was very slow ... When I was five, an important marker in my dyslexic case history emerged. The use of my left and right hands became more or less even, and in places, alternated, a fact that puzzled my class teacher ... I was physically weak and uncoordinated. My contemporaries at school concluded that I wasn't one of them. I wasn't any good at throwing a ball, reading, or beating someone up for no apparent reason ...

> Despite my wide literary knowledge, I was no good at my English class, something that rather upset me. My spelling was bad, and handwriting slow and abominable. It hurt to write, because I had to write so quickly to keep up ... I did badly in English and Maths and it was suggested my qualities were incompatible with the next part of the school. I was humiliatingly sent down in the period before lunch to the bottom class to be taught how to write letters properly ...

> Official confirmation that I had dyslexia came in 1990, when I was seven ... When I was still in the pre-prep, I got my parents' Othello cassettes and fully-illustrated text, and set about reading and listening to it simultaneously (a method which was later to serve me in good stead). My parents asked me to talk about the play on tape. They then showed me more new texts and plays which expanded my mind and helped me to see that life cannot just be tackled by attacking

a surface but by digging out the root ... At the beginning of the spring term in 1992, when I was nine, my parents finally let out the secret to me – all the reading of Shakespeare and Donne had had a purpose: I had been doing a GCSE. I felt a sense of achievement unlike anything before.

By this time I had entered the lower school ... My form teacher, who took me for Maths, gave me a 'D' at the end of term, and told me to try harder, for I was using my dyslexia as an excuse for laziness and that it wasn't the problem my parents and I were making it out to be ... My handwriting got worse as I was expected to write at speed. A normally well-meaning and kind science teacher ripped out several pages of my work in front of the entire class because he thought them insufficiently neat. I felt humiliated and dejected ...

I received my GCSE results during the summer. It was a very special day. Taking a GCSE had raised my standard of thinking and helped me put the concerns of my contemporaries in perspective. They would feel great sorrow if they kicked a football the wrong way, but I had learned about the real sorrows of death, love, hate, kindness, greed, treachery, avarice, power and corruption. I could learn more about life from poetry than I could by trying to kick a large spherical object between two posts.

(Faludy, 1998, p.3)

An example of Alexander's handwriting, aged 9, the same year he got his GCSE in English literature

Activity 5.2

Make notes on which difficulties experienced by Alexander were the result of his condition, and which were 'constructed' by having to fit in to 'normal' ways of doing things?

Comment

In some senses dyslexia itself is a 'construction' because it was not identified as a difficulty until there was a societal expectation that everyone should be literate. The difficulties in learning to read and in physical coordination (including writing) experienced by Alexander are genuine problems, but the negative social and emotional consequences of them are not: they result from expectations of the level of performance he should attain and limited tolerance by others to his 'being different'. This is evidenced not just in the bullying, but also in the way that his teachers responded to his work, as they wanted him to conform to the 'normal' set of skills and abilities defined as appropriate to his age and culture. Alexander's success in English using his technique of listening to book tapes and dictating his work suggests that there was limited need for such an emphasis on traditional forms of literacy to demonstrate his competence in the subject.

The comments of Alexander's mathematics teacher illustrate another aspect of having dyslexia: having a label that effectively says 'this person is not normal'. You might like to look back to the earlier discussion of labelling in Chapter 1 of Book 1. People react to labels in different ways, sometimes positively, sometimes negatively. Labels relate to stereotypes and can result in prejudicial attitudes towards the individual concerned. The teacher here suggests such an attitude: the idea that dyslexia is used by parents as an excuse for little more than laziness on the part of their child. It also suggests that the teacher may be sceptical about dyslexia itself. This scepticism persists in some quarters because there has been debate about the nature and causes of dyslexia, whether it differs from general reading difficulties, and how. In this chapter we consider the evidence that dyslexia exists as a distinct syndrome with a biological basis.

What is dyslexia?

Dyslexia involves difficulties in learning to read and write. However, this is not the only form of difficulty that people with dyslexia experience. They usually have particular difficulties with *coding*: learning and retrieving associations between verbal and visual information. The most obvious example is when we have to learn what sounds the letters of the alphabet make, but this difficulty can also affect the speed with which dyslexic people are able to learn and recall the names for objects. Generally, people with dyslexia have difficulty dealing with phonological information (speech sounds) in short-term memory, so any task that requires the processing of verbal information will prove difficult. For this reason mental arithmetic is also often difficult, and mathematics generally can suffer because of the coding that is often necessary when learning mathematical symbols and their functions. Another general area of weakness is the sequencing of information. Poor sequencing can affect the written expression of ideas, or methods of working in mathematics, but it most obviously affects information that is usually learned by rote, such as the months of the year, or multiplication tables. Directional confusions are also common, and people with dyslexia often have difficulty remembering left from right.

Key characteristics of people with dyslexia compared to people without dyslexia

- A delay or deficit in understanding letter-sound correspondences.
- A delay in learning to read.
- Poor spelling.
- Difficulty generating written language.
- Some initial difficulty in recognizing rhyme.
- Poor short-term memory.
- Poor mental arithmetic.
- Difficulty in learning labels (e.g. names for new objects).
- Difficulty naming objects and word finding.
- Difficulty learning sequences (e.g. months of the year, the order of a sequence of tasks).
- Slowness in learning text or verbal information.
- A subtle difference in form and function of some areas of the brain.

Dyslexia is relatively common, with an estimated prevalence of around 5 per cent in its severe form, and as much as 10 per cent if milder cases are included. Prevalence depends on the definition used and there are several different ways in which the identification of dyslexia can be approached. There is a wide variety of terms used to describe specific difficulties in learning to read. The original term 'word blindness' was rejected in the 1960s and replaced by the more familiar term dyslexia, which is preferred by people with dyslexia and their families. However, it is disliked by many psychologists, who believe that it implies a degree of certainty about the existence of a *distinct* syndrome. In fact, there is continued debate about the core symptoms of dyslexia and its potential causes. The terms **specific learning difficulty** or **specific reading difficulty** are preferred because they are more neutral and less suggestive of a distinct and cohesive 'medical' syndrome.

1.4 Defining dyslexia

The ongoing debate about dyslexia is reflected in the different approaches that have been taken to formally defining it. Clearly this impacts on how

Specific learning difficulty
Used to refer to specific difficulties in one area of learning such as reading or mathematics.

Specific reading difficulty
Used to refer to specific difficulties in learning to read, but in no other areas of academic study.

dyslexia is defined in practice. The next three sections summarize how definitions of dyslexia have changed as our knowledge has increased. In short, there have been three main approaches to defining dyslexia: **definition by exclusion**, **discrepancy definitions** and the identification of **positive indicators**.

Definition by exclusion

> *A person is 'dyslexic' if no alternative explanation can be offered for their reading and writing difficulties.*

In the UK, interest in children who showed a specific lack of ability in literacy grew as all children became entitled to a basic education. For the first time there was an expectation that all adults should be literate. Initially, it was proposed that specific difficulties in learning to read and write were visual in nature, and the term **congenital word blindness** was used by James Hinshelwood (a Scottish eye surgeon) to refer to:

> *... a congenital defect occurring in children with otherwise normal and undamaged brains characterized by a difficulty in learning to read so great that it is manifestly due to a pathological condition, and where the attempts to teach the child by ordinary methods have completely failed.*
>
> *(Hinshelwood, 1917, p.40)*

Notice that Hinshelwood identifies the dyslexic population by reference to two norms: the children have normally functioning brains, and that normal methods of teaching result in failure. What this quote reflects is how little was understood about the causes of reading difficulties. This lack of knowledge resulted in dyslexia being defined and diagnosed by exclusion. One example of this is the definition from Critchley:

> *A disorder manifested by difficulty in learning to read despite conventional instruction, adequate intelligence, and sociocultural opportunity. It is dependent upon fundamental cognitive disabilities which are frequently of constitutional origin.*
>
> *(Critchley, 1970, p.11)*

That is, if the children's disability could not be attributed to other potential causes (i.e. the children are apparently 'normal' in key respects), then they were given the label of 'dyslexic' – diagnosis by exclusion.

Diagnosis by exclusion is problematic as it is based on assumptions about what factors might affect one's ability to learn to read. The most problematic exclusionary criterion is that of 'adequate intelligence'. While IQ tends to correlate with reading ability, a low IQ is not a barrier to learning to read. The idea that someone with a low IQ is 'expected' to fail to read is no longer socially acceptable. Dyslexia is not a set of difficulties that can only be experienced by the intelligent. Similarly, the criterion of sociocultural opportunity implies that people from households with few books, or children who are read to less by their parents, either because of financial, cultural or linguistic reasons can also be 'reasonably expected' to fail to learn to read.

You may find that you yourself satisfy one of these criteria. Did you experience difficulties learning to read and write? How reasonable do you believe these criteria to be? Think also about what they say about our expectations of children from diverse social and cultural backgrounds, in terms of standards that are being set concerning the conditions necessary for 'normal' development?

More fundamentally, definition by exclusion is unsatisfactory on logical grounds. If dyslexia represents a particular 'abnormal' pattern of development with a biological basis, then there is no reason why it could not coincide with other factors that may also be disadvantageous to the development of literacy skills. Dyslexia can in fact be found across the whole range of intelligence, although it may be more easily recognized in a child who otherwise appears to be highly talented, and it occurs at fairly similar rates in all countries and cultures where universal literacy is demanded. Social, economic, cultural and personal factors can certainly influence the rate and extent of someone's development in literacy skills, as we shall discuss later. However, these factors may also be quite independent of the predisposition to dyslexia. The fact that they have often been used to 'explain away' reading failure amongst children whose background does not conform to desired standards may account for why dyslexia has been mocked as a 'middle-class disease'.

Discrepancy definitions

> *The label is given if there is a discrepancy between perceived potential to learn to read (as indicated by general ability) and actual level of reading achievement.*

The most common way of diagnosing dyslexia is to look for a discrepancy between someone's general ability as measured by an IQ assessment and his or her performance on standardized measures of reading and spelling. However, there are many variations in the procedures for measuring a discrepancy between potential and actual reading ability, and the precise boundaries that may be chosen as 'cut-offs' will also vary depending on the purposes of the measurement. Different criteria may be used, for example, in research studies (where strict statistical boundaries may be needed for scientific reasons) than in educational or other settings (where diagnoses may be used to guide more personal and/or practical decisions).

Notice that this approach to defining dyslexia reflects a psychometric perspective. To remind yourself of the details of this perspective look at Chapter 5 in Book 1.

Discrepancy based definition and diagnosis of dyslexia assumes that an IQ assessment indicates a person's potential for learning to read. However, IQ is only weakly related to reading achievement, and assessment will involve some 'measurement error', so any predictions of 'expected' reading achievement will be insensitive at best. Keith Stanovich (1991) has argued for a different approach to discrepancy based diagnosis of dyslexia, where reading ability is compared to *listening comprehension* rather than IQ. Despite the academic support for such an approach, IQ based assessment remains the 'gold standard' method for identifying dyslexia, but educational psychologists do not simply look for a discrepancy in scores. Instead they examine a person's performance on each IQ subtest as well as overall performance. This information is combined with evidence from other sources, such as the person's case history, before dyslexia is identified.

An overall discrepancy between IQ and reading ability will identify a broad range of people with *specific reading difficulties*, but depending on the population studied, reading problems will in some cases arise entirely from social, emotional or cultural influences. This means that specific reading difficulties are not to be equated with dyslexia, as this term refers to a broader developmental syndrome proposed to have a (biological) basis.

If you recall Section 1.2, you will recognize that discrepancy definitions reflect the statistical approach to defining 'abnormality'. As we saw then, other criteria are usually required for any meaningful definition of 'abnormal' functioning – and the methods used for assessment, their reliability and their validity are crucial issues.

If someone's reading improves through special help and there is no longer a discrepancy, would that make him or her less dyslexic? If we accept that dyslexia has a biological basis which impacts on skills other than literacy, then even if the reading difficulties 'go away' the underlying cause of the dyslexia and other associated symptoms may remain.

Positive indicators

Dyslexia is recognized if the person shows various core behavioural symptoms or other features associated with dyslexia.

As mentioned in the previous section, contemporary approaches also involve identifying positive indicators that signal potential dyslexia by their presence. Dyslexia involves specific weaknesses in areas that relate to written language, but because it is not associated with a general lack of ability it also often involves compensatory strengths. For example, Alexander Faludy was verbally gifted from a young age (see Box 5.1). For this reason, in addition to assessing the discrepancy between ability and written language skills, psychologists usually take particular note of the profile of strengths and weaknesses on cognitive tests. Discrepancies between verbal and non-verbal IQ may be significant. People with dyslexia often show lower verbal than non-verbal ability, but the reverse pattern is also found, illustrating the variability within dyslexia. Particular profiles on the sub-tests of IQ assessments have been suggested as characteristic of dyslexia. One such profile emphasizes deficits on Arithmetic, Coding, Information (general knowledge) and Digit Span (short-term memory capacity) sub-tests. This is called the **ACID profile** (Thomson and Grant, 1979). However, not all children diagnosed show deficits in all these areas. Bannatyne (1971) advocated grouping the sub-tests according to the kinds of abilities they tap. Studies using this procedure suggest that dyslexic people typically show a profile of above average *spatial* and *conceptual abilities*, and below average *sequential abilities* and *acquired knowledge*. However, none of these procedures results in clear diagnosis, again emphasizing the variation within any dyslexic population.

Behaviours that are indicative of dyslexia include a mixture of weaknesses and strengths, with some factors related to reading and writing, and others apparently unrelated. For example, among his list of positive indicators, Tim Miles (1983) cites directional confusions, poor auditory sequential memory, problems with word repetition and other members of the family with reading or writing problems. Screening for dyslexia usually includes assessments of a wide range of skills, such as visual and auditory perception, integration of different types of sensory information, and aspects of motor function such as balance. If dyslexia really is a neurodevelopmental syndrome, it is highly implausible that this would *only* affect written language skills, and the evidence does implicate a broader range of abilities. Kinsbourne *et al.* (1991) assessed dyslexic and non-dyslexic adults on a wide range of neuropsychological tests. They found many differences on tasks bearing no apparent relation to reading, such as rapid alternating movements of the hands or feet, and judging which came first of two simple auditory or visual stimuli presented in quick succession.

Miles (1983) has argued that dyslexia should not be seen as a form of reading disability but as a **syndrome**: a set of symptoms with a neurological basis.

ACID profile
Refers to the observed deficit in arithmetic, coding, information (general knowledge) and digit span (short-term memory) that is associated with dyslexia by some researchers.

Syndrome
A combination of symptoms which regularly occur together and may have a shared neurological basis.

Although each of these individual 'signs' (such as problems telling left from right) may also be found in some people with a 'normal' reading ability, the presence of more than a certain number of these indicators would suggest a dyslexic profile. When used together with standardized measures of reading and spelling, these kinds of screening measures can provide useful information to guide both research and educational practice.

Simple examples of assessments that focus on positive indicators rather than discrepancies are the checklists often used for initial screening before a formal dyslexia assessment takes place. Table 5.1 shows the one used by the British Dyslexia Association.

Table 5.1   **British Dyslexia Association – adult dyslexia checklist (1994)**

		YES	NO
1	Do you find difficulty telling left from right?		
2	Is map reading or finding your way to a strange place confusing?		
3	Do you dislike reading aloud?		
4	Do you take longer than you should to read a page of a book?		
5	Do you find it difficult to remember the sense of what you have read?		
6	Do you dislike reading long books?		
7	Is your spelling poor?		
8	Is your writing difficult to read?		
9	Do you get confused if you have to speak in public?		
10	Do you find it difficult to take messages on the telephone and pass them on correctly?		
11	When you have to say a long word, do you sometimes find it difficult to get all the sounds in the right order?		
12	Do you find it difficult to do sums in your head without using your fingers or paper?		
13	When using the telephone, do you tend to get the numbers mixed up when you dial?		
14	Do you find it difficult to say the months of the year forwards in a fluent manner?		
15	Do you find it difficult to say the months of the year backwards?		
16	Do you mix up dates and times and miss appointments?		
17	When writing cheques do you frequently find yourself making mistakes?		
18	Do you find forms difficult and confusing?		
19	Do you mix up bus numbers like 95 and 59?		
20	Did you find it hard to learn your multiplication tables at school?		

Nine or more 'yes' responses on the questionnaire could be indicative of dyslexia-type difficulties.

Source: Vinegrad, 1994

You may answer yes to several of these questions, but not have dyslexia. This is why they are termed 'indicators' and are only used for screening purposes. They cannot 'diagnose' dyslexia on their own, and must be used in conjunction with background information and a psychometric assessment.

The need for a balance between identifying dyslexia by a discrepancy between potential and actual achievement, and by the presence of clear symptoms is reflected in a more recent definition from the Orton Dyslexia Society, now known as the International Dyslexia Association:

> *It is a specific language-based disorder of constitutional origin characterized by difficulties in single word coding, usually reflecting insufficient phonological processing abilities. These difficulties in single word coding are often unexpected in relation to age and other cognitive and academic abilities; they are not the result of generalized developmental disability or sensory impairment. Dyslexia is manifested by variable difficulty with different forms of language, often including, in addition to problems of reading, a conspicuous problem with acquiring proficiency in writing and spelling.*
>
> *(Miles and Miles, 1999, p.169)*

1.5 Dyslexia as a distinctive condition

Differentiating dyslexia from other reading difficulties

The idea that dyslexia is distinctive from other forms of reading difficulty is still debated. One viewpoint is that reading ability is a simple continuum, with exceptionally gifted readers at one end and people with dyslexia at the other. However, as we have already seen, dyslexia involves more than just difficulties in reading and writing. Reading difficulties must be specific and accompanied by a variable profile of cognitive abilities. It is the presence of other characteristics unrelated to reading that makes dyslexia distinctive.

Activity 5.3

If dyslexia were simply part of a continuum (i.e. it was dimensional), can you suggest how we might go about identifying people with dyslexia?

Comment

Section 1.2 mentioned that conditions that are part of a normally distributed continuum lend themselves to identification by statistical means, perhaps using the standard deviation as a boundary between 'normal' and 'dyslexic' readers.

Differentiating within dyslexia - acquired versus developmental dyslexia and the search for subtypes

There has also been continued debate regarding the variability *within* any dyslexic population, the apparent variety of forms that dyslexia can take. Given the complexity of the skills required to develop fluent reading and spelling perhaps this is not surprising. The variability within dyslexia may simply reflect the fact that this complex process can go wrong in different ways and for different reasons.

Acquired dyslexia
A form of dyslexia which is acquired as the result of neurological damage.

The term 'dyslexia' was originally used to refer to the **acquired dyslexias** – specific disorders of reading or writing that can follow from brain injury in adults. The study of people with such acquired difficulties has provided invaluable insights into how written language may be processed in the brain (recall the discussion of 'double dissociation' in Chapter 8 of Book 1). These people often suffer selective impairments, where some abilities are lost while others are preserved. For example, people with acquired *phonological dyslexia* may have no problem reading familiar words by sight, but they can no longer 'sound out' unfamiliar words, or find a pronunciation for nonsense words like 'flad'. Conversely, some people with *surface dyslexia* may have no trouble with regularly spelt words such as 'bat' or pronounceable nonsense words such as 'pux', but they seem to have lost the ability to recognize words purely by sight (i.e. without decoding each letter). They tend to misread even familiar words like 'pint' – which they would pronounce to rhyme with 'flint'. Even more bizarre are the errors made by people with *deep dyslexia*, who may misread 'lion' as 'tiger', or 'symphony' as 'orchestra'. They seem to have difficulties with both the visual and phonological components of reading, and yet their errors suggest that they still have some access to the meaning of words they cannot read.

The different patterns of impairment found in the acquired dyslexias indicate that skilled reading requires the interplay of many sub-processes. It is therefore not surprising that the search for subtypes in developmental dyslexia has been modelled on the different kinds of acquired dyslexia. However, there are good reasons why comparisons between acquired and developmental reading disorders may not be appropriate. For example, there is evidence that the development of literacy skills is not an additive process (where the earliest skills are extended and elaborated upon in later stages), but may involve substitution, with later stages or processes replacing earlier ones (Morton, 1989). If so, the development of reading and writing skills may be more akin to a metamorphosis, such that the mature written language processing system bears little relation to its early components. There are likely to be important differences between a system that developed 'normally' but was then damaged, and one where the process of development itself was abnormal.

The search for subtypes within developmental dyslexia has engendered much research, but no clear and consistent subgroups have stood the test of time and experimental investigation. The most frequent distinction has been between auditory problems (i.e. difficulties in identifying and manipulating letter sounds within words) and visual problems (difficulties in visually recognizing and remembering words). These categories broadly resemble the phonological and surface forms of acquired dyslexia. However, many people with developmental dyslexia show both types of impairment. It has even been suggested that both kinds of difficulties have a common basis, as we shall see later. The truth is that no simple picture emerges from attempts to define subgroups, and it may be more appropriate to think about several distinct but overlapping components to dyslexic type difficulties. We shall return to the issue of subtypes in Section 2.

Differentiating dyslexia from other developmental conditions

While dyslexia is distinctive, there are other developmental syndromes that often co-occur with it. Examples include:

- developmental dysphasia – specific difficulties with spoken language
- attention deficit/hyperactivity disorder – involving particular problems with concentration and/or behaviour
- developmental dyspraxia – developmental coordination disorder.

Developmental dysphasia

Developmental dysphasia involves primary problems in the development of speech and language skills. Despite abilities in other areas, some children are slow to achieve the usual milestones in the development of spoken language, such as uttering their first words, putting together meaningful sentences, and/or understanding complex verbal instructions. It is perhaps unsurprising that these children can go on to show specific difficulties in acquiring the ability to write language.

Attention deficit/hyperactivity disorder (ADHD)

This refers to persistent and age inappropriate difficulties in regulating attention and/or behaviour. This diagnosis remains somewhat controversial, but it involves specific difficulties in either or both of two distinct dimensions:

- *inattention* – difficulties maintaining concentration on the task in hand, high distractibility, working memory problems and tendencies to daydream
- *hyperactivity-impulsivity* – excessive motor restlessness, and apparent difficulties in the inhibition of impulse, leading to inappropriate and often reckless behaviour.

Children may be diagnosed with ADHD if they show either or both of these kinds of problems, so there is considerable variability within such populations.

The overlap between dyslexia and ADHD is high (between 30 to 50 per cent in both directions), but it appears to be stronger for attentional problems than it is for the purely hyperactive-impulsive form of ADHD.

Developmental dyspraxia

This broadly refers to specific difficulties in motor coordination (corresponding to the diagnosis used in the US of 'developmental coordination disorder') but the term strictly refers to problems in the planning and execution of any complex, sequenced actions (including speech and writing). Dyspraxic children typically have difficulties in learning to do up buttons or tie their shoelaces, in balance and ball skills, and in copying and handwriting. Mothers often report that as babies they never went through the crawling stage, but simply got up and walked. At play or sports they appear 'clumsy', and they often show specific weaknesses in visual-perceptual skills and visual-motor coordination (relative to their other abilities) as well as marked attentional and organizational problems. The dyspraxia syndrome remains less widely recognized than dyslexia, but the overlap between the two appears to be very high, as around 50 per cent of dyspraxic children typically show dyslexic difficulties, and vice-versa.

In summary, there is considerable overlap between dyslexia and other abnormal developmental conditions such as dysphasia, ADHD and dyspraxia, although each syndrome can also occur in isolation. As well as their frequent co-occurrence in the same individual, these conditions also tend to associate within families, suggesting that there may be some common predisposing factors. We will return to this issue in Section 2.

Activity 5.4

Reread the case study of Alexander Faludy presented in Box 5.1. As well as dyslexia, does his account suggest features of any of the other conditions discussed here?

1.6 Reflecting on definitions of 'abnormality'

The main thing to remember is that the way that 'abnormality' is defined will have consequences for the method of identification. It will also impact on people's expectations of their future development. For example, we discussed the way that dyslexia is defined in relation to a person's IQ. Does that mean that if someone has a low IQ and an even lower reading age we should adjust our expectations of what that person can achieve with help, or let IQ influence how much help is offered? Similarly, if positive indicators suggest that the problem is neurologically based, do we assume that it cannot be overcome? Moreover, do the individuals themselves believe that they cannot overcome their difficulties? Definitions can be powerful influences on people's beliefs and expectations.

Finally, it is worth reflecting on what dyslexia has told us about the way we think of people who experience disability. It is easy to assume that everyone with a particular difficulty will have highly similar characteristics but in practice these groups are much more heterogeneous than you might first expect. Again, this often reflects the difficulties associated with identifying the precise nature of a psychological difficulty and differentiating it from other types of problems. More fundamentally, individuals differ in all kinds of ways, and the key issue is that deviation from the 'norm' is not always 'abnormal' in the sense of pathological. The same characteristics that are disadvantageous in one situation can be advantageous in others. It may also be, as we saw in the sub-section on positive indicators (see Section 1.4), that lesser ability in some skills may go hand-in-hand with greater ability in others.

Meanwhile, there is increasing recognition that people should not be defined or characterized by the difficulties they experience, but rather understood as people who have been affected by them. This is why you will notice that psychological texts increasingly talk about '*people with dyslexia*', rather than '*dyslexics*', '*people with autism*' rather than '*autistics*' and so on. It shows that we realise that people do not conform to some kind of stereotype just because they experience difficulties in certain areas, and helps us to remember that they are all individuals first and foremost. However, even this terminology suggests that dyslexia and autism are clear 'entities' that people do or do not have (and they also sound like medical labels, to which many people still object). In fact, all the evidence suggests that labels such as dyslexia and autism are just that – labels. They are useful descriptions of collections of characteristics that can affect different people in different patterns to different degrees. To capture this dimensionality, it would probably be more accurate to identify people as slightly, very or not at all dyslexic (or whatever condition is under consideration), and include plenty of additional information about the precise pattern of strengths and weakness that they show in relevant situations.

By now you might realise that during our discussion of dyslexia the different approaches discussed in Section 1.2 have been reflected in the way that dyslexia has been defined. For example, discrepancy definitions of dyslexia are based on a statistical definition of 'normality'. Definition by exclusion, in emphasizing the biological basis of dyslexia, is subscribing to a medical definition of normality, as does the notion of 'positive indicators'. Finally, the identification of dyslexia as a 'problem' in itself is the result of cultural expectations of literacy being part of an adult's 'normal' repertoire of skills.

Summary   Section 1

- 'Normality' and therefore 'abnormality' may be defined in a variety of ways: in relation to statistical frequency, perceived disability, cultural expectations or personal distress. No single definition is appropriate for all purposes.
- Dyslexia is a label used to describe a condition involving, but not confined to, specific difficulties in learning to read and write. The term 'dyslexia' has been used by approaches which propose that there is a (constitutional) biological basis to those difficulties.
- Definitions of dyslexia were originally based on exclusion criteria, but are now based on the discrepancy between potential and actual literacy ability. Modern assessments also identify positive indicators of the presence of dyslexia.
- As a result of the heterogeneous nature of people with dyslexia, there have been attempts to classify different combinations of symptoms into discrete subtypes of dyslexia. These attempts have been unsuccessful because people often show the characteristics of more than one subtype.
- Dyslexia is known to co-occur with other developmental conditions.

2   Explanations of dyslexia

So far we have discussed what contributes to our ideas of 'abnormality' and these issues have been illustrated by examining the real life example of dyslexia.

We will now consider the different potential explanations that have been offered to account for the observed symptoms of dyslexia.

Uta Frith (1999) has provided a useful framework for thinking about the nature of developmental difficulties (see Figure 5.2).

Frith suggests that there are three main perspectives on any given developmental condition: a behavioural, cognitive and biological one. In addition to this there are

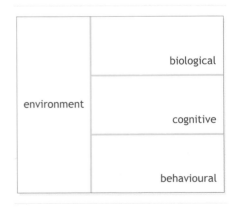

Figure 5.2   Frith's three level framework (Source: Frith, 1999, p.193)

environmental factors (literally referring to the environments, biological or otherwise, that we are exposed to) that can have a role in the accounts offered from these perspectives.

- *Behavioural perspectives* provide a model of the difficulty by describing the nature of the behavioural symptoms experienced, much as we have done in Section 1 of this chapter.
- *Cognitive perspectives* describe what mental processes are involved in and affected by the difficulty (e.g. memory, perception, attention). As such, these descriptions offer a cognitive 'explanation' of what may cause the types of behavioural symptoms observed.
- *Biological perspectives* offer descriptions of the behavioural difficulties in terms of their potential biological origins, which can cover genetic, biochemical and neurophysiological explanations.

Thus, biological and cognitive perspectives offer theoretical explanations that require experimental validation, whereas behavioural perspectives tend to be less debated because the behaviours can be directly observed. Cognitive perspectives describe cognitive processes that might explain how the biological and behavioural accounts map onto each other. For example, damage to one area of the brain (*biological perspective*) may result in an inability to store new long-term memories (*behavioural perspective*), because the person is no longer able to transfer information from short-term to long-term storage (*cognitive perspective*).

The chapters of this book have explored in different contexts the extent to which perspectives in psychology can be seen as complementary, conflicting and co-existing. Frith's framework echoes the same ideas and suggests that when discussing explanations of 'abnormal' development it is wrong to think that biological and cognitive perspectives are competing with each other. In fact, cognitive and biological models can be complementary rather than conflicting.

We can use this framework to think about theoretical explanations of dyslexia. As we have already provided a behavioural account of dyslexia in Section 1, we will now consider cognitive and biological explanations of what may cause these behaviours and acknowledge environmental influences on their development. After examining each explanation individually we suggest how different perspectives can be put together to offer a complete account.

2.1 Cognitive explanations of dyslexia

The phonological processing deficit

Recall Alexander Faludy's difficulties in learning to read and write, and the other behavioural characteristics associated with having dyslexia. You might have noticed that many features of dyslexia point to a difficulty with some aspects of memory. That is, people with dyslexia have difficulty with tasks that require short-term memory processing such as mental arithmetic, writing and learning new information. However, these tasks have an additional feature in common: they contain a phonological component. That is, they involve the processing of speech sounds in short-term memory. It is therefore possible to suggest that a deficit in phonological processing may provide an explanation of dyslexia. To understand why a phonological deficit would impact on reading and writing we need to understand how people typically learn to read (see Box 5.2).

5.2 Learning to read (after Frith 1985)

Logographic strategy
A holistic approach to identifying written words via their overall visual appearance, sometimes also referred to as 'sight word reading'.

Alphabetic decoding strategy
An analytical approach to identifying written words by translating letters and letter-strings ('graphemes') into the sounds that they represent ('phonemes').

Orthographic strategy
The approach skilled readers use to identify written words, employing both alphabetic and logographic strategies a well as their existing knowledge of grammatical forms and similar words.

It has been suggested that initially we adopt two strategies. One strategy, widely suggested to be the first to develop in beginning readers, is the whole word, or **logographic strategy**. This refers to the way children learn to associate a spoken word with its written form, without showing any awareness of the sounds that each of the individual letters make. This strategy is often encouraged in early years classrooms where objects are labelled with their names and teachers use 'flashcards' to teach children a core 'sight vocabulary' of common words. This technique is useful in enabling children to build a large sight vocabulary quickly, which will enable them to begin reading with some degree of fluency. However, this approach places huge demands on visual memory and does not provide children with a strategy for coping with unfamiliar words.

To address these limitations, children also need an **alphabetic decoding strategy**. This requires them to learn the sounds that each letter of the alphabet makes, and then learn how to blend those sounds together during reading to work out how to pronounce the word. Alphabetic decoding is also needed during spelling to analyse spoken words and break them down into their corresponding letter sounds.

A skilled reader is one who moves beyond letter by letter decoding and rapidly processes longer 'strings' of letters that recur across different words (an **orthographic strategy**).

Did you notice how these strategies reflect what we know about reading processes from the acquired dyslexias?

The alphabetic decoding strategy draws heavily on phonological processing – both in the learning of **letter-sound correspondences**, and in the manipulation of those sounds during reading and spelling. People with dyslexia often find it difficult to move beyond a logographic strategy and problems with spelling usually persist into adulthood.

Letter-sound correspondences
The associations between individual letters, and the sounds that those letters can make in a given language.

The severity of the phonological deficit is best demonstrated by the awareness of rhyme by children with dyslexia. Recognizing that two words rhyme is a skill that most children acquire at an early age. However, studies have repeatedly shown that children with reading difficulties have trouble identifying words that rhyme (e.g. Bradley and Bryant, 1978). This is just one finding from a large literature showing that children with reading difficulties find it difficult to isolate and manipulate sounds in words.

What is still not clear is whether the phonological deficit is related to the *encoding* or *retrieval* (see Book 1, Chapter 8) of phonological representations in memory. While there is evidence of difficulties in processing phonological information in short-term memory, there is also speculation that the way this information is represented and stored in long-term memory could further explain the poor performance of people with dyslexia on phonological tasks.

Much of the research into phonological awareness and reading disability has centred on English speaking children. However, this presents a misleading picture, as letter-sound correspondences in English are complex. Often, the same sound can be spelt a number of different ways (e.g. /f/ can be spelt f and ph), and the same letter can make a variety of different sounds (consider the sound that 'a' makes in 'bat', 'part' and 'apron'). Furthermore, it is not a simple case of one letter per sound: mouse has five letters but only three sounds: /m/ / au/ /s/. The phonological awareness deficit that has been demonstrated with English speakers may not be a universal characteristic of reading disability, as many other European languages have much more predictable letter-sound correspondences. Research into phonological deficits in other languages is ongoing, but there does seem to be evidence of phonological deficits in people with dyslexia (and at risk of dyslexia) who learn to read in more regular languages (see Courcy, Béland and Pitchford, 2000; Müller, Saarenketo and Lyytinen, 2000). It has also been suggested that measuring the speed *of performance on tests may be a more universal indicator of reading difficulties across languages.*

Almost *all* types of reading difficulty appear to be characterized by a phonological processing deficit, not just dyslexia. However, this does not mean that because it appears to have the same underlying cognitive deficit as other reading difficulties, dyslexia is the same as other types of reading difficulty. While the phonological processing deficit may 'explain' the *reading and writing difficulties* associated with dyslexia, it cannot account for the full range of behavioural symptoms that are observed, and that make dyslexia a distinctive condition. Other cognitive accounts are needed to explain the origins of the other behavioural symptoms of dyslexia. We have already proposed in the previous section that dyslexia can be thought of as consisting of several overlapping dimensions – it seems likely that a phonological deficit may be just one of several cognitive components associated with the condition. Moreover the phonological deficit hypothesis is exactly that, a *hypothesis*. While it has a good deal of empirical support, it is a theoretical proposal – but not something that we know definitely exists.

'Visual deficit' hypotheses

Samuel Orton was one of the earliest and most influential researchers into dyslexia, although he used the term **strephosymbolia** – literally meaning 'twisted symbols'. He noticed that children with specific reading difficulties often wrote letters back to front, confused letters such as 'b' and 'd', and would swap the position of letters within a word during spelling (e.g. 'was' might be written 'saw'). From these and other observations, he suggested that their reading difficulties might reflect some kind of visual processing impairment involving incomplete specialization between the left and right sides of the brain. You may recall from Chapter 4 in Book 1 that the left hemisphere of the brain is specialized for processing language.

As we saw in Section 1.4, the original observations by Hinshelwood about what he called congenital word blindness also emphasized a visual-perceptual contribution. Much early research was therefore focused on trying to identify perceptual factors that could contribute to dyslexia. Visual deficit explanations fell out of favour during the 1970s and 1980s when psychologists increasingly adopted a phonological deficit model of dyslexia, arguing that reading difficulties reflect primary problems with language processing. While the phonological deficit explanation is still popular and widely researched, there has been a resurgence of interest in the idea that there may be an underlying visual deficit that could explain difficulties in learning visual-phonological correspondences (see Everatt, 1999; Whiteley and Smith, 2001).

More recently, the evidence for visual-sensory processing deficits in dyslexia has become robust. The challenge now is to determine whether these visual-perceptual problems affect the development of visual processing required for

Strephosymbolia
The term coined by Orton to describe dyslexic-like symptoms (literally – 'twisted symbols').

fluent and skilled reading, and if so how. Seymour (1986) has re-emphasized the obvious point that the cognitive systems specifically required for *written* language (as opposed to spoken language) are actually in the visual domain. He and others have shown that the reading performance of many dyslexic people reflects weaknesses in visual processing that can occur independently of phonological difficulties.

It has been claimed that phonological deficits are more common than visual deficits in dyslexia, and the fact that many dyslexic people show superior visual-spatial abilities is cited as supporting evidence. The trouble with this argument is that the psychological tests used to assess visuo-spatial abilities do not actually measure the same kinds of visual processing that Seymour refers to, which is more perceptual in nature. In fact, mild visual disturbances are consistently found in up to 70 per cent of people with dyslexia, and more importantly, these typically co-occur with phonological problems (Lovegrove, 1991). It has even been suggested that both types of problem might have a common cause.

As we have already seen, it is misleading to think either that visual-perceptual and phonological problems must be mutually exclusive, or that all people with specific reading difficulties are the same. What is more, variation in the 'clinical' picture of dyslexia (at either the behavioural or the cognitive level of Frith's model) does not in fact rule out some common underlying 'cause' at the biological level. The complex interactions between biology and environment mean that the same biological 'problem' can result in different cognitive and behavioural consequences for different people.

'Automaticity' and 'rate of processing' hypotheses

A proposal that attempts to address the broader picture of dyslexic functioning is that dyslexia may be caused by problems in the **automatization** of skills. The concept of automatization refers to the gradual reduction in the need for *conscious* control as a new skill is learned. This leads to greater speed and efficiency and a decreased likelihood of breakdown of performance under stress, as well as the ability to perform a second task at the same time with minimal disruption to either behaviour. Nicolson and Fawcett (1990, 1994) have pointed out that even highly competent dyslexic readers show a distinct lack of fluency in written language skills: their reading and writing is more laboured, more prone to error, and more susceptible to interference from other tasks. They also suggest that 'incomplete mastery' characterizes many other features of dyslexic performance, such as problems learning to ride a bicycle or tie shoelaces. However, a general 'automatization deficit' would be most evident during complex, highly demanding, multi-sensory tasks such as learning to read and write.

Automatization
The process of making a skill 'automatic', so that performance no longer needs conscious monitoring. (If fully automatized, a task can be carried out with no interference to another task being performed simultaneously.)

One way of assessing the presence of an automaticity deficit is through the use of a **rapid automatized naming task** (RAN). For example, individuals may be presented with a set of fifty stimuli consisting of five rows of 10 pictures of a given type in a random order and asked to name each picture as quickly as possible (see Figure 5.3). People with dyslexia typically show a deficit in speed on this type of task.

Figure 5.3   An example of a RAN task for pictures

These results have been interpreted as further support for a phonological deficit in reading, as the task does require some phonological processing during the retrieval of the picture names. However, more recently Wolf and Bowers (1999) have suggested that difficulties in rapid naming are a separate, additional deficit to phonological difficulties, and that such a deficit is sufficient to explain reading difficulties even if the person has good phonological awareness. They suggest that people with reading difficulties fall into one of three subtypes, depending on the underlying cause of their problem:

- phonology group: shows a phonological deficit, but no real problems on the RAN task
- (slow naming) rate group: shows a RAN task time deficit, but no phonological problems
- double deficit group: shows signs of a deficit in both phonology and naming rate and therefore has the greatest reading difficulties.

Because the most common form of treatment recommended for reading difficulties in children focuses on improving phonological awareness, evidence for different forms of cognitive deficit in dyslexia is important. If visual processing deficits do play an important role, or if there are rate and double deficit subtypes as described above, then training in phonological awareness alone would be unlikely to address all reading difficulties.

However, it is always important to look carefully at the nature of tests used to diagnose reading difficulties. RAN tasks come in two forms: **serial presentation** where the person is timed from start to finish, and **discrete presentation** where the symbols are presented one at a time and a reaction time for each item is recorded. Only serial presentation procedures are consistently associated with reading difficulties. This may be because serial tasks usually require more sustained concentration in comparison to discrete presentation tasks (where there is no need to follow a line of text or keep one's place in the grid of symbols). In other words, the apparent difference between 'normal' and dyslexic readers on tasks of this kind could be due to perceptual, attentional or fatigue effects rather than differences in RAN ability. This would undermine the case for a separate 'RAN deficit'. However, it also raises a different, interesting question: why should dyslexic people be particularly susceptible to these kinds of effects? It would certainly be difficult to explain this fully in terms of a pure 'phonological deficit' hypothesis.

We can see how the cognitive accounts 'explain' many of the behavioural symptoms of dyslexia. However, even when taken together, they cannot explain dyslexia fully, nor its variability between individuals. As Frith suggests, cognitive accounts taken in isolation are incomplete: we also need to consider biological explanations.

Serial presentation
The presentation of test items one after the other in the form of a list (or grid) that the participant has to work through in a systematic fashion.

Discrete presentation
The presentation of test items one at a time. None of the other test stimuli are visible at the same time.

2.2 Biological explanations of dyslexia

Some physical characteristics appear to be 'typical' of people with reading difficulties, although their relevance is debated. These include being male, tendencies towards left-handedness or mixed-handedness (i.e. *inconsistency* of hand preference across different tasks), and a variety of neurological **'soft' signs** and minor physical anomalies. We will consider each of these in detail in the sections that follow. There is also some evidence that people with dyslexia (and their relatives) may show higher rates of allergic conditions such as asthma and eczema as well as other autoimmune disorders. On the surface these factors may appear to have little to do with dyslexia. However, by relating these physical characteristics to the observed behavioural symptoms of dyslexia we may identify clues to the possible biological mechanisms underlying the condition.

'Soft' sign
Any behaviour or response that may be linked to an underlying cause (like brain damage) but which is difficult to establish or open to interpretation.

Sex differences

Referral bias
Any influence on the
composition of a study
sample that arises from
the particular method or
source by which
participants are recruited.

An intriguing aspect of dyslexia is the apparent excess of males who are affected. This could simply reflect **referral bias** – a tendency for boys to be *identified* as dyslexic more readily than girls. In the past, society's expectations of boys and girls were very different with respect to educational achievement. There is now much less overt stereotyping of this kind, but there may still be other reasons why dyslexia might be more readily identified in boys. For example, evidence suggests that in mixed-sex classes, boys often dominate classroom interactions. This might bring their general ability to the attention of teachers, who could fail to notice the abilities of some quieter girls whose reading attainment is equally discrepant. Another possibility is that boys and girls may respond differently to the experience of reading failure, with boys perhaps more likely to 'externalize' their frustrations over their reading difficulties than girls. Even awareness that dyslexia is more common in boys could serve to influence the expectations of parents, teachers and others, thereby creating something of a 'self-fulfilling prophecy'.

Nevertheless, the evidence does suggest that as many as three or four males may be affected for every female (James, 1992). This apparent sex difference still awaits adequate explanation, especially given evidence from a recent twin study that found no gender difference in heritability of reading difficulties (Wadsworth *et al.*, 2000). In some respects, the excess of males with dyslexia appears to be an exaggeration of the usual slight advantage that females, on average, tend to show for language-related skills. You may recall from Chapter 3 that boys appear to show greater visual-spatial awareness than girls do, and you may wonder why these skills do not offer any advantage for processing written language. However, as we have already observed, visual-*spatial* awareness does not prohibit the development of visual-*perceptual* difficulties that are associated with dyslexia. Males are over-represented to varying degrees across a whole range of developmental disorders. These include not only dyslexia, but also dysphasia, dyspraxia, ADHD and the autistic spectrum of disorders. What is more, all of these conditions tend to run in families, suggesting that they might share at least some common elements at the level of biological predisposition.

Why are boys more vulnerable to some conditions?

In some conditions that affect more males than females (such as colour-blindness), the explanation has been found to lie in genes on the X chromosome. Most females have two X chromosomes (one inherited from each parent) while most males have an XY combination. This means that if someone should inherit an X-linked gene predisposing to a particular condition, compensation for this will be easier for a female (whose other X chromosome may have a 'normal' copy of the gene) than for a male. However, as yet no X-linked genes have been identified in connection with dyslexia, dyspraxia, ADHD or autism. As we shall see later, a combination of many different genes is probably involved in the predisposition to these conditions, and environmental factors are also crucial, because genes alone do not dictate outcome. What the evidence from family studies does suggest is that females may need a higher 'genetic loading' (i.e. a stronger 'family history') than males for these conditions to be 'expressed'. Some protective factors therefore seem to be operating in females, but we do not yet know what these are.

Lateralization

It has long been suspected that unusual patterns of **cerebral lateralization** (i.e. the 'division of labour' between left and right hemispheres of the brain) may have some connection with dyslexia. Early researchers noticed an apparent excess of left-handedness in children with specific reading difficulties (and their relatives). However, most dyslexic people are in fact right-handed, and most left-handed people are not dyslexic. Nonetheless, large-scale analyses of the research findings have shown that mixed-handedness is more common than usual in dyslexic people (Eglington and Annett, 1994). You will recall how Alexander Faludy used his left and right hands interchangeably. Although the relationship between handedness and other aspects of cerebral lateralization is far from clear-cut, these findings are consistent with Orton's original proposal that dyslexia may involve a relative lack of specialization between the hemispheres.

Neuroanatomical studies, in which brain structure is studied either from post-mortem samples or via brain imaging techniques such as magnetic resonance imaging (MRI) in live participants, also provide some support for this view. The typical human brain has a number of well-known structural asymmetries, which

> **Cerebral lateralization**
> Refers to the asymmetries found in many brain structures and functions, and/or the developmental processes by which these differences between the left and right sides of the brain usually emerge.

Figure 5.4   A cross section of a 'normal' brain showing asymmetry of the planum temporale region across hemispheres (Source: adapted from Kalat, 2001, Figure 14.8, p.402)

are more often reduced or reversed in dyslexic people (Hynd and Semrud-Clikeman, 1989). In particular, brains of people with dyslexia often show an unusual symmetry across hemispheres of a region called the *planum temporale* (see Figure 5.4), which is typically larger in the left hemisphere. This finding has attracted considerable attention, because this area is involved in auditory and language processing. This planum symmetry appears to distinguish dyslexic from ADHD children (Hynd *et al.*, 1990) and there is some evidence that it may relate to poor phonological skills (Larsen *et al.*, 1990).

So could this reduced brain lateralization be a 'biological marker' for dyslexia? And could it be considered 'abnormal' in the 'medical' sense that we discussed in Section 1? It would seem not. Firstly, general population studies have shown that this 'abnormal' pattern of planum temporale symmetry is shared by up to one person in every four (Galaburda *et al.*, 1987). This means that it cannot be a feature that is *specific* to dyslexia (but it could perhaps be one 'risk factor' among others). Secondly, the degree of planum temporale asymmetry in the general population is normally distributed on a continuum. If you recall our discussion in Section 1 about defining 'abnormality', you will remember that for dimensional traits, any cut-off chosen to distinguish 'normal' and 'abnormal' is essentially arbitrary. Another interesting point is that the 'normal' asymmetric pattern involves a large planum temporale on the left, and a smaller one on the right – in keeping with the usual left hemispheric specialization for language processing. However, the symmetry associated with dyslexia appears to reflect two large regions (rather than two small ones): the total area of these brain regions may actually be *greater* in people with dyslexia (and others who share this symmetrical pattern). This might possibly help to explain the very *superior* language abilities shown by some people like Alexander Faludy.

Differences in brain architecture

Some findings that do appear to be more specific to dyslexia are various microscopic anomalies in the actual organization of brain cells, reported from post-mortem studies (Galaburda *et al.*, 1985). These include collections of slightly 'misplaced' cells (called **ectopias**) and some minor disordering of the usual very regular layering of cells in the cortex. They are often particularly concentrated in left hemisphere regions involved in language processing, although their distribution varies considerably between individual cases. Another interesting feature of these ectopias is that they are typically accompanied by an unusually rich and diverse pattern of connections to other brain regions, which may account for the apparent increased creativity that is sometimes observed in people with dyslexia.

These minor disturbances of brain architecture are known to arise during prenatal development, and although the reasons for their origin are still unclear, it is thought that they could reflect unusual immune system effects on the

Ectopia
A collection of misplaced cells.

developing brain. Research into their significance for brain function suggests that they could interfere with the coding of rapidly changing auditory stimuli, like sounds in speech. If so, this could be relevant to the phonological deficits already discussed. However, it is particularly interesting to note that these anomalies have so far only been associated with auditory processing problems in males (Herman *et al.*, 1997).

The discovery of minor structural differences in the brains of people with and without dyslexia would support the idea that the predisposition to dyslexia is constitutional, particularly if these differences are present before birth. However, a major difficulty is that these differences can only be observed post-mortem, so only a limited number of brains have so far been studied in this way. This means that we should be very cautious about generalizing these findings to all people with dyslexia.

If these anomalies do have any causal significance for dyslexia, then the fact that their regional distribution varies so much between individuals could help to explain some of the variation observed in behavioural symptoms. For example, if this unusual brain micro-architecture were to occur in left hemisphere areas important for auditory or language processing, would we expect a more 'phonological' form of dyslexia than if it occurred in right hemisphere areas important for rapid visual processing?

Finally, some speculation can also be offered regarding these apparent differences in the 'hardware' of the dyslexic brain. Two points seem particularly relevant:

- the brain symmetry associated with dyslexia may reflect an increase in the total number of neurons
- the microscopic disturbances of cellular organization are associated with greater connectivity between different regions.

There is evidence from the study of artificial 'neural networks' that this kind of arrangement (i.e. one with more cells and more interconnections) may be disadvantageous for some tasks – such as learning associative 'rules' – but it may actually be *more efficient* at tasks which require less automatization and more creativity.

Differences in sensory, perceptual and motor function

As we saw in our discussion of cognitive explanations, there has been longstanding debate over the possible contribution of perceptual problems to dyslexia. Subjectively, many children and adults with dyslexic difficulties do report 'visual symptoms' when trying to read. These include letters and words appearing to move or 'blur' on the page, particular difficulties with small, crowded print, and complaints of 'glare' or other kinds of visual discomfort.

If you want to remind yourself of the 'neural networks' model, reread Chapter 2, Section 3 of this book.

Robinson and Conway (1988, unpublished) reported significant improvement in subjects using Irlen lenses in attitude toward school, basic academic subjects, reading comprehension, reading accuracy, but not in rate of reading. Alliter and Atwood (1987) evaluated the results of fifteen lenses on 23 remedial high school students and a matched control group. Significant improvement for the experimental group was noted for time needed to locate words on a printed page, timed reading scores, length of time for sustained reading, and span of focus, as well as other perceptual tasks. Additionally, seven of the 23 experimental found employment, but none of the control group was employed by the end of the semester.

In contrast, Winters (1987) was unable to find differences in his study. Winters gave 15 elementary school children four minutes to locate and circle 68 examples of the letter "b" on three pages, each page of which contained 600 random letters in 20 lines of

As any parent, grandparent, or baby-sitter knows, some babies are adaptable, placid, and regular in their habits, while others are difficult and unpredictable. Differences in temperament show up from the first day of life: some infants sleep very little, others sleep a lot; some infants are highly sensitive and cranky, others are quiet and accommodating.

Since newborns have not been exposed to the world for long, environmental influences beyond the womb can hardly account for such differences in temperament. Rather, these differences must be largely as a result of genetic influences. Yet there have been few, if any, attempts to reduce differences in temperament at birth to genetics.

Examples of visual disturbances experienced by some people with dyslexia

Experimental studies now provide evidence of some perceptual difficulties in dyslexia for tasks involving the processing of rapidly changing information, such as the perception of flicker or motion (Stein, 1994). Such difficulties in processing rapid visual information implicate the **magnocellular visual system** (Stein and Walsh, 1997). Furthermore, neuroanatomical abnormalities relating to this visual pathway have been reported in the brains of dyslexic people post-mortem (Livingstone *et al.*, 1991). The magnocellular system is particularly important for the control of eye movements and visual attention.

Similar difficulties in processing rapidly presented auditory information have also been observed in people with dyslexia. Some have argued that this is evidence of general difficulties with rapid auditory perception, which would account for the difficulties in acquiring phonological awareness in dyslexia (Tallal *et al.*, 1997). However, an alternative explanation that has increasing support suggests that the phonological awareness deficit is the result of a specific problem with speech sounds only, perhaps associated with difficulties in speech perception (Mody *et al.*, 1997).

Magnocellular visual system

A visual sub-system specialized for processing information that changes very rapidly over time, characterized by large cells with fast responses. (Strictly, this refers to a specific sub-cortical pathway from retina to primary visual cortex, but it can also include further cortical areas to which these cells project.)

Attention has also turned to the possible role of the **cerebellum** in dyslexia. This brain structure is important for motor coordination and planning, but is now recognized to play an important role in cognitive development, particularly in the automatization of skills and 'rote' learning (i.e. learning facts 'off by heart', like multiplication tables). Brain imaging studies using positron emission tomography (PET) have shown differences in the activity of the cerebellum in dyslexic versus non-dyslexic adults during motor learning tasks (Nicholson *et al.*, 1999). In our discussion of cognitive explanations we noted that an 'automatization' deficit could help to explain a wide range of features of dyslexic functioning, including (but not confined to) phonological deficits. Furthermore, because the cerebellum is known to act as a 'timing' device, a

Cerebellum
A part of the brain (situated underneath the rear cerebral cortex) involved with motor and balance functions, and recently shown to be involved in the automatization of many cognitive skills.

Cerebellum

'cerebellar deficit' theory is also highly compatible with the idea of problems in very rapid sensory processing (the 'magnocellular' hypothesis).

If you recall our discussion of Frith's model (see Figure 5.2), we emphasized that variability at the behavioural or the cognitive level (e.g. phonological or visual problems) need not rule out some single underlying cause at the biological level. It is perfectly possible that microscopic differences in brain architecture could have different effects according to the particular brain areas affected.

Figure 5.5 The cerebellum (Source: adapted from Martini *et al.*, 2000, Figure 15-9 (a), p.395)

Biochemical factors

As we saw in Section 1, 'medical' approaches to some psychological conditions have focused on biochemistry and the use of corresponding drug treatments. Very little research of this kind has been applied to dyslexia. However, emerging evidence suggests that there may be a biochemical contribution involving abnormal metabolism of **highly unsaturated fatty acids** (HUFA) – essential substances that play a key role in brain development and the maintenance of normal brain function. In fact, just two fatty acids make up 20 per cent of the brain's dry mass, as they are essential components of the membranes surrounding every cell (and structures within each cell). HUFA are also needed to produce other substances that are crucial for regulating a very wide range of brain and body functions including cell signalling, immune system responses and cardiovascular function.

Highly unsaturated fatty acids
Lipid molecules which make up 20 per cent of the brain's dry weight, and are crucial for normal brain development and function.

These essential fatty acids – from the so-called omega-6 and omega-3 series – are found in a wide range of natural foods. However, they are often seriously lacking from modern diets, especially if these are high in saturated fats or processed foods with a high level of artificial fats. In fact, only fish and seafood provide significant quantities of the crucial omega-3 fatty acids. Most of us therefore rely on being able to build our own HUFA from simpler compounds. However, this conversion process may be inefficient in some people, who would therefore have a higher dietary requirement. There is some evidence that this (and/or other inefficiencies in fatty acid metabolism) may be a factor in the biological predisposition to dyslexia, as well as related conditions such as ADHD and dyspraxia (Richardson *et al.*, 1999; Richardson and Ross, 2000).

Fatty acid deficiency leads to minor physical symptoms such as excessive thirst, frequent urination, rough dry skin and hair, and soft or brittle nails. Research has shown that these characteristics are common in children with ADHD, and adults and children with dyslexia. Magnetic resonance (MR) imaging is a safe and non-invasive technique involving the use of radiowaves within a very strong magnetic field. It can be used to obtain either structural images (the well-known MRI) or information on the chemical composition of tissues (magnetic resonance spectroscopy, or MRS). MR brain imaging has also revealed differences in lipid metabolism in dyslexic versus non-dyslexic adults that are consistent with HUFA deficiency, and increased levels of an enzyme that removes HUFA from cell membranes have been reported from blood biochemical studies of dyslexia. If some features of dyslexia and related conditions like ADHD reflect fatty acid deficiency, then supplementing the diet with these fatty acids could be helpful in the management of these conditions. We will return to this in Section 3.

Genetic explanations

Earliest investigators noted that dyslexia tends to run in families, and studies involving extended families or twins have confirmed this. The heritability of dyslexia is estimated at around 50 per cent –about half of the variability in dyslexic traits found in the general population could be attributable to genetic variation. However, the mode of inheritance is not known, and as with most behaviourally defined conditions, genetic studies of dyslexia are complicated by a number of factors. The most obvious of these is the difficulty in arriving at a satisfactory definition of dyslexia, as we have seen in Section 1. Another complication arises when individuals with the genetic tendency for dyslexia fail to develop the condition, or when individuals without the genetic predisposition show problems that resemble dyslexia. Moreover, the same condition in different people may each be 'caused' by a different gene. All these factors can make heritability estimates unreliable. It is most likely that a combination of different genes are involved in dyslexia.

Why there can be no such thing as 'a gene for dyslexia'?

In terms of human evolution, reading is a recent acquisition. The demand for literacy has largely arisen within the last 100 years, and is still confined to 'developed' societies. We can therefore be confident that no specific neural mechanism can have evolved for dealing with written language. Skilled reading is also a highly complex process, drawing on a wide range of abilities and requiring integration across many different domains of perception and cognition. Whatever genes are involved, they may include those associated with the structures necessary for language development in general, certain aspects of visual perception and cross-modal integration. Given the wide range of component processes involved, it seems evident that variation in reading ability (to the extent that this is genetically determined at all) will depend on interactions between many different genes. At most, what is inherited is a predisposition towards reading difficulties, but to explore this further we need to understand much more about the actual brain processes involved in such difficulties.

2.3 Environmental explanations of dyslexia?

'Environment' is often used to refer to only social or non-biological influences. However, it actually also refers to the biological, cognitive and behavioural environments that we may be exposed to. If you refer back to Frith's framework (see Figure 5.2) you will remember that the environment can be heavily involved in each perspective. An example of a biological environmental influence is a dietary deficiency such as insufficient consumption of fatty acids. The idea that dyslexia has a non-biological environmental explanation has been excluded: you may recall that external environmental factors were explicitly rejected in exclusion based definitions of dyslexia. However, Spear-Swerling and Sternberg (1998) believe that there is some evidence to suggest that while such factors may not explain dyslexia, they can dramatically affect the nature and extent of the difficulties experienced. For example, Adams (1990) has suggested that reading aloud to preschool children results in real benefits in later reading development. Snow (1991) found that children who have a 'literate home environment' were more likely to progress in reading than peers whose were exposed to less 'literate' contexts. MacLean *et al.* (1987) have also shown that children's knowledge of nursery rhymes can predict both reading performance and phonological awareness.

Just as the home environment can influence reading development, so too can school environments. For example, children are exposed to different methods of reading instruction and it has been argued that some instructional methods can effectively prevent reading difficulties (Clay, 1990). Similarly, the overemphasis on either phonic (alphabetic) or whole word (logographic) approaches to reading can exacerbate existing reading difficulties, because of the need for both skills to compensate for the relative weaknesses of each approach (Chall, 1996). Anderson *et al.* (1985) have also found evidence that children who are 'streamed' into low ability groups receive less effective instruction due to lower expectations of what they can be expected to achieve. There is also often a higher incidence of behavioural difficulties in such groups, which can disrupt opportunities for learning.

> *... we cannot blame reading failure – especially extreme disability – on either the child or the initial method alone. Severe disability seems to result when a child has a predisposition (a set of characteristics that make it difficult for him to associate printed symbols with their spoken counterparts) and is exposed to an initial method that ignores this predisposition.*

> *(Chall, 1996, p.175)*

2.4 Reflecting on explanations of 'abnormal' development: the case of dyslexia

We can draw the following general conclusions about cognitive and biological explanations of abnormality from the material presented above.

- Both cognitive and biological accounts of dyslexia are offered as theories which explain the behavioural difficulties that are observed. While some theories may dominate accounts of a given condition (e.g. the phonological deficit hypothesis), and may result in influencing the nature of interventions, they are still only theories and always need to be validated by consistent empirical evidence.
- Any single level of description, taken in isolation, will provide an incomplete account of what may cause the behavioural symptoms. Evidence and theories from different levels of description give a fuller account of a condition and better reflect the systemic nature of dyslexia.
- Research evidence provided at one level of description can support a theoretical idea offered at a different level. For example, the evidence suggesting that people with dyslexia show neurological abnormalities in the magnocellular visual pathway (biological evidence) lends support to the visual deficit hypothesis (cognitive explanation).
- The case of dyslexia illustrates a general finding that few conditions are caused by a single biological problem, which affects a single cognitive process, which in turn results in a consistent set of behavioural symptoms. Within most conditions there will be a good deal of potential variability in the symptoms manifested, the cognitive processes affected and the biological factors proposed to explain them. This is because human behaviour is the product of the complex interplay between cognitive and other processes, influenced by a whole range of interconnected and

modifiable biological systems. Our 'environment' (physical, psychological and biological) can impact on all these levels and either exacerbate or temper the severity of the condition as a result.

Summary Section 2

- Theoretical explanations of 'abnormal' development conditions need to take into account behavioural, biological, cognitive and environmental evidence.
- Cognitive explanations of dyslexia include deficits in phonological awareness, visual perception and automatization of skills.
- Biological explanations of dyslexia refer to observed abnormalities in brain architecture, perceptual pathways and biochemistry.
- *External* environmental explanations are specifically excluded from current definitions of dyslexia. However, evidence suggests that certain home and school environments can contribute to successful reading development.

3 Treatment and management

3.1 Thinking about intervention

So far we have looked at issues relating to how we define 'abnormal' behaviour, and how we think about explanations. Now we will consider the more practical issue of how to approach the treatment of such difficulties. As in the previous section, we will discuss behavioural, cognitive and biological perspectives on treatment and consider specific techniques from each perspective that are applicable to the management of dyslexia.

Treatment or management?

In the preceding paragraph you will notice that we talked generally about the treatment of conditions, but referred to 'managing' dyslexia. Why did we do this? It relates to the following important general issues:

Is treatment (i.e. intervention) warranted? We mentioned this issue when we were discussing sociocultural or personal distress based definitions of abnormality. Intervention is not always desirable or sought by the individual, who may feel that what other people perceive as 'abnormal' is little more than an individual difference that simply requires increased awareness on the part of other people. For example, some people with hearing impairment do not use hearing aids, which they find unnecessary or distracting. A hearing aid may make life easier for hearing individuals speaking to someone with a hearing impairment because it means that they do not have to adjust their own behaviour to accommodate the other person's difficulties. But it may not make life easier for the hearing impaired person. From this perspective, such an intervention is just as unnecessary as it would be if all hearing people were required to communicate in sign language. Alexander Faludy's case study provides a good illustration of someone who has found a way of managing his difficulties, most of which are only perceived as 'difficulties' because of the constraints and expectations that he is expected to work within.

Are all conditions 'curable'? In many cases it is simply not possible to treat the condition in the sense of 'curing' it, and so the individual often has no choice other than to find a way of managing his or her symptoms. As already noted, few psychological conditions have a single cause that would respond to appropriate treatment and disappear, because of the complex interaction of different factors and the difficulty in altering some types of biological difference. Moreover, it is worth considering what might be lost as well as gained if some types of psychological functioning were 'corrected'. Dyslexia is often associated with compensatory strengths (as described in Box 5.1). If all children could be inoculated against developing dyslexia, then these strengths may also fail to develop. A crucial point to consider is whether the gains of any intervention might outweigh the potential losses.

What caused it? Choice of intervention is often influenced by what is believed to cause the condition. For example, if the primary difficulty is believed to be cognitive then the strategy for intervention may also centre on addressing cognitive rather than biological or social aspects of the situation. As we shall see, dyslexia is a good example of a condition where intervention strategies have been largely cognitive in nature, but increased understanding of its biological basis is leading to new possibilities. In contrast, children with ADHD are already offered drug based treatments simply because these appear to calm their disruptive behaviour, despite the lack of any clear evidence for corresponding biological theories of what causes this 'syndrome'. However, the idea of prescribing such drugs to young children has proved controversial in the UK and raises issues to do with the appropriateness of some treatments. Do the ends really justify the means? As we have seen, most 'problem' behaviours are usually sustained by many influences operating at different levels. This means that in some circumstances any intervention that helps to break what is sometimes a vicious cycle may be beneficial. Although it is helpful if a clear 'primary cause' can be identified and tackled, this is not always necessary for treatment or management strategies to be effective.

3.2 Behavioural approaches

Behavioural therapies are based on principles of classical conditioning and operant conditioning (the latter being more properly referred to as behaviour modification therapy). If you recall Book 1, Chapter 3, you will remember that operant conditioning is about the presentation of a reinforcement being dependent (*contingent*) on the appearance of a given behaviour. Based on this idea, Skinner (1953) suggested that sometimes 'abnormal' behaviour is the result of bad **contingency management**, where inappropriate behaviours have been reinforced. He suggested that such behaviours could be modified by a process of more appropriate contingency management to become 'normal'. A simple form of this is the so-called 'token economy', often used by schools in the UK to encourage children to engage in good work or behaviour, for which they receive awards such as gold stars. Behavioural therapies are also well suited to the treatment of conditions such as phobias where unwanted emotional reactions can sometimes be extinguished by behavioural means (see Box 5.3).

> **Contingency management**
> An alternative term to 'behaviour modification therapy', used to describe a behavioural intervention that is based on principles of operant conditioning.

5.3 *The three stages of a contingency management programme (Klein, 1996)*

1   Observations are made of the client, and the frequency of the inappropriate behaviour is noted along with the characteristics of the situations that it occurs in. From this it is possible to generate hypotheses about what is reinforcing these behaviours inappropriately.
2   Based on the data from stage one, an intervention is designed which seeks to establish new contingent relationships between desirable behaviours and suitable reinforcement.
3   The situation is monitored as in stage one to ascertain whether the new relationships are having the desired effect. Changes to the contingent relationships are made if necessary.

There are emotional consequences of dyslexia which can also be treated using a programme of this kind. Although there has been little research in this area, the studies that have been conducted do show that poor self-esteem and high levels of stress are real problems (Riddick 1996; Riddick *et al.*, 1999). If this is the case, remediation programmes need to address both the direct symptoms of dyslexia and the emotional difficulties that people with dyslexia often experience. One example of a study that has done this was the summer camp programme devised by Westervelt *et al.* (1998) outlined in Box 5.4 below.

5.4 *The Westervelt et al. (1998) summer camp study*

Over a six-week residential summer camp in the USA, 48 dyslexic students aged between 9 and 14 years received daily tuition in phonics using the Orton-Gillingham multisensory method (see Section 3.3) and oral reading. Student progress was monitored and individual achievements were shared in a weekly newsletter. Psychosocial difficulties were addressed by praising the children, encouraging them to praise and support each other and by creating opportunities for each child to demonstrate success and receive recognition for it. Awards were presented daily to children who had shown progress in socializing. At the end of the summer camp the children showed significant gains in phonetic reading, spelling skills and self esteem. However, it was noted that children who also had ADHD showed little gain in self-esteem, despite showing the same degree of improvement on the literacy measures. It would seem that the additional difficulties experienced by these children prevented them from receiving praise as readily as the other children with dyslexia did.

You will notice that this programme of intervention has a behavioural element to it. It was observed that much of the children's low self-esteem was associated with failed attempts at reading and writing, and with socializing with other children who might judge them. The researchers attempted to break this cycle by praising the children when they worked hard, rather than criticizing them for their errors, and by rewarding the children with awards when they started to engage socially with other children. While this benefited many children, the ADHD/dyslexic children were not benefiting emotionally from the programme, and so some modification to the contingency management programme would be needed for these children in future.

Can you think of any modifications that might increase opportunities for praise for the children with ADHD/dyslexia?

3.3 Cognitive approaches

Cognitive approaches to therapy involve interventions that focus on addressing aspects of cognitive processing. For example, **cognitive therapy** is frequently used to treat stress, depression or phobia, and involves working with a therapist who highlights maladaptive beliefs that an individual may

Cognitive therapy
Involves working with a therapist who highlights maladaptive beliefs that an individual may have about their situation. The individual is retrained to monitor their own thoughts, recognize when their thoughts are based on emotion rather than reality, reject biased cognitions and learn to change whatever beliefs have caused them to distort their interpretation of reality.

have about their situation. The individual is retrained to monitor their own thoughts, recognize when their thoughts are based on emotion rather than reality, reject biased cognitions and learn to change whatever beliefs have caused them to distort their interpretation of reality. Another approach, referred to as **cognitive behaviour therapy** (CBT) involves observing the therapist 'modelling' the desired behavioural response to a situation, and the individual trying to copy that response and receiving feedback on their attempt. This behavioural rehearsal is repeated until the behaviour has been mastered. It is claimed that this process, whereby the person realises that they can now do something that they had previously been unable to, leads to the development of a sense of self-efficacy, will also encourage the person to cope with new situations.

Interventions that directly address the cognitive deficits of a condition (i.e. rather than emotional difficulties) through training may also be thought of as 'cognitive therapy'. As the primary difficulty for people with dyslexia is with acquiring literacy, the most common approach to remediation is to develop programmes that teach reading and writing in a way that addresses the cognitive deficits associated with dyslexia. The difficulty shown in acquiring alphabetic and phonological awareness has led to the development of phonic teaching programmes. **Phonic approaches** to reading teach students how to break words down into their composite sounds, e.g. "cat" = /k/ /a/ /t/ (phonic analysis) and how to blend individual sounds together to form words (phonic synthesis).

At the time of writing, all English and Welsh children are routinely taught phonic strategies as part of the National Literacy Strategy. Phonic strategies are also included in reading programmes in other countries in Europe and in America. Earlier we noted that phonic strategies should not be taught to the exclusion of other approaches if they are to be successful, and they rarely are although they are an especially important technique for children with dyslexia to focus on due to their difficulties in achieving 'alphabetic' reading. Moreover, phonic strategies alone are not enough to improve dyslexic symptoms if they are taught in normal classroom contexts – so the *way* that they are taught to students with dyslexia is an important feature of remedial programmes. One approach known as the **Reading Recovery System**, developed by Marie Clay in New Zealand, emphasizes the need for regular periods of one-to-one tuition that focuses on the types of error each child typically makes. There is evidence that this level of individual support is effective in bringing poor readers up to age appropriate levels of performance, especially when combined with tuition in phonics (see Iversen and Tunmer, 1993), but such programmes are expensive to maintain. They also lack thorough evaluation of the long-term performance of children after the intervention period has finished. Other projects have found that parental tuition and peer-support (where more able friends teach struggling readers) can also be effective,

Cognitive behaviour therapy
Involves observing the therapist 'modelling' the desired behavioural response to a situation, and the individual trying to copy that response and receiving feedback on their attempt. This *behavioural rehearsal* is repeated until the behaviour has been mastered.

Phonic approaches
An approach to teaching reading that emphasizes the relationships between letters (graphemes) and their corresponding sounds (phonemes).

Reading Recovery System
An intensive individualized technique for teaching reading devised by Marie Clay.

although specific guidance on how to support the student must be given to the tutors.

Clearly, one-to-one tuition is not always a practical option. The more common approach to teaching phonics is known as **multisensory teaching**. The origins of this idea appear to be with Hinshelwood (1917) who recommended that when teaching reading to dyslexic children, the teacher should simultaneously provide input to verbal, visual, motor and tactile memory centres. This sensory integration is intended to maximise the child's ability to make associations between visual and verbal information by linking them via the other available senses. However, this idea is more widely credited to Samuel Orton who, along with Anna Gillingham, developed the **Orton-Gillingham Technique**. This involved '... the constant use of associations of all of the following: how a letter or word looks, how it sounds and how the speech organs or the hand in writing feels when producing it' (Gillingham and Stillman, 1956, p.17).

A wide variety of multisensory teaching strategies have been developed based on this principle (e.g. the *Hickey Multisensory Language Course* in the UK, or the *Wilson Reading System* in the US). Studies have shown the multisensory technique to be especially effective in helping students with dyslexia and it has also been applied to the teaching of mathematics (Kibel, 1992).

Multisensory teaching for students

Guyer *et al.* (1993) tested the effectiveness of the Wilson Reading System for improving spelling in higher education students with dyslexia. They compared this technique to a non-phonic approach that teaches visual memory techniques to help students to remember frequently misspelled words. A control group of students with dyslexia but who had specifically requested no intervention formed the control group. Both intervention groups were tutored in the given technique for two, one-hour sessions per week, for 16 weeks. Only the multisensory group showed a significant improvement in spelling ability at the end of this period.

Activity 5.5

What is significant about the students in the control group regarding (1) the ethics of conducting intervention studies of this kind and (2) the interpretation of the study's results?

There are normally ethical problems in excluding people from an intervention in order to form a control group. When this happens it is normally necessary to offer the treatment to the control group after the study has concluded to make

---

Multisensory teaching
A technique that involves teaching children via the simultaneous stimulation of as many senses as possible.

Orton-Gillingham technique
A specific multisensory technique for teaching reading.

sure that they have not been unfairly disadvantaged. However, Guyer *et al.* (1993) avoided this problem by using people who did not want any help for their dyslexia as his control group. However, this does raise some issues regarding the interpretation of their results because we do not know the reasons why this group did not want support. For example, the control group may have achieved less because they were less motivated to improve, or because their primarily difficulties had been successfully addressed elsewhere. In other words, an important factor to consider when designing an intervention is to use a closely **matched control group**.

As we have already mentioned, phonic approaches do not address the wider difficulties of visual or attentional processing, physical coordination or automatization associated with dyslexia. There may be some individuals with no primary problems in phonological awareness who need programmes specifically tailored to address their particular difficulties.

Matched control group
A control group that has been matched to the participants in the experimental group on various key characteristics.

3.4 Biological approaches

Certain kinds of psychological disturbances may be seen as 'malfunctions' of the brain. If a psychological problem has an obvious biological explanation, then it may be possible to direct therapeutic approaches at this level. However, as we have seen, it is difficult to identify precise biological causes for complex psychological phenomena. Even if this were possible, it would not always be practicable to use treatments to change the underlying biological factors. Genetic 'explanations' provide the most obvious example of this problem. As we have seen, the genetic factors underlying complex patterns of behaviour are rarely simple, usually involving many different genes. Even if a single malfunctioning gene *could* be identified, the likelihood of successful 'gene therapies' remains highly theoretical and would be fraught with both ethical and practical difficulties.

The most common medical method of treating psychological problems is through biochemistry. Numerous pharmacological (drug) treatments are already in use for conditions such as anxiety, depression, schizophrenia and ADHD. However, prescription of these kinds of treatments lies in the province of psychiatry, not psychology, because their safe use requires specialized medical knowledge and training. Nutritional treatments offer a possible alternative to drugs for correcting biochemical imbalances that contribute to psychological problems. It is easy to forget that what we consume can have powerful effects on brain function, both in the short-term (e.g. the way that coffee or sugary foods provide a temporary 'lift' in energy) and in the long-term, because our diet provides the substances we need to fuel, maintain and repair our brain and body.

Pharmaceuticals or nutraceuticals?

Nutraceuticals refers to the use of food supplements or herbal remedies for health purposes. For example, certain ingredients of the herb St John's Wort can be as effective in managing depression as conventional anti-depressants, with fewer negative side effects (Greeson *et al.*, 2001). However, research also shows that this supplement can interact negatively with some commonly prescribed drugs, such as the contraceptive pill. This highlights the need for:

- proper research into food supplements and herbal remedies
- consulting a medical practitioner before taking any of the supplements.

Similarly, doctors sometimes 'prescribe' vitamins and minerals (e.g. vitamin B6 for depression, poor concentration or memory problems). Evidence has also emerged that supplements of fish oil, which contains certain highly unsaturated omega-3 fatty acids, may help to reduce the symptoms of serious mood disorders (Stoll *et al.*, 1999). As discussed earlier, deficiencies in highly unsaturated fatty acids are also suspected of playing a part in behavioural and learning problems like ADHD, dyslexia and dyspraxia.

Even apparent evidence of benefits does not mean that the treatment is really addressing the underlying problem. For example, sleeping pills may render someone unconscious, but can we really say that this is addressing the underlying problem? You may ask: 'does it matter if we don't know how something works, as long as it works?' The answer depends on a careful evaluation of both the costs and the benefits associated with a particular treatment. However, even if a treatment appears to 'work', it can still be difficult or impossible to know whether the benefits observed result from the treatment. The problem of evaluating interventions, be they biological, cognitive or behavioural, is discussed in Section 3.5.

As we saw in Section 2, we still know comparatively little about the physical brain differences that may contribute to developmental dyslexia, and what we do know suggests limited scope for direct biological interventions. Related conditions such as ADHD are often treated using drugs, but there has been little investigation of possible biochemical contributions to dyslexia. However, as discussed, there is some evidence of deficiencies in certain highly unsaturated fatty acids, and case studies suggest that nutritional therapy may be helpful in some cases (see Box 5.5). Large scale double-blind trials should soon reveal whether dietary supplementation may be of more general benefit in the management of dyslexia.

5.5 A biochemical approach to dyslexia (Baker, 1985)

This report describes the case of a boy diagnosed with dyslexia, for whom biochemical testing revealed various imbalances. Correcting these with nutritional supplements led to clear improvements in his schoolwork. His story illustrates the importance of treating the individual child rather than the apparent problem of his dyslexia (which had not responded to conventional remedial teaching methods).

Deficiencies in certain fatty acids were considered the single most important factor in this case, but some vitamins and minerals were also lacking. Furthermore, to anyone familiar with the signs, this child's fatty acid deficiency was evident from simple observation (although biochemical testing was needed to confirm it).

> *Michael had very dry, patchy, dull skin. Like a matte finish on a photograph, his skin, as well as his hair, failed to reflect light with a normal lustre. His hair was easily tousled and when pulled between the fingers it had a straw-like texture rather than a normal silky feel. He had dandruff. The skin on the backs of his arms was raised in tiny closed bumps like chicken skin. His fingernails were soft and frayed at the ends. All of these findings point to an imbalance of fatty acids.*
>
> *(Baker, 1985, p.583)*

This biochemical approach apparently angered some specialists, who took the view that 'Nutrition has nothing to do with dyslexia'. However, as the author notes:

> *Improvement in Michael's school work coincided with the return of normal lustre and texture to his skin and hair. If he had been a cocker spaniel his family would have accepted the connection between his 'glossier coat' and better disposition more readily. The timing was convincing. Although it is never enough to establish 'proof' in a given person, Michael was convinced. He saw and felt the changes together, and he understood the idea behind the work we did with him. With a twinkle in his eye, he told his grandmother that dandruff had been the cause of his dyslexia.*
>
> *(Baker, 1985, p.583)*

The doctor emphasized that he was simply treating the individual child, and did not regard dyslexia as any kind of 'disease'. Instead it was the non-medical specialists who seemed pre-occupied with the 'dyslexia' label. Recall too our discussion of 'explanations', where we saw that a proper understanding of any psychological problem requires an appreciation of three levels – behavioural, cognitive and biological, as well as the way that environment (in this case diet) can impact on each of these. This report also shows the value of a well-documented single-case study, although randomized controlled trials are necessary to provide unequivocal evidence of benefits from biochemical treatments.

Placebo
Any therapy that is used for a specific symptom or disease, but which is actually thought to be ineffective for that purpose. A placebo is usually employed in clinical trials for comparison with the 'active' treatment under study. A study with no placebo is an 'open study' (see Box 5.6).

Some visual treatments, such as covering one eye when reading, have shown benefits in double-blind trials (Stein *et al.*, 2000). However, this kind of specialist treatment is only appropriate for children who have particular visual deficits, and it requires proper professional supervision. Others, such as using coloured lenses or overlays for reading, are popular amongst some people with dyslexia and lead to improvements in reading ability in open studies (Sawyer *et al.*, 1994), but as yet there is limited evidence from **placebo** controlled studies to suggest that they are effective (Francis *et al.*, 1992). A few other unconventional treatments for dyslexia are widely advertized by private clinics as 'based' on biological evidence, but have no reliable evidence of their efficacy. One unorthodox approach that has support from randomized, double blind placebo controlled trials involves special physical exercises designed to improve aspects of motor coordination thought to reflect neurological immaturities in dyslexia (McPhillips *et al.*, 2000). Benefits to physical coordination, reading and attention were reported.

3.5 Evaluating intervention studies

Expectancy versus effect

One of the biggest problems in evaluating psychological interventions is that even if a treatment appears to 'work' it can still be difficult to ascertain whether the results were a consequence of the treatment itself. The improvement might have occurred anyway, with or without the treatment, or the apparent benefits might have resulted from other factors, such as being able to discuss the difficulties with a professional who understands. *Any treatment* can lead to expectations of improvement that can be self-fulfilling. Even a treatment with absolutely no benefits for the condition in question can be followed by substantial improvements if the person *believes* that it will help. This is the so-called placebo effect (see Book 1, Chapter 4).

For biochemical interventions, professionals evaluate treatments via randomized, double-blind, placebo controlled trials (see Box 5.6). This kind of trial remains the benchmark of 'evidence-based medicine', as the most objective way to find out whether a treatment is effective. It can also be used to evaluate other types of intervention strategy where it is possible to develop a suitable placebo.

5.6 *Randomized, double-blind, placebo controlled trials – some definitions*

Placebo-controlled – the treatment being tested (known as the 'active' treatment) is compared with another treatment (the 'placebo') that is believed to be neutral with regard to the underlying specific basis of the condition in question, but is otherwise indistinguishable from the active treatment. Studies with no placebo are known as *open treatment* studies.

Double-blind – to eliminate as much bias as possible, it is crucial that neither the participants nor those carrying out the study know which people are receiving the 'active' treatment and which the placebo (i.e. everyone involved in the study must be 'blind' to treatment status until all data have been collected and analysed). Sometimes it is not possible to achieve this owing to the nature of the treatment, in which case the next best option is the *single-blind* study, in which the participant does not know what kind of treatment they are receiving but those carrying out the trial do.

Randomized – the kind of treatment that each participant receives must be determined by pure chance, otherwise there is an opportunity for bias (conscious or unconscious) in the allocation of treatments that could influence the results.

Proof of efficacy is required before any new drugs are licensed for prescription, but inevitably this evidence is often obtained under rather limited conditions. Individual differences in the metabolism of many drugs can mean that not everyone reacts biochemically in the same way to a given dosage. For ethical or other reasons, clinical research trials often do not include particular groups such as children or women. Many drug-based interventions also have undesirable side-effects that have to be weighed against the possible benefits. Since psychological problems usually have a wide range of possible interacting causes, in many cases drugs may not be the primary treatment option.

There are difficulties inherent in carrying out placebo-controlled trials, particularly for non-pharmacological treatments, including:

- *deception – can it be justified?*

- *double-blind trial – can this be achieved when the experimenter is administering a cognitive or behavioural 'placebo' therapy?*

- *homogeneity – for some medical problems it may be possible to ensure close similarity of symptoms experienced across all participants. However for many complex psychological conditions this is much more difficult.*

Pre-post test studies

Another method for evaluating the effectiveness of a therapy is to use a **pre-post test design**. This is where a group of people is assessed before and after a programme of intervention. Ideally, these people would be matched to a control group who are also tested twice, but do not receive the same (or any) intervention during that period. However, as with randomized controlled trials, there are ethical issues if it becomes clear that the intervention is having an adverse affect on the experimental group. Even if the intervention is successful, there may be ethical issues as the control group could be seen as 'disadvantaged' by not receiving the intervention. Finally, it is always important to assess the long-term effects of any intervention programme to see if the apparent benefits are sustained long after the study has concluded.

Single participant interventions

A single participant intervention study, studies the effects of an intervention in the case of one person, with the aim of establishing those elements of the intervention which would work with the majority of people. This is because the method assumes that in all important respects, all human beings are the same, and the effects of the intervention in one case should be the same in all cases. It is a method that belongs to objectivity, which is discussed in Methods Booklet 1, *Introduction to Research Methods*.

5.7 FEATURED METHOD

Single participant experimental designs

Single participant experimental designs are used to assess the effectiveness of an intervention on a case by case basis. What may be effective for some people may not work well for others, and given the heterogeneous nature of people with reading difficulties it would seem appropriate to adopt a single case strategy to the design and assessment of interventions for this and similarly varied samples. This approach is also used in other areas of psychological intervention such as psychotherapy and psychoanalysis.

There are a variety of designs that are used within this method, one of them being the ABAB Design (opposite).

A baseline measure is taken several times before the intervention is introduced (A), and then during the intervention itself (B). The intervention is then withdrawn for a sustained period (A) and reintroduced (B). This alternating pattern enables the researcher to see if the intervention has any genuine effect on the individual, whether the benefit is reliable (i.e. is it reproduced the second time the intervention is applied), and whether it has a continued benefit after the intervention is withdrawn. The participant also acts as his or her own 'control' in a design of this nature. This design gives a richer picture of what is going on than a simple pre-post test design would.

number of sessions

Figure 5.6   ABAB Design

3.6 Reflecting on dyslexia

Throughout the chapter, dyslexia has been evaluated as an example of 'abnormality', a difficulty, a problem in need of an intervention. However, research has shown that some adults with dyslexia are distinctive, not just in their difficulties, but also in their increased levels of creative reasoning compared to 'normal' people (Everatt 1997). West (1997) reports that Nicholas Negroponte, the founding member of the Media Lab at the world renowned *Massachusetts Institute of Technology* has joked that dyslexia is 'the MIT disease', because so many of the individuals at the forefront of their fields have dyslexia.

The following are some of the strengths associated with dyslexia (Reid and Kirk, 2001):

- Good visual and spatial skills in areas such as engineering and the physical sciences.
- Ability to recognize patterns of information and represent three dimensional images.
- A facility for mentally rearranging designs and information.
- A holistic way of viewing the world, which aids the discovery of problem solutions.
- Rich colour memory and ability to use fast multisensory combinations.
- Creativity.
- Critical thinking skills.

What is problematic in one situation can be advantageous in another. In Section 2.2 we saw that the brain anomalies associated with dyslexia can result in rich neural connections, and that computer models with similar patterns of connectivity are more efficient at tasks that require creativity but not automaticity. Similarly, the ease with which people with dyslexia transpose letters like *b*, *d*, *p* and *q*, reflects an ability to manipulate and match images that can be helpful in engineering. Rather than viewing it as a deficiency or abnormality, it has been proposed that dyslexia can be thought of as a unique cognitive style that favours parallel/holistic reasoning over sequential processing of information (Aaron *et al.*, 1993).

Remember what we discussed at the beginning of the chapter about social or historical factors constructing 'normality'? Dyslexia was not recognized as a problem until there was a social expectation of and need for literacy, even though the condition probably did exist before then and affected people's lives in other ways (e.g. poor memory). Written language is a technology, but technologies change – as we become more dependent on one, we will become less dependent on others. The increase in new technologies is prompting a re-examination of the sorts of skills society needs. This might highlight a need for the creative thinking that computers are unable to do, but which many dyslexic people are skilled in.

As a final postscript, not just to the ideas we have examined to do with dyslexia, but with 'normality' generally, consider once more the case of Alexander Faludy (Box 5.1). His story is worth reflecting on in terms of what it tells us about 'normality' and 'abnormality' and the way that society responds to individuals who are exactly that – individual.

Summary Section 3

- There are important distinctions between 'treating' and 'managing' a condition.
- Therapies can be directed at behavioural, cognitive and biological levels.
- Interventions require effective evaluation.
- Successful approaches to managing dyslexia include multisensory teaching of phonics, the promotion of self-esteem through rewards, and addressing nutritional deficiencies though dietary supplementation.

4 Concluding remarks

This chapter has been about understanding the idea of psychological abnormality and its implications. What we have learned is that 'normality' is defined in a variety of ways, and it is important to ask what model of 'normality' is being subscribed to when looking at 'abnormal' populations. Are we judging someone's behaviour according to medical, statistical or social definitions of 'normality'? The point of giving a detailed example like that of dyslexia is to show that in practice there are difficulties in applying any one model of 'normality', and that they all have implications for defining a condition, which in turn will have implications for diagnosis and management. Our discussion has shown that it is important to integrate the different psychological accounts of the condition in order to provide a full explanation of potential causes and strategies for remediation. Moreover, it is important to consider what can and should be addressed during remediation and which behaviours, however 'abnormal', are valuable and even desirable in particular contexts. In Book 3 you will be introduced to other types of 'abnormal' psychology, remember to reflect on the issues that you have been introduced to here when reading about them.

If you believe that you may suffer from dyslexia, we advise you to contact a national charity that will be able to offer assistance and guidance in the first instance. If you are based in the UK, you may wish to contact the British Dyslexia Association, the Dyslexia Institute or the Adult Dyslexic Association.

Further reading

Claridge, G. (1985) *Origins of Mental Illness: Temperament, Deviance and Disorder*, Oxford, Blackwell.
A classic text on 'abnormal' psychology.

Faludy, T. and Faludy, A. (1996) *A Little Edge of Darkness: A Boy's Triumph Over Dyslexia*, London, Jessica Kingsley.
This is the personal account written by Alexander Faludy and his mother, Tanya, of their experiences of understanding and managing Alexander's dyslexia.

Miles, T.R. and Miles, E. (1999) *Dyslexia: A Hundred Years On* (2nd edn),
Buckingham, Open University Press.
A good introduction to the history, issues and research that relates to
developmental dyslexia.

References

Aaron, P.G., Wleklinski, M. and Wills, C. (1993) 'Developmental dyslexia as a
cognitive style', in Joshi, R.M. and Leong, C.K. (eds) *Reading Disabilities:
Diagnosis and Component Processes*, Dordrecht, Kluwer Academic Publishers.

Adams, M.J. (1990) *Beginning to Read: Thinking and Learning About Print*,
Cambridge, MA, MIT Press.

Anderson, R., Hiebert, E., Scott, J. and Wilkinson, I. (1985) *Becoming a Nation
of Readers: The Report of the Commission on Reading*, Champaign, IL, Center
for the Study of Reading.

Baker, S.M. (1985) 'A biochemical approach to the problem of dyslexia', *Journal
of Learning Disabilities*, vol. 18, no.10, pp.581–4.

Bannatyne, A.D. (1971) *Language, Reading and Learning Disabilities*,
Springfield, IL, Thomas.

Bradley, L. and Bryant, P.E. (1978) 'Difficulties in auditory organization as a
possible cause of reading backwardness', *Nature*, pp.271 and 746–7.

Chall, J.S. (1996) *Learning to Read: The Great Debate* (3rd edn), Fort Worth, TX,
Harcourt Brace College Publishers.

Clay, M.M. (1990) 'Learning to be learning disabled', *ERS Spectrum*, vol. 8, pp.3–
8.

Courcy, A., Béland, R. and Pitchford, N.J. (2000*) Phonological Awareness in
Preliterate French-Speaking Children*, Paper presented at the Society for the
Scientific Study of Reading Annual Conference, Stockholm, July 2000.

Critchley, M. (1970) *The Dyslexic Child*, London, Heinemann.

Dancey, C.P. and Reidy, J. (2002) *Statistics Without Maths for Psychology* (2nd
edn)*,* Harlow, Pearson Education.

Eglington, E. and Annett, M. (1994) 'Handedness and dyslexia: a meta analysis',
Perceptual and Motor Skills, vol. 79, pp.1611–6.

Everatt, J. (1997) 'The abilities and disabilities associated with adult
developmental dyslexia', *Journal of Research in Reading*, vol. 20, pp.13–21.

Everatt, J. (1999) (ed.) *Reading and Dyslexia: Visual and Attentional Processes*,
London, Routledge.

Francis, M., Taylor, S. and Sawyer, C. (1992) 'Coloured lenses and the Dex
frame: new issues', *Support for Learning*, vol. 7, pp.25–7.

Faludy, A. (1998) 'How I faced the bullies and won', *The Guardian*, 29th August 1998, p.3.

Frith, U. (1985) 'Beneath the surface of developmental dyslexia', in Patterson, K., Marshall, J.C. and Coltheart, M. (eds) *Surface Dyslexia: Neuropsychological and Cognitive Studies of Phonological Reading*, London, Laurence Erlbaum Associates.

Frith, U. (1999) 'Paradoxes in the definition of dyslexia', *Dyslexia*, vol. 5, no.4, pp.192–214.

Galaburda, A.M., Corsiglia, J., Rosen, G.D. and Sherman, G.F. (1987) 'Planum temorale asymmetry: reappraisal since Geschwind and Levitsky', *Neuropsychologica*, vol. 25, pp.853 and 868.

Galaburda, A.M., Sherman, G.F., Rosen, G.D., Aboitiz, F. and Geschwind, N. (1985) 'Developmental dyslexia: four consecutive patients with cortical abnormalities', *Annals of Neurology*, vol.18, pp.222–33.

Gillingham, A. and Stillman, B.W. (1956) *Remedial Training for Children with Specific Disability in Reading, Spelling and Penmanship*, (5th edn), Bronxville, NY, A. Gilligham.

Greeson, J.M., Sanford, B. and Monti, D.A. (2001) 'St. John's Wort (Hypericum perforatum): a review of the current pharmacological, toxicological, and clinical literature', *Psychopharmacology*, vol. 153, no. 4, pp.402–14.

Guyer, B.P., Banks, S.R. and Guyer, K.E. (1993) 'Spelling improvement for college students who are dyslexic' *Annals of Dyslexia*, vol. 43, pp.186–93.

Herman, A.E., Galaburda, A.M., Fitch, R.H., Carter, A.R. and Rosen, G.D. (1997) 'Cerebral microgyria, thalamic cell size and auditory temporal processing in male and female rats', *Cerebral Cortex*, vol. 7, pp.453–64.

Hinshelwood, J. (1917) *Congenital Word-Blindness*, London, H.K. Lewis.

Hynd, G.W. and Semrud-Clikeman, M. (1989) 'Dyslexia and brain morphology', *Psychological Bulletin*, vol. 106, pp.447–82.

Hynd, G.W., Semrud-Clikeman, M., Lorys, A.R., Novey, E.S. and Eliopoulos, D. (1990) 'Brain morphology in developmental dyslexia and attention deficit disorder/hyperactivity', *Archives of Neurology*, vol. 47, pp.919–26.

Iversen, S. and Tunmer, W.E. (1993) 'Phonological processing skills and the reading recovery program', *Journal of Educational Psychology*, vol. 85, pp.112–6.

James, W.H. (1992) 'The sex ratios of dyslexic children and their siblings', *Developmental Medicine and Child Neurology*, vol. 34, pp.530–3.

Kalat, J.W. (2001) *Biological Psychology* (7th edn), Belmont, CA, Wadsworth Thomson.

Kibel, M. (1992) 'Linking language to action', in Miles, T.R. and Miles, E. (eds), *Dyslexia and Mathematics*, London, Routledge.

Kinsbourne, M., Rufo, D.T., Gamzu, E., Palmer, R.L. and Berliner, A.K. (1991) 'Neuropsychological deficits in adults with dyslexia', *Developmental Medicine & Child Neurology*, vol. 33, pp.763–75.

Klein, S.B. (1996) *Learning: Principles and Applications* (3rd edn), New York, McGraw-Hill.

Larsen, J.P., Hoien, T., Lundberg, I. and Odegaard, H. (1990) 'MRI evaluation of the size and symmetry of the planum temporale in adolescents with developmental dyslexia', *Brain and Language*, vol. 39, pp.289–301.

Livingstone, M.S., Rosen, G.D., Drislane, F.W. and Galaburda, A.M. (1991) 'Phonological and anatomical evidence for a magnocellular defect in developmental dyslexia', Proceedings of the National Academy of Sciences (USA), vol. 88, pp.7943–7.

Lovegrove, W. (1991) 'Spatial frequency processing in dyslexic and normal readers', in Stein, J.F. (ed.) *Vision and Visual Dyslexia*, London, Macmillan.

McPhilips, M., Hepper, P.G. and Mulhern, G. (2000) 'Effects of replicating primary-reflex movements on specific reading difficulties in children: a randomized, double-blind, controlled trial', *The Lancet*, vol. 355, pp.537–541.

MacLean, M., Bryant, P.E. and Bradley, L. (1987) 'Rhymes, nursery rhymes, and reading in early childhood', *Merrill-Palmer Quarterly*, vol. 33, pp.255–81.

Martini, F.H., Timmons, M.J. and McKinley, M.P. (2000) *Human Anatomy*, Upper Saddle River, NJ, Prentice Hall.

Miles, T.R. (1983) *Dyslexia: The Pattern of Difficulties*, Oxford, Blackwell.

Miles, T.R. and Miles, E. (1999) *Dyslexia: A Hundred Years On* (2nd edn), Buckingham, Open University Press.

Mody, M., Studdert-Kennedy, M. and Brady, S. (1997) 'Speech perception deficits in poor readers: auditory processing or phonological coding?', *Journal of Experimental Child Psychology*, vol. 64, pp.199–231.

Morton, J. (1989) 'An information processing account of reading acquisition', in Galaburda, A.M. and Landau, E. (eds) *From Reading to Neurons*, Cambridge, MA, MIT Press.

Müller, K., Saarenketo, A. and Lyytinen, H. (2000) 'The role of rapid naming in spelling and reading speed among adult dyslexia readers in a transparent orthography', Paper presented at the Society for the Scientific Study of Reading annual conference, Stockholm, July 2000.

Nicholson, R.I. and Fawcett, A.J. (1990) 'Automaticity: a new foundation for dyslexic research?', *Cognition*, vol. 30, pp.159–82.

Nicholson, R.I. and Fawcett, A.J. (1994) 'Comparison of deficits in cognitive and motor skills among children with dyslexia', *Annals of Dyslexia*, vol. 44, pp.147–64.

Nicholson, R.I., Fawcett, A.J., Berry, E.L., Jenkins, I. H., Dean, P. and Brooks, D.J. (1999) 'Association of abnormal cerebellar activation with motor learning difficulties in dyslexic adults', *Lancet*, vol. 353, pp.1662–7.

Reid, G. and Kirk, J. (2001) *Dyslexia in Adults: Education and Employment*, Chichester, John Wiley.

Richardson, A.J., Easton, T., McDaid, A.M., Hall, J.A., Montgomery, P., Clisby, C. and Puri, B.K. (1999) 'Essential fatty acids in dyslexia: theory, evidence and clinical trials', in Peet, M., Glen, I. and Horrobin, D.F. (eds) *Phospholipid Spectrum Disorder in Psychiatry*, Carnforth, Marius Press.

Richardson, A.J. and Ross, M.A. (2000) 'Fatty acid metabolism in neurodevelopmental disorder: a new perspective on associations between ADHD, dyslexia, dyspraxia and the autistic spectrum', *Prostaglandins Leukotr Essential Fatty Acids*, vol. 63, pp.1–9.

Riddick, B. (1996) *Living with Dyslexia: The Social and Emotional Consequences of Specific Learning Difficulties*, London, Routledge.

Riddick, B., Sterling, C., Farmer, M. and Morgan, S. (1999) 'Self-esteem and anxiety in the educational histories of adult dyslexic students', *Dyslexia*, vol. 5, pp.227–48.

Sawyer, C., Taylor, S. and Wilcocks, S. (1994) 'Transparent coloured overlays and specific learning difficulties', *Educational Psychology in Practice*, vol. 9, pp.217–20.

Seymour, P.H.K. (1986) *Cognitive Analysis of Dyslexia*, London, Routledge and Kegan Paul.

Skinner, B.F. (1953) *Science and Human Behaviour*, New York, Macmillan.

Snow, C.E. (1991) *Unfulfilled Expectations: Home and School Influences on Literacy*, Cambridge, MA, Harvard University Press.

Spear-Swerling, L. and Sternberg, R.J. (1998) *Off Track: When Poor Readers Become 'Learning Disabled'*, Boulder, CO, Westview Press.

Stanovich, K.E. (1991) 'The theoretical and practical consequences of discrepancy definitions of dyslexia', in Snowling, M.J. and Thomson, M.E. (eds) *Dyslexia: Integrating Theory and Practice*, London, Whurr.

Stein, J. (1994) 'Developmental dyslexia, neural timing and hemispheric lateralization', *International Journal of Psychophysiology*, vol.18, pp.241–9.

Stein, J., Richardson, A.J. and Fowler, M.S. (2000) 'Monocular occlusion can improve binocular control and reading in developmental dyslexics', *Brain*, vol. 123, pp.164–70.

Stein, J. and Walsh, V. (1997) 'To see but not to read: the magnocellular theory of dyslexia', *Trends in Neuroscience*, vol. 20, pp.147–52.

Stoll, A.L., Severus, E., Freeman, M.P. (1999) 'Omega-3 fatty acids in bipolar disorder: a preliminary double-blind, placebo-controlled trial', *Archive of General Psychiatry*, vol. 56, pp.407–12.

Tallal, P., Miller, S.L., Jenkins, W.M. and Merzenich, M.M. (1997) 'The role of temporal processing in developmental language-based learning disorders: research and clinical implications', in Blachman, B.A. (ed.) *Foundations of*

Reading Acquisition and Dyslexia: Implications for Early Intervention, Mahwah, NJ, Lawrence Erlbaum Associates.

Thomson, M.E. and Grant, S.E. (1979) 'The WISC subtest profile of the dyslexic child', in Newton, M.J., Thomson, M.E. and Richards, I.L. (eds) *Readings in Dyslexia*, Wisbech, Bemrose UK.

Vinegrad, M. (1994) *A Revised Dyslexia Checklist*, Educare, no.48, March 1994, British Dyslexia Association.

Wadsworth, S.J., Knopik, V.S. and DeFries, J.C. (2000) 'Reading disabililty in boys and girls: no evidence for a differential genetic etiology', *Reading and Writing: An Interdisciplinary Journal*, vol. 13, pp.133–45.

West, T.G. (1997) 'Slow words, quick images – dyslexia as an advantage in tomorrow's workplace', in Gerber, J. and Brown, D.S. (eds) *Learning Disabilities and Employment*, Austin, TX, Pro-Ed.

Westervelt, V.D., Johnson, D.C., Westervelt, M.D. and Murrill, S. (1998) 'Changes in self-concept and academic skills during a multimodal summer camp program', *Annals of Dyslexia*, vol. 48, pp.191–212.

Whiteley, H.E. and Smith, C.D. (2001) 'The use of tinted lenses to alleviate reading difficulties', *Journal of Research in Reading*, vol. 24, pp.30–40.

Wolf, M. and Bowers, P.G. (1999) 'The double deficit hypothesis for the developmental dyslexias', *Journal of Educational Psychology*, vol. 91, pp.415–38.

Index

external and internal influences
on 5
fixity and change in 6–7
and friendships 6
genes, hormones and the brain
127, 128
later life 3, 37–49
organismic approaches to 51–4,
57–8
perspectives on ix, 3, 4–6
themes in ix, 3–8
see also attachment theory
logographic strategy, in learning to
read 242, 243, 255–6
longitudinal studies, of intelligence
in later life 48–9
Lorenz, K. 72
Luzzatti, L.L. 180–1

Mac an Ghaill, M. 143
McClelland, J.L. 84, 85, 86
Maccoby, E.E. 121
McGinn, Colin 211
macrosystem, 'ecological' theory of
56
magnetic resonance imaging (MRI)
249–50, 254
magnocellular visual system, and
dyslexia 252, 256
Main, M. 26–7
male primates, and optimal
reproductive style 132
Mandela, N. 99–100, 105
Marshall, J. 180, 181
masculinity
attribution of 118–19
boys and academic achievement
143–4, 145
matched control groups 263
maternal deprivation 29–30
mathematics, and dyslexia 228–9
Mayer, D.E. 83
Maylor, E.A. 44
me, and the self 14–15
Mead, G.H. 14–16
medical approaches to 'normality'
222–3
and dyslexia 239
memory
autobiographical 105, 172, 173
and consciousness 172, 175–6,
188, 191, 195
and global workspace theory
198, 199, 201

post-traumatic amnesia 184,
194
and discursive psychology 105–6
and dyslexia 228, 229
phonological processing
deficit 243
in later life 43–6
psychological perspectives on 5
men
sexual behaviour and attitudes
133–7, 156
and 'womb envy' 151, 152
see also boys
mental health, sex-role stereotypes
in clinical judgements of 120–1
mesosystem, 'ecological' theory of
56
meta-analysis 35
of attachment research 34
meta-cognitive skills, and
collaborative work 18
metacommunication, and pretend
play 10–11
metapresentations
and consciousness 203
in conversation 93, 94
and the evolution of language
80–1
methodological reflexivity 108
methods
case studies 72–3
coexisting methodologies viii, 5,
116, 122, 154–5, 160–2
cross-sectional versus
longitudinal designs 48–9
discourse analysis 101–2
ethnomethodology 97–8
guidelines for non-sexist
research on gender differences
121–2
and lifespan psychology 59
meta-analysis 35
single participant experimental
designs 268–9
subjective and objective
approaches to viii
thought experiments 189–90
microsystem, 'ecological' theory of
56
middle age
Erikson's characterization of 41
Peck's characterization of 41–2
Miles, E. 235
Miles, T.R. 233, 235

mind-body problem, and
consciousness 186–8, 189, 206
monitoring consciousness 193, 201,
204, 211–12
Moss, H.E. 83, 87
mother-infant relationships
and attachment theory 21, 22,
29–32, 34, 37
and Oedipal theory 147–50
motherhood, discourses of 100–1
motor skills, and dyslexia 253
MRI (magnetic resonance imaging)
249–50, 254
Müller-Lyer illusion 173
multisensory teaching for dyslexic
children 262–3
mysterianism 211–12, 213

Nagel, T. 192, 205, 206, 207
natural selection, of language 76–8,
80
nature-nurture distinction vii
and gender 159–60
and lifespan development 21
Necker cube, and consciousness
199–200
Negroponte, N. 269
neuroscience, and attachment
theory 28
Nicolson, R.I. 245
non-fluent aphasia 79
'normality' 219, 220–5, 271
cultural approaches to 223–4,
239, 257
and managing or treating
dyslexia 257–8
medical approaches to 222–3,
239
and personal distress 224, 257–8
statistical approaches to 220–2,
239
nutraceuticals, in the treatment of
dyslexia 264–5

object relations theory 152
and attachment 29
Oedipal conflict 147–50
and changing gender relations
153
critics of 150–2
old age
Erikson's characterization of 40,
42
Peck's characterization of 42

Acknowledgements

Grateful acknowledgement is made to the following sources for permission to reproduce material in this book:

Chapter 1

Text

pp.39–40: From Lemme, B.H., *Development in Adulthood*, Copyright © 1995 by Allyn & Bacon. Reprinted/adapted by permission by Allyn & Bacon; p.57: Ford, D.H. and Lerner, R.M. (1992) *Developmental Systems Theory – An Integrative Approach*, Sage Publications, Inc. Copyright © 1992 by Sage Publications, Inc. Reprinted by permission of Sage Publications, Inc.

Figures

Figure 1.1: Maylor, E.A. (1996) 'Older people's memory for the past and the future', *The Psychologist*, October 1996, British Psychological Society; Figure 1.2: Adapted from Baltes, P.B. (1987) 'Theoretical propositions of life-span developmental psychology: on the dynamics between growth and decline', *Developmental Psychology*, vol.23, no.5, American Psychological Association. Copyright © 1987 by the American Psychological Association. Adapted with permission; Figure 1.3: Adapted from Schaie, K.W. and Willis, S.L. (1991) *Adult Development and Aging*. Copyright © 1991 by K. Warner Schaie and Sherry L. Willis. Reprinted by permission of Pearson Education, Inc., Upper Saddle River, NJ; Figure 1.4: Adapted from Ford, D.H. and Lerner, R.M. (1992) *Developmental Systems Theory – An Integrative Approach*, Sage Publications, Inc. Copyright © 1992 by Sage Publications, Inc. Reprinted by permission of Sage Publications, Inc.

Chapter 2

Figures

Figure 2.1: From J.L. McClelland (1985) 'Putting knowledge in its place: a scheme for programming parallel processing structures on the fly', *Cognitive Science*, 9, 115, Ablex Publishing. Reprinted by permission of Cognitive Science Society, Inc.; Figure 2.2: From 'An interactive activation model of context effects in letter perception: Part 1. An account of basic findings' by J.L. McCelland and D.E. Rumelhart, 1981, *Psychological Review*, 88, p.380. Copyright © 1981 by the American Psychological Association. Reprinted with permission; Figure 2.3: Picture context for the 'balloon story' from J.D. Bransford and M.K. Johnson, 'Consideration of some problems in comprehension', in *Visual Information Processing*, p.396, edited by W.D. Chase. Copyright © 1973 by Academic Press, reproduced by permission of the publisher.

Illustrations

p.73: Copyright © Language Research Center, Georgia State University.

Chapter 3

Illustrations

p.148: Science Photo Library; p.151: Detail of sculpture by G. L. Bernini, The Ecstacy of Saint Teresa, 1647–1652. Photo: Alinari Archives, Florence.

Chapter 4

Figures

Figure 4.1: Carter, R. (1998) *Mapping the Mind*, reprinted by permission of MoonRunner Designs Ltd; Figure 4.3: Baars, B.J. (1998) *A Cognitive Theory of Consciousness*, Cambridge University Press.

Chapter 5

Text

pp.226–7: Faludy, T. and Faludy, A. (1996) *A Little Edge of Darkness*, Jessica Kingsley Publishers.

Figures

Figure 5.1: Dancey, C.P. and Reidy, J. ((2002) *Statistics Without Maths for Psychology: Using SPSS for Windows*^{TM}, 2nd edn, Pearson Education Limited. Copyright © Pearson Education Limited 2002, reprinted by permission of Pearson Education Limited; Figure 5.2: Frith, U. (1999) 'Paradoxes in the definition of dyslexia', *Dyslexia*, vol.5, no.4, December 1999. Copyright © 1999 John Wiley & Sons, Ltd. Reproduced by permission of John Wiley & Sons, Ltd; Figure 5.4: Reprinted with permission from 'Human brain: left-right asymmetries in temporal speech region' by N. Geschwind and W. Levitsky, *Science*, 161, pp.186–7. Copyright © 1968 by American Association for the Advancement of Science.

Tables

Table 5.1: *AO3. Adult Dyslexia Checklist*, 1994, http://www.bda-dyslexia.org.uk, British Dyslexia Association.

Illustrations

p.227: Faludy, T. and Faludy, A. (1996) *A Little Edge of Darkness*, Jessica Kingsley Publishers. Courtesy of Tanya and Alexander Faludy; p.252: Reprinted from *Reading by the Colors*, by Helen Irlen, Penguin-Putnam/ Perigee Publishing, New York, 1991, with permission.

Every effort has been made to trace all the copyright owners, but if any has been inadvertently overlooked, the publishers will be pleased to make the necessary arrangements at the first opportunity.